HANDLING QUALITATIVE DATA
A PRACTICAL GUIDE

SAGE was founded in 1965 by Sara Miller McCune to support the dissemination of usable knowledge by publishing innovative and high-quality research and teaching content. Today, we publish more than 750 journals, including those of more than 300 learned societies, more than 800 new books per year, and a growing range of library products including archives, data, case studies, reports, conference highlights, and video. SAGE remains majority-owned by our founder, and on her passing will become owned by a charitable trust that secures our continued independence.

Los Angeles | London | Washington DC | New Delhi | Singapore

THIRD
EDITION

HANDLING QUALITATIVE DATA
A PRACTICAL GUIDE

LYN RICHARDS

Los Angeles | London | New Delhi
Singapore | Washington DC

Los Angeles | London | New Delhi
Singapore | Washington DC

SAGE Publications Ltd
1 Oliver's Yard
55 City Road
London EC1Y 1SP

SAGE Publications Inc.
2455 Teller Road
Thousand Oaks, California 91320

SAGE Publications India Pvt Ltd
B 1/I 1 Mohan Cooperative Industrial Area
Mathura Road
New Delhi 110 044

SAGE Publications Asia-Pacific Pte Ltd
3 Church Street
#10-04 Samsung Hub
Singapore 049483

Editor: Katie Metzler
Editorial assistant: Lily Mehrbod
Production editor: Ian Antcliff
Copyeditor: Sarah Bury
Proofreader: Andrew Baxter
Marketing manager: Ben Griffin-Sherwood
Cover design: Shaun Mercier
Typeset by: C&M Digitals (P) Ltd, Chennai, India
Printed in Great Britain by Henry Ling Limited at
The Dorset Press, Dorchester, DT1 1HD

Library of Congress Control Number: 2014939150

British Library Cataloguing in Publication data

A catalogue record for this book is available from
the British Library

MIX
Paper from
responsible sources
FSC
www.fsc.org   FSC™ C013985

ISBN 978-1-4462-7605-1
ISBN 978-1-4462-7606-8 (pbk)

At SAGE we take sustainability seriously. Most of our products are printed in the UK using FSC papers and boards.
When we print overseas we ensure sustainable papers are used as measured by the Egmont grading system.
We undertake an annual audit to monitor our sustainability.

Summary of contents

Contents

List of tables

Companion website

Handling Qualitative Data, third edition, is supported by a companion website: **https://study.sagepub.com/richards3e**. Visit the website to access two sets of useful resources to accompany the book:

- **Methods in Practice:** the stories of ten projects (from eight countries and as many qualitative methods), are told in the researchers' own voices. How was the project set up, what data were sought and created, how did the researcher work with the data, what actually happened during analysis and reporting?
- **Qualitative Software:** this is not a summary of the current state of the various software products aimed at qualitative researchers. But it does tell you where to go for such summaries. And more importantly, it advises you before you go shopping for software. Should you use qualitative software, and how? How to find impartial, useful and non-marketing advice about software products? It then provides help on how to manage your relationship with your software, including a brief handbook of advice to help you ask the necessary questions as you start stepping into software.

About the author

Lyn Richards has a highly unusual range of relationships with qualitative research. After undergraduate training as a Historian and Political Scientist, she moved to Sociology. Her early work as a family sociologist addressed both popular and academic audiences, with a strong motivation always to make the funded research relevant to the people studied, and the qualitative analysis credible to those affected. Each of her four books in family sociology was a text at university level but also widely discussed in popular media and at community level. During her tenure as Reader and Associate Professor at La Trobe University in Melbourne, she won major research grants, presented and published research papers, was a founding member of a qualitative research association and taught qualitative methods at undergraduate and graduate level, supervising Masters and PhD students.

She strayed from this academic pathway when challenges with handling qualitative data in her family and community studies led to the development, with Tom Richards, of what rapidly became the world's leading qualitative analysis software. They left the university to found a research software company, in which for a decade Lyn was Director of Research Services, writing software documentation and managing international teaching of the methods behind the software. Designing and documenting software taught her to confront fuzzy thinking about methods, and to demand straight talking, clarity of purpose, detail of technique and a clear answer always to 'Why would we want to do that?' Teaching methods to thousands of researchers in dozens of disciplines in 14 countries, she learned what worked and what didn't. From those researchers, graduates and faculty in universities and research practitioners in the world beyond, she learned their many ways of handling data, on and off computers, and their strategies for making sense of data.

Handling Qualitative Data is a direct result of this experience. It offers clear, practical advice for researchers approaching qualitative research and wishing to do justice to rich data. Like her previous book, with Janice Morse, *Readme First, for a User's Guide to Qualitative Methods* it strongly maintains the requirements of good qualitative research, assumes and critiques the use of software and draws on practical work, helping researchers whose progress has been hindered by confusion, lack of training, mixed messages about standards and fear of being overwhelmed by rich, messy data.

Throughout this hybrid career, Lyn continued contributions to critical reflection on new methods, as a writer and a keynote speaker in a wide range of international conferences. She has life membership of the International Sociological Association and its Methodology section. Her writing aims always to cut through barriers to high quality qualitative research and to assist researchers and teachers in making the inevitable shift to computing whilst maximizing the benefits for their research processes and outcomes. On leaving software development, she took an Adjunct Professorship at RMIT University where she is now Associate Research Fellow of the Centre for Applied Social Research (CASR) and coordinates an active, informal and splendidly supportive qualitative research network group.

Preface

Are you at risk of acquiring qualitative data, whether by careful, theoretically based research design, by practical need or by accident? Are you prepared for rich, complex, unstructured data records, which may rapidly appear in confusing profusion? Are you doubting you can do justice to those records, and to the people whose accounts you have been privileged to acquire? Are you prevented from starting by messages about the difficulty of doing good qualitative work, the debates about epistemology, or the necessity to learn confronting specialist software?

This book is designed to assist when qualitative data have to be handled, and to guide you through those barriers to doing it. In decades of helping researchers worldwide, I have learned that those who come to qualitative research 'data first' rather than 'methods first' are often the most motivated and critical. But they are also held back by lack of preparation in ways to handle data records, and by messages about the mystique of doing, or even thinking about doing, qualitative research and the heavy tasks of doing it in a digital age. So too, often, are those who have had some training in the study of the theory of methods – methodology. However adequate their understanding of the philosophy behind what they are trying to do, they may have no practical idea of how they would handle data if they ever had some.

This book starts there. It is, therefore, very different from most texts on qualitative methods.

Firstly, it is about *handling data* – working with data in order to produce adequate and useful outcomes. The title carries two messages. Qualitative data don't speak for themselves, but have to be handled if they are to be analysed. And handling data is something you can learn and do well as you get started.

It's amazing how little of the methodological literature is in this area. Even texts with titles about 'analysing' or 'doing' qualitative research spend considerably more time on ways of making data than on what you would do with such data if you ever actually had any. From the perspective of those who have to do it, texts on qualitative method are often inaccessibly high up in the misty mountains of academic discourse. By horrid contrast, literature on the tools you need for qualitative research, and particularly on digital tools, suggests you might never get started if burdened with learning software functions and with very negative messages about their results for research. In this third edition, these messages have been strongly pursued.

Secondly, this book is about the *agency* of the researcher. The researcher designs and creates a project and then also creates data, collaboratively with those studied, and it is the researcher who then does the analysing of that data. In this new edition there is increased emphasis on issues of ethics as you negotiate that collaboration. In every section, the book confronts the critical issues of reflexivity, alerting the reader to their relationship with their research questions, design, conduct and records, and advising on how these reflections can be recorded and used in validating analysis.

Thirdly, the book aims to provide practical advice and build confidence so that, by following it, a good job can be done. An irony of our time is that just as qualitative research has become acceptable and required across most areas of research practice in social enquiry, it has been shrouded in clouds of debate about reality and its representation. These debates enthral and entice those of us with time and training to engage in them, but send a strong message to many practitioners that qualitative research is possibly a futile endeavour from the start. It seems to me that, since the world undoubtedly needs good qualitative research (and does not need bad research), all researchers require assistance in designing projects and handling data thoughtfully, reflexively, ethically and successfully. This book is for students of qualitative methods who have been taught to reflect on their data and their relationship to data, but it is also for the many (out of and inside academia) who have neither access to courses on epistemological issues nor time to do them, yet are confronted with a project and wish to learn how they can best deal with it. They need practical, accessible and informed advice on how to do their task well, reflecting on their relationship to their data, on what would be a credible account and how properly to produce one.

Fourthly, the book covers neither the range of qualitative methods nor how different methods derive from different epistemological positions, nor does it teach any particular method. Instead, it daringly assumes that handling data well and producing a good research outcome does not *require* knowing the range and rules of any particular method, let alone all.

Most texts start with the assumption that qualitative data are accessible only via a researched understanding of all or at least some methodologies, and that a project must be located within a coherent methodology. I started there too and I strongly hold a commitment to what I term methodological fit, the ways in which question, data, ways of handling data, ways of constructing an outcome and ways of justifying it *fit* together. I wrote about that in *Readme First* (Richards and Morse, 2013). In the present book, however, I aim to convey this fit to researchers whether or not they have the time or opportunity to learn from or engage in methodological debates. My prime goal is to help them to do justice to data. And I aim to encourage them, whatever their methodological persuasion, to reflect on their relationship to their project and their data. Since the first edition of this book appeared, the feedback has consistently told me this was useful.

You will find here no specification of the rules for working in any particular method. Texts that do address the tasks of data handling usually do so from within one method, providing detailed rules for the processes associated with, for example, a particular version of discourse analysis, grounded theory or phenomenology or preparation for an ethnography. Such learning will of course provide a firm basis for research, and as a teacher and writer I have set it as a goal for students. This book consistently urges the reader who can do so to pursue literature within the appropriate method for their study. But it also assumes that there is much to be learned for any study from many methods. Methodological ghettoism serves neither those outside nor those working inside the closed world of a particular method. All qualitative researchers need basic skills for handling data, and these skills are used across methods. Methodological fit and skills for handling data can be learned by those working in any particular method or by those who are not steeped in the literature particular to one method. All novice researchers need pragmatic, informed and understandable assistance in the processes of making useful data records, in handling and working with the data on the road to a good analysis, and in showing that it is good.

And finally, this book confronts directly the undeniable fact that qualitative research is now done on computers. Unlike most texts (see review by Paulus et al., 2013), it assumes that you will use computer software when handling qualitative data and consistently offers advice on maximizing the benefits of doing so, and dealing with the challenges, particularly the challenge of having your project confined to the 'box' of a dedicated software product. All researchers use computers in at least some context and those who do not also use tools that assist qualitative research are clearly restricted. For methods texts to treat computer handling of qualitative data as an optional extra (most do), makes it far harder to discuss practically what we can now do with data. But the constraining of research by software packages is a recently recognized challenge which this new edition addresses in every chapter.

Software has transformed the tasks of handling qualitative data. This book advises of course on techniques that can be done on paper or in your head, alongside ones that can be undertaken only by using software. It warns of and tackles the challenges of computer-assisted handling of data, and the issues to be considered. But it assumes you will use software, and urges you to use many digital tools. It does not teach any particular software – learning software is another task (there's help for this task on the website). Nor does the text assume that any particular software is to be used. And it firmly avoids assuming that the techniques made available by qualitative software necessarily improve research practice. Indeed, as you'll discover from the warnings in each chapter, and from the website, I have serious concerns about the ways accepted specialist software shapes and constrains research.

Moreover, very importantly, this book does not assume that software use will be limited to the small group of commercial packages specifically marketed to qualitative researchers and which I refer to simply as 'qualitative software' (but which also go under the acronym of CAQDAS: Computer Assisted Qualitative Data AnalysiS). The story of the development of these packages spans a quarter of a century, and in many ways they are still set in the same methodological approaches. A decade of my research life was spent in the fascinating tasks of qualitative software development and teaching research strategies with software. Of course, this work is reflected in my advice to researchers and my take on the challenges and pitfalls this book aims to rescue you from. And, of course, the software I helped develop (QSR NUD*IST and NVivo) reflected the methods I teach and the approaches I take to data. But I now have no connection with any software company and, since leaving that field, I have watched from the sidelines as the adventure of inventing qualitative software became, in my view, routinized, innovation too often dampened, at least for some developers, by commercial goals and competitive pressures and the inertia of research institutions, which have limited the variety and exploratory range of products. On the website for this book you'll find a strong message that it's time for innovation and encouragement to explore options beyond the CAQDAS stable. In the chapters of this book you'll find that discussion of the powerful possibilities of advanced packages is balanced by warnings about the ways software can constrain your research. A strong message is to avoid having your enquiry contained within the box of the project you build in qualitative software. It's a nice coincidence that this edition coincides with the 25th anniversary of the first international gathering of qualitative software developers. My hope is that this will mark a new spurt of innovation for qualitative computing, and new thinking outside the 'box' for researchers.

Meanwhile, you can use this book with no computer software (if you must!) or with any qualitative software, and/or with any combination of the increasingly familiar other digital tools. Where the techniques described require software, this is noted, as are the few places where the techniques suggested are particular to one software package. Where challenges are greater, or risks higher, because of what you can do with software, this too is discussed.

Each of these goals has been expanded in the website accompanying this third edition: study.sagepub.com/richards3e. There are two parts to the website – 'Methods in Practice' and 'Qualitative Software'. The first is designed to offer, as few published accounts do, a vivid picture of qualitative research as it happens. There you will find a set of project accounts giving brief but detailed stories of research experience – what really did occur, what worked and the strategies developed to deal with challenges. The contributors have returned to those accounts for this third edition, reflecting on their practice then and what they now see as important.

The website's second part advises on software. These pages are designed to help novice researchers approach the tasks of reviewing and critiquing the qualitative software available, assessing its usefulness for their own projects and, if they wish, selecting and learning a package. Because no software is ever static, and the needs of researchers are dynamic and varied, there are no specific descriptions here of current software. Rather, the reader is directed to sites where they will find regularly updated descriptions and tutorials.

This book is written in the conviction that handling qualitative data well beats handling them badly, and that it can be done. If you are approaching data via qualitative methods courses, it offers detailed advice at each step as you prepare for a project and design the processes of analysis. If you are meeting qualitative methods via data, you will not be burdened here with a message that to do so is morally bad or practically unwise. But you will be urged to pause and reflect on your relationship to that data, and advised how to set up and competently conduct a project.

Novice researchers can always achieve new understanding from data, however they come to the task, by thinking through their relationship to the data, by using good tools and by learning simple skills. Many readers will wish to do no more than this. Some may go on to learn the varieties and rules of different qualitative methods and to participate in the discussions of what they represent. Others will go on to approach positively the puzzles of qualitative data, to meet the challenge of sensitively managing larger bodies of more complex data records, and to enjoy the accessible achievement of making sense of a 'real' project and even to contribute to the next stage of innovation with methods and software tools. On finishing this book, your data records may not be fully accessible and analysed, but the goal is to end this book, and the first stage of a real project, with the knowledge that access and analysis are achievable.

Lyn Richards

Acknowledgements

In preparing the third edition of this book, I have been greatly helped by generous feedback from students, teachers and researchers around the world, and from the editorial team at Sage and their anonymous reviewers – my thanks to all.

One theme was dominant among the responses to the book, as in the stories from researchers I had taught and helped in 20 years of teaching qualitative methods in academia and outside, across countries and disciplines, and all levels of seniority and experience. This was the difficulty novices find at the start of research, in picturing what it would be like to *be there*, doing a qualitative project, and what they could realistically hope to achieve – what it would be like to *get there*. I was encouraged by this feedback, and by several close colleagues, in pursuing a maverick project I'd talked of for years – putting together an informal body of accounts of research experience, accessible online. Unlike most refereed publications and thesis chapters, such a website could tell it as it is, with live accounts of what really happened and what it was really like to face the challenges, how ways around obstacles were devised, what worked and what didn't, and the extraordinary experience of arriving at an adequate account of your data.

My thanks to those who backed me in this project, to Sage for seeing it as not just ambitious but useful, to the many who responded to the call for contributions but for one reason or another were turned away, and above all to the ten researchers who finally ran the whole course. It wasn't an easy task (or for many academics, a familiar one) to write succinctly, briefly, honestly and clearly about the real story of a project. I greatly appreciate their persistence in reworking drafts, their tolerance in accepting my critical editing and suggestions, and my goals for the project. The outcome is a unique research resource, and a good read. And I thank those who spent time writing a postscript section to their account for the present edition, reflecting on what they now know, looking back.

I wrote this book for all the researchers I have tried to help around the globe, in decades of university teaching at undergraduate and graduate level, then workshop teaching and project consultancy. They taught me to set aside assumptions about research goals and experience that make sense only in academia (and possibly, now, not there). I also learned new practical ways of tackling the myths and monsters of qualitative methods, and discovered or invented techniques that worked for those confronted with data and the task of doing justice to messy records.

This book was dreamt long back. I kept thinking, as the acceptability of qualitative research grew, and I tried to help researchers with important questions and no training, that a straightforward text would appear to show researchers how to handle data. As I waited, both teaching and literature increasingly shifted away from such purposes, to theoretical discussions about representations of reality. Meanwhile, it was more and more evident that the world needed good qualitative research to address the clamouring questions of health and social justice. With few books advising what one would do with data if one ever got any, the need for balance increasingly concerned me, as did the continuing irrelevance of texts to those normally using software. Can you think of another profession in which the majority of practitioners are untrained, and the majority of texts and teachers teach methods long overtaken by technology?

This third edition is a next step in my attempts to fill that gap. The first was *Readme First* (2013), written with Jan Morse to address a related need: that of researchers who meet methodological choice without any training and have to find their way to an understanding of methodological congruence. This book followed, aimed to help them handle the data that results, and to assist those other researchers who meet qualitative methods 'data first'. With the second edition, it moved to include the website accounts of methods in practice, live examples and sharing of experiences. This new edition asked for more reflection from those contributors. And it also asks of the reader another level of reflection, on their agency in doing the research and the ethical implications.

My thanks to the professionals at Sage, particularly to Commissioning Editor Katie Metzler, who advised wisely, tracked progress and checked from the northern winter if I'd survived bushfires in Australia, to Anna Horvai, who prepared the excellent and encouraging detailed report on referee feedback and performance of the second edition and to Lily Mehrbod who took the new edition through to the finishing post.

Thanks also to the Qualitative Interest Group at RMIT University, who gave me a new understanding of the needs of researchers, at all levels of experience and an amazing range of disciplines, for windows on the research process.

In preparing each edition, I have always been greatly helped by Tom Richards, to whom I originally dedicated this book. It is a small by-product of our shared belief in the importance of qualitative research and of helping people to do justice to data, of the shared adventure of developing software tools, and of Tom's ability to design and create tools that would remove barriers to research and create entirely new ways of doing it, first for my work, and then for the research of many thousands of others.

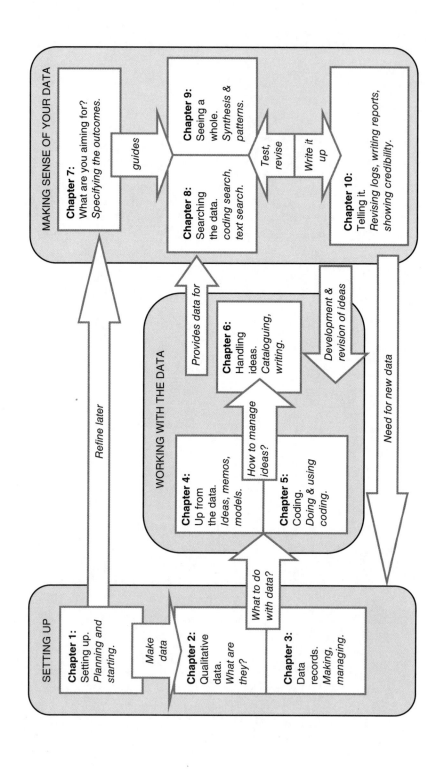

Introduction

Since the first publication of this book, much – and little – has changed. The literature available to researchers has expanded greatly, as has the variety of methodological approaches to qualitative research. The popularity of qualitative methods has soared, in an ever-widening range of disciplines. But judging from feedback to this book and other help resources, little has changed for embattled novice researchers meeting qualitative data before they have training in techniques for handling such records. This book was written for them, and has now been expanded in response to their needs.

In this book you will find practical help in designing and using basic strategies for making sense of qualitative data. And the book now links with a website (https://study.sagepub.com/richards3e that carries more detailed advice and an extraordinary online goldmine of ten researchers' open and practical stories of their experiences in real projects. The 'Methods in Practice' web-pages take you into each project with the voice of the researcher recounting it. There you can read stories of strategies developed and challenges met in projects from eight countries, including many methods, contexts and disciplines, what it was like working this way, what worked and what didn't.

STARTING POINTS

Qualitative Methods and Qualitative Data

The first two chapters of this book concern the preparation for and design of qualitative studies, and the nature of and challenges in handling qualitative data. Here, I offer some starting definitions.

Qualitative *methods* are ways of studying people and their social worlds by going there, observing them closely, in their natural setting, and learning how they understand their situations and account for their behaviour. There are many, very different, qualitative research methods, but all attempt understanding of individuals or small numbers of cases. Analysis aims to generate new accounts or explanations out of this rich data, rather than test existing theories. A qualitative method is needed for researchers who are trying to learn something new, rather than test something that is known. If you are planning a qualitative project, it is probably because you don't know what you will find. Qualitative methods seek surprises.

So qualitative *data* is messy stuff! If you are working qualitatively it is usually because the question being asked does not clearly indicate what data you need to answer it. Whatever the qualitative method chosen, the researcher will be seeking people's own understanding, in their own words, of their own and others' behaviour and its social context. The records of observations or discussions are most often textual, sometimes visual or audio files. Those records ideally include data about the social context, and are usually unstructured, since the goal was to gather people's own accounts, in their own words, rather than record answers to the researcher's prepared questions. The researcher is part of those data, not an outside observer. Qualitative data are the results of interaction between the researcher and 'subject'. Qualitative data records are thus typically *records of observation or interaction that are complex and contexted.*

These starter definitions may surprise you, as both qualitative methods and qualitative data are more usually defined negatively – the method is *not* quantitative, the data *not* expressed numerically. Such definitions can be confusing, since most qualitative studies, like most social observations, involve some counting, and most data can be summarized numerically. More usefully, qualitative data can be described as *data that are not easily reducible immediately (or, perhaps ever) to numbers.*

Data First: Meeting Qualitative Methods

The majority of those first meeting qualitative data are unprepared by training to handle such data. This problem is encountered at all levels and locations of research practice, by policy analysts, postgraduate students, evaluators, research assistants, contract researchers, consultants, undergraduates, senior colleagues and supervisors. Meeting data without training can happen for any of several perfectly good reasons.

This may be your first meeting with qualitative data because you are being taught the methods by first working with data. Some teachers prefer to show students the richness and interest of qualitative data, and to introduce the challenges of handling data, before they tackle the philosophical basis for methodologies. Early in a course about research, the emphasis may be on what social researchers do to record social interaction. The student is immediately making data records, and needs to know both that records must be handled in order to be analysed and that *they* could handle such data. Later, if they go on to a more advanced level, distinctions between different methods may be explored, and detailed instructions may be given in a particular method.

Or it may be that you are unprepared with data-handling skills because you simply didn't *mean* to make qualitative data. Practitioners trained in other methods, or with no research training, may be confronted, in an academic task or a contract research setting, with an issue requiring qualitative data. Such data happen when you ask questions like 'What's going on?' or 'How do they see their situation?' or simply when you leave space for 'write-ins' in a questionnaire. Perhaps the meanings people put on their actions or experiences have to be understood because a statistical analysis has failed to explain the patterns discovered. Answers may then be sought by talking to people or observing them.

You may have happened on qualitative data, even a lot of data, as a result of a project that was not designed to be qualitative. In recent years, the use of qualitative data has spread rapidly, and in areas where qualitative data have not hitherto been used, projects are designed to inform researchers needing to understand medical problems 'on the ground', political issues at the grass roots or the needs of local action groups, to advise government, businesses or marketing strategists, to prepare legal evidence or evaluate programmes. Across disciplines, many researchers strive to handle qualitative data records far more numerous (though not, often, as rich) as were handled in traditional small-scale projects. The methodological disadvantages of bulk data are massive, but saying so doesn't help the researcher who has to handle the data. Throughout this book, there are notes on how particular techniques can be adapted to bigger projects.

Or perhaps you did plan to do a qualitative project, and you prepared yourself by reading about methodology, but delayed the challenge of learning how to deal with the material. The graduate student who embarks upon a dissertation without a plan for handling data can be overwhelmed by a sense that the well-honed research design has failed them. Records soon pile up when (amazingly!) everyone wants to talk to you. Just as the material becomes both exciting and informing, it also threatens to get away from your control. Records you could hold in your hand moments ago expand to a massive body of complexity that could knock you over.

In all of these situations, the data may prove splendidly relevant and very exciting, but the challenges of doing justice to these records look formidable. Wasting such material, whose acquisition took time and trust, is not an option. In the field, when researchers are dealing with qualitative data for the first time, or are confronted with data they do not know how to handle, the need is for pragmatic, achievable techniques for data management, data reduction and data analysis. The following chapters offer a basic set of such handling skills, to maximize the chance that qualitative data will be well handled and well used. The website offers real experiences of researchers' efforts to do justice to qualitative data.

I am not here debating the disadvantages (or surprisingly, sometimes, advantages) of meeting data before methodology. This book is simply responding to the fact that many researchers do.

If your starting point was to get a glimpse of ways of handling data before gaining an understanding of the *why* of qualitative research, this book will leave you still needing that understanding. *Why* would you locate your study thus, *why* would you have such data, *why* would you seek different sorts of data for another study, *why* is this not a quantitative study? My strong advice is not to avoid those questions. The present book leaves them still to be addressed, in the appropriate way for your research context, at the appropriate time for your project.

Such wider questions are the focus of the methodological map-book I wrote with Janice Morse, *Readme First for a User's Guide to Qualitative Methods* (Richards and Morse, 2013), hereafter *Readme First*. Like the present book, it assumes little prior training. *Readme First* is about the *why* questions that apply to method, why one would use one method rather than another, and why good qualitative research requires a fit of question to method, method to data and data to analysis and outcome. It sketches for different methods what the experience of using them would be like, and offers a wide list of readings for each method and its justification. To inform the choice of methods, and direct the reader who wishes to go there to the relevant literature and to ways of learning methods without mystique, I refer to *Readme First*. Each chapter in this book, and also each of the projects on the website, ends with suggested further readings.

Here, the emphasis is on *how* to do the data handling. With class exercise data or 'real' projects, the first hurdle is often to gain understanding that such data *can* be handled – and that data handling is the first step to analysis. The next hurdle is seeing that being able to deal with qualitative data does not require interminable time or sophisticated skills. Once these hurdles are cleared, researchers can immerse themselves in their rich records and seek subtle understanding and adequate explanations of the situation studied.

The handling is also done, hands-on, with computers. Working without computers is no longer an option for qualitative (or indeed any) researchers. Handwritten records like diaries or letters may stay on paper, but any typed text will be in electronic format, as will your report. Researchers now use software to handle such records, because, once software is learned, they can achieve much more in considerably less time and at far less risk if they do. If you or someone with power over you still prefers to work with coloured pens and copied extracts, most of the advice about the goals of handling data in this book will still be relevant to your work, but the goals will be much harder to achieve. As mentioned in the Preface, where software is necessary for the techniques discussed, this is noted. The 'Methods in Practice' reports on the website offer honest accounts of what it is like to work with any of several software packages – or none.

HANDLING DATA

Handling data? There are books and workshops on *collecting* data and *analysing* data – ways of making and doing things to data. The emphasis here is more on the craft of creating and working with data records and the book is intended for those doing such work, hands-on. Like any craft, it has guidelines for setting up and working skilfully with the materials.

Using those guidelines, a researcher can rapidly build a live, changing body of material from which new understanding can be created. To get there requires that the ideas and the data records are not just managed but *handled*, and handled skilfully.

Qualitative researchers deal with, and revel in, confusing, contradictory, multi-faceted data records, rich accounts of experience and interaction. The researcher confronted by such data records almost always talks in terms of dilemmas. How to tame the data without losing their excitement, get order without trivializing the accounts, or losing the reflections about the researcher's role in making them happen? How to exert control without losing vivid recall? How to show a pattern that respects the data without prematurely reducing vivid words to numbers?

So think in terms of handling the records of data that you collaboratively create in interaction with those you study. We use 'handler' to refer to interaction with animals we respect, and with whom we expect to form a relationship – whoever heard of a fish handler? The verb indicates understanding and control, or lack of it ('I have to learn to handle change better'). It is about coming to grips with a challenge. (The slang phrase 'I can handle that' means it's good.) The goal of the rest of this book is that the reader will finish it confident that they can handle qualitative data and that the experience is good.

Real Data and Real Projects?

This book can be read without data, or used with provided data, classroom exercise data or the first stages of data for a 'real' project.

But you also need to know real projects, ones that work and ones that don't. In this book, each chapter has a running 'example' of a research project. There are no references to publications on these projects, because I made them up, to avoid loading the text with detail. The real projects are on the website, where the 'Methods in Practice' reports offer something you don't get from referred journals – a sense of what projects are really like. Many have links to project sites, publications and online reports.

For more hands-on experience, find an experienced researcher who will let you work alongside them, perhaps as a volunteer assistant. Like any craft, qualitative research is well learned in apprenticeship, so long as the apprentice retains the ability to question what they observe in practice.

If you are not working in a 'real' project, consider finding or making a very small body of your own data, by observing and taking notes, by talking to people and recording recollections or by taping and transcribing interviews. Learning about techniques and achieving competence in them is easier if you are genuinely interested in the data being handled.

THE SHAPE OF THIS BOOK

The following chapters take the reader through ten research processes that are always involved in qualitative data handling, though not always in that order. For convenience they are grouped in three parts: on setting up, on working with the data and on making sense.

In each chapter, references to the projects on the 'Methods in Practice' website are indicated by an icon in the margin.

Practical tasks to do, uses of the website material and suggested readings, round off each chapter.

Part I: Setting Up

Part I is about starting the project. Its message is to think forward, think ethics, think project goals, think making good records and think from the start about how you will later justify and account for your research processes.

Chapter 1 is about setting up your project. It advises on qualitative research design, ethical issues in qualitative work and the thinking through of project purpose, goal and outcomes.

Chapter 2 discusses the meanings of 'qualitative' and 'data', the differences between qualitative and quantitative, the importance of complexity and context and of reflection on your part in making your data. It covers readying for data, gaining familiarity with the research field and with the ongoing tasks of writing of qualitative research, and logging the records to establish validity and reliability.

Chapter 3 is about making data *records*, the different ways of making data, and the importance of avoiding wastage and data loss, the necessity for data reduction, skills for doing it and ways of ensuring a smooth flow of data. It deals with access to information and recording of the decisions that affect what the project will later be able to claim. And it confronts the tasks of choosing software tools and becoming competent in using them.

Aim to end this part with a project set up and a sense of data as manageable.

Part II: Working with the Data

In all qualitative methods, data making and analysis are simultaneous, not sequential, stages. The next three chapters explore what this means in practice.

Chapter 4 explains ways of exploring data to get 'up' from the mass of your data to a clearer picture of what's going on. It looks at processes of interpretation, during reading, reflection, review. It sets out ways of recording what happens in annotations and memos.

Chapter 5 is on qualitative coding, starting with why it is so different from quantitative coding and the purposes of qualitative coding. It explains how to use coding to store information about cases, gather material on a topic, and the all-important ways in which coding can open up meaning, allowing you to develop categories or explore dimensions in the data. It warns of the traps of over-coding, especially with software assistance, and advises on how to avoid them.

Then Chapter 6 deals with the ideas that result from working up from the data and coding: the discovery and handling of ideas, how to catalogue the categories for thinking about your project, and what to do with the ideas emerging from the data.

Aim to end this part with a growing project within which ideas emerging from the data are catalogued and accessible, linked to well-coded data and documented as they develop.

Part III: Making Sense of Your Data

The final part is on handling the processes of analysis and reporting.

As you work through the book, it will become evident that each of the analysis processes will probably occur throughout a project, as, of course, does writing. The ways of searching and seeing your data send you back to revisit processes of making data, interpreting, coding and handling ideas. Writing about your project aids analysis.

Chapter 7 invites you to reconsider the outcome you want from the project, and firm up what you are aiming for. It tackles two challenges of qualitative research: understanding how theory can be constructed and not knowing what sort of an outcome you might be able to construct. Possible constructs seeking synthesis and patterns are discussed, with ways of assessing what would be satisfactory and how the researcher will know when they get there.

Searching for, interpreting and validating patterns in the data are covered in Chapter 8, with an emphasis on the many ways of searching either the text or your coding, or both. It discusses how to use these tools to question themes and build understanding, and how to use the results to establish and explore patterns and test hunches.

Seeing the project as a whole requires different skills, the subject of Chapter 9. It indicates the array of techniques for seeing an overall 'whole' or seeing a pattern and for testing what is seen, including modelling, displaying relationships and developing interpretations.

Finally, Chapter 10 maps the paths to concluding a project satisfactorily. The emphasis is on establishing the strength of the argument by using your writing from the start of the project and using the data purposively. It discusses the ways of usefully telling your project to others and establishing that your research has been rigorous and your conclusions deserve interest and respect.

Feedback Loops and Forward Planning

These ten chapters do not represent discrete, sequential stages of a project. Nor do the website materials fit neatly into them. This is because of two core characteristics of qualitative research.

Firstly, the techniques of qualitative research are not linear but looping. The researcher learns from the data, returning to revise or revisit steps taken before that understanding developed.

The non-linear nature of qualitative research is sometimes a problem to novices. The method is often described as 'cyclical', and the researcher can be pardoned for wondering how they can ever get anywhere other than where they started. Along the way, they discover that the feedback process is never cyclical; it always takes them somewhere else. But its uncertainty remains a challenge.

This book is designed to show that at each step, well-planned feedback loops drive the project forward rather than dragging it back. The looping of a project occurs throughout the book, from the discussion in Chapter 1 of the essential process of designing for feedback loops, to the use of them in Chapter 10 for validating the outcome in your final report. These journeys are illustrated in the diagrams that commence each chapter, maps of the book showing you where you are now, where you came from and where you can go next.

Secondly, the techniques of qualitative research work only if they are purposive, and can be highly dysfunctional if they become ends in themselves. You are urged to move around the book and follow leads to the website purposively, with your own goals in mind. Use the maps to see how the processes described draw on or feed into processes in other chapters. Jump forward where a process makes sense because it is preparatory for another technique to be discussed later, or back to check why you would want to be doing this. (Do you really need to code this data at this stage, for example? You may need to know how you can use coding in questioning and pattern discovery.)

However you get there, you are advised to read the whole book before you seriously commence making data in a 'real' project. The methods of qualitative research are many and often messy. You'll hear researchers bemoan the load of 'all that data' and the threat that 'it will never make sense'. You will also hear critics question whether there's a method in this madness. My aim in this book, and our aim in providing the website examples, is to show that qualitative researchers can make sense of disparate and challenging data, and justify their accounts, because they have flexible, adaptable but rigorous and trusted methods that work.

I
Setting up

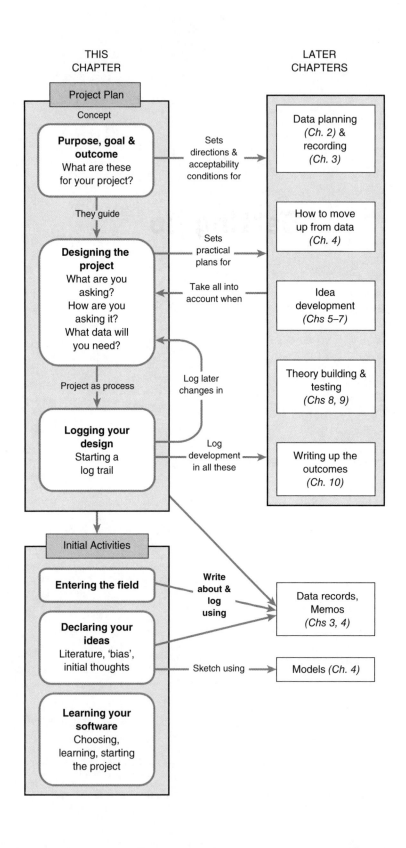

THIS CHAPTER

LATER CHAPTERS

Project Plan

Concept

Purpose, goal & outcome
What are these for your project?

They guide

Designing the project
What are you asking?
How are you asking it?
What data will you need?

Project as process

Logging your design
Starting a log trail

Sets directions & acceptability conditions for

Sets practical plans for

Take all into account when

Log later changes in

Log development in all these

Data planning (Ch. 2) & recording (Ch. 3)

How to move up from data (Ch. 4)

Idea development (Chs 5–7)

Theory building & testing (Chs 8, 9)

Writing up the outcomes (Ch. 10)

Initial Activities

Entering the field

Declaring your ideas
Literature, 'bias', initial thoughts

Learning your software
Choosing, learning, starting the project

Write about & log using

Sketch using

Data records, Memos (Chs 3, 4)

Models (Ch. 4)

ONE

Setting up your project

This chapter is about starting out sure-footed. It advises on ways of specifying what you are setting out to do, why, and how you will do it. It urges that in setting up you should be usefully reflecting on your research question, whether it requires qualitative research and the data needed to answer it well. How might you acquire such data and what are the ethical implications of doing this? These are all questions that should be asked before you start even planning to acquire data. It proposes as first steps clarifying your own relationship to the topic and the intended data, and declaring the assumptions you bring with you.

Starting can be the hardest part of any new task. In any social research project, putting off starting is easy because of the risks of starting unprepared. If you change your approach once you have entered the research field, you may not get a second attempt. This is particularly salient if you are intending to do a qualitative project, which is likely to be focusing closely on a fairly identifiable group of people. Moreover, there is a special challenge for the qualitative researcher; rarely can a project be specified in advance. If you are working qualitatively it's because you don't know what you will find. Even riskier than putting off starting is starting too soon, by making data without clear goals and procedures in mind. The risks are ethical and practical. Ethical risks are huge. If you have not reflected on what you wish to do and its impact on those involved, you may harm those you wish to study, impact their lives and damage your own reputation and chances of constructive research. And if you have not reflected on your relationship to the question, the people involved and the data, you may skew the study irreparably, and seriously damage those relationships. Practically, if you have not organized your project, considered the design, the data needed and the ways they will be handled, you will find yourself swamped by a flood of complex, contradictory accounts of experiences that are only partially relevant to your question.

So start by thinking first. The first stage is to *frame* your project – placing it in context, forming it, fitting the parts together, constructing them into a plausible, doable whole, so you can see it before you start. This opening stage of a project is undoubtedly the most under-emphasized and indeed often overlooked stage in qualitative work. Far too often, novice researchers just start, assuming the project will just happen, as they enter (or blunder into!) the research field. The practical and ethical challenges of beginning that way are massive, and projects can be doomed from the start if they are not framed at the start.

PLACING THE PROJECT IN CONTEXT

For most new researchers the early stages of proposing and starting a project are fraught by regulation. All these regulations have purposes. (Many are designed to rescue you and/or those you propose to study from your own lack of preparation, or from approaches that are unthinking or ill-informed), but they may appear as barriers to getting going, and are often resented. Treat those requirements as positive steps, helping you to do a thorough job of framing your project, reporting on its ethical implications and presenting a design.

The Literature as Context

For most research, a first essential step will be to find out what's already known, and what sorts of studies have been done, in the area. This comes early not just because a committee requires it before you get approval, but because your own project must be informed by other studies, your own question by the answers to others' questions and, importantly, your own research design by what has been done, what it offered, and especially, what's not yet known.

There is a substantial literature on doing a literature review! (See references at the end of this chapter, and, as for any topic, do a web search for new ones.) But novices often lack advice on how to approach it, and regrettably it's too often seen as a necessary chore, and a hurdle to get over before the study can commence. Resist that attitude! This is a precious chance to locate your project. Consider approaching the task this way:

- Literature reviewing is a qualitative data task. You are seeking to understand unstructured text documents, to distil the important themes in them, to come up with your own account of what they offer. So treat it as a starter project, exploring tools for coding and analysis.
- Literature reviewing (like qualitative research) is detective work – you are seeking the explanation of priorities, the story of how things are seen. Don't allow your review to become merely descriptive, a list of who said what when. Make it critical, incisive, new. Aim to say something surprising about what isn't known and how you could help. Aim to become the new authority in this field.
- Literature reviews, like qualitative projects, are ongoing. Don't get trapped into seeing your review as a once-off exercise prior to starting. Once you start, you'll see that paper you overlooked as

suddenly significant, you'll understand why other studies omitted this major issue, you'll need to seek out what's known in areas you didn't see as mattering.

- Literature reviewing is a task generously supported by a variety of computer tools (Paulus et al., 2014). Find bibliographic software, use web searches, chase discussion groups and blogs around important themes.

- If you are intending to use a qualitative software package, consider putting your literature review into a project in that package. It offers a safe container for your reflections and explorations. Seek out current papers or workshops on the use of your chosen qualitative software in this way. (Jump to Chapter 5 for discussion of coding. If you code the material in the literature, or your interpretative notes, you'll be starting a category system that will point to the things you will later look for in your own data.)

The Social Context

All social research occurs somewhere. Before you start, consider where you will place your project, both geographically and socially. Where will you need to go and do you have the resources to do this? If you can't physically go there, will online data suffice? And socially, will you be acceptable and accepted where you wish to go, and adequately informed about the context?

Is there a location that is accessible, practically, socially and (in both regards) ethically, for your purposes? Simply asking this question may cause you to reframe the project!

If on the other hand you already know where you are heading, because you are there, do some hard thinking about whether this is the best place. Researchers often propose a project where they are already – studying an issue or process in their place of work, or a community they belong to, a problem they face or an experience they share. These proposals may be admirable – you know a problem that needs to be solved or strongly feel for those dealing with an issue and want to help. They may also be practical – you are accepted in the area and known, people will talk with you, indeed have already offered to do so. But beware the assumption that the location is advantageous because you know the context! See Chapter 2 for more on the relationship of you to your data.

PURPOSE, GOAL AND OUTCOME

At the early stages of project proposal, it is easy to confuse the purpose of your project with its specific goals, and easy to leave out of consideration what sort of an outcome is required. These are three very different aspects of the 'results' you are aiming for. A first step towards design is to put yourself into the picture. What are your purposes, your goals and what outcome do you seek?

- **Purpose:** Why this study? Will it help ameliorate some societal problem? Will it inform the literature? Will it drive policy making and decision making? Is it more generally to add to our understanding of the social world? Or – be careful here – is its purpose to justify some action or back some proposal you are committed to? Clear answers are needed here, to set the context, to establish clearly where you stand, and to justify the enquiry, the intrusion on people's lives and the time and money it will involve. Here's a possible answer for an (imaginary) project.

Our purpose is to assist the health authority to improve child health delivery in the community.

- **Goal:** What question are you going to try to answer? What would be involved in answering it, and what shape do you think the answer might have? This is a different question from your purpose. (The purpose of a game may be winning, achieving team spirit or fitness. A goal can be kicked at.) Your purpose may in fact require multiple outcomes.

We are investigating for the health authority whether and how parents bypass health authority instructions for their children's health. We expect to provide an explanation of why some parents ignore advice, in terms of parental attitudes, ideologies and beliefs.

- **Outcome:** What sort of an outcome would achieve that purpose, and that goal? Are you producing a report for an action group or a client, a thesis for a supervisor or a string of papers for a journal or perhaps all three? What do these (possibly diverse) recipients expect, so how will you shape your results into reports, presentations, papers, etc.?

The health authority is concerned that there seem to be inefficiencies and poor targeting in this area of its health budget, and wants a brief report with a half-hour audio-visual presentation for senior planners on practicalities. The doctoral programme requires a dissertation, in an appropriate theoretical context. And you want to make a real contribution to what seems to you to be a most unsatisfactory literature in this area, so others may use your theories.

It is quite usual (though never required) that qualitative projects start without a firm and fixed *goal*. But research without a clear and honest statement of *purpose* is a major practical and ethical problem. And it is highly risky to start with no idea whatsoever about the sort of *outcomes* that would be satisfactory.

Thinking It Through

If you don't know the *purpose* of your project, ask seriously, why are you doing this? The question is an entirely practical one. (I don't mean 'How dare you do this?', though I have been tempted to say that to researchers using intrusive methods in highly sensitive areas when there is no apparently useful purpose.) Practically, you are less likely to succeed if you don't know why you are starting. You will need a purpose to drive your project, and it will need to be better than 'to get through this course'.

Now, do you have more specific goals? Is there something you want to answer? If so, is it answerable? Thinking through these questions will help you design the project.

Think Ethics

The ethical challenges come from the first conception of a project and appear until the final report – and often for some time after. From the framing of purpose and goal, get into the habit of constantly asking 'Is it ethical?'

In most research contexts, before you commence doing a project, you will have to gain what is usually termed approval or clearance from an ethics committee. This is not a mere irritation and the task of preparing an ethics report is not simply an obstacle to getting started. Rather, it's a necessary first step. Thinking about the ethical implications of your purpose, your goals and your intended outcomes should come first. It should also inform the entire project. Having your proposal approved gives you no clearance from concern about the ethical implications of situations that will arise in the future.

Qualitative researchers are far more likely to impact and impede people's lives than are researchers whose data are collected impersonally and recorded numerically. Their questions are more intimate, and their methods more intrusive. Training qualitative interviewers, I was always aware that I was teaching them how to get people to say things they would not normally say to a stranger.

And the outcomes of qualitative research are more likely to risk harm or exposure than are reports that are less personal, less contextualized and detailed, more easily anonymized. So qualitative researchers must start by thinking about the ethics of what they are proposing, design the project in that context and reflect on the ethical implications of everything they report and conclude. You will need constant awareness of the ethical challenges of asking this question, probing this way, for this purpose, and doing your best to report fully and vividly what you learn. That awareness will define for you the limitations to your enquiry, where you can't or shouldn't go and what you can't or shouldn't ask or report, as well as what you must achieve.

If these issues are new to you, pause to read detailed discussions that will alert you to risks for your own work. (See references at the end of the Chapter.)

Think Outcomes

Now, importantly, what do you intend and expect to offer as an outcome? Ideally:

- It should offer something more than the participants in your research could have reported. (Otherwise, you've wasted their time and yours.)
- It should present conclusions that account for your data in terms of the project's goals. This has to be an adequate account, so you will be able to claim that it 'makes sense' of what's going on in the data. (This is your overall duty as a researcher.)

It should also, if possible, be usable; you or others should be able to do something with the outcome. (Otherwise, why do the project? This is an ethical, not merely a practical, question.) You can't at this stage predict how the project outcome will in fact be used, but you can aim from the start to make it usable. If it is well informed by the literature, perhaps it will be used to improve existing approaches and theories, or to compare with other studies. If the scope of your study is sufficient, and the data sufficiently rich and well analysed, maybe it will find a practical use. But your study will be better and your motivation maintained, your demands on those you are studying more justifiable and your explanations to them more acceptable if you are intending to produce something usable.

It is very helpful at this earliest stage to write about the outcome you aim for. In many ways this will inform your design. The outcome wanted will indicate the scope of data needed for representing all the views on a problem; for example, you may need to seek data on contrasting types of cases (e.g. institutes of technical education as well as academic education). The desired outcome will also set requirements for the coding needed (Chapter 5) in order to ask the questions demanding answers (Chapter 8). *Is it only the working-class parents who bypass diet education programmes? How differently do working-class and middle-class parents see the relevance of these programmes?*

Just Checking: Is This Best Done as a Qualitative Project?

Isn't it a bit late to ask that? No, it's never too late. Indeed, it's worth asking throughout your project, whether each part of it requires the ways of making and handling data that this book is about.

In the Introduction, I defined qualitative *methods* as ways of studying people and their social worlds by going there, observing them closely, in their natural setting, and learning how they understand their situations and account for their behaviour. This is a challenging task. Qualitative research should never be regarded as the default, the best or the 'normal' way of finding out. It sounds 'normal' that if you want to know something, you should just go and ask, and then look in detail at what people tell you. But as I argued above, to do so is by far the most intrusive and ethically charged of social research approaches. And qualitative data are also the most time-consuming to acquire and challenging to analyse.

It's not too late to wonder if some or all of your project can be conducted by other means. Take a simple example: most interview projects require that the researcher records 'base data' like participants' age and where they were born. It's unlikely you need to record that in their own words, transcribe the dialogue and then code and analyse it. Why not save their time and yours by giving them a simple sheet of questions to fill in before or after you start the interview? This will be easier for them, and, importantly, less embarrassing, and save time and money for you. What will be lost are hesitations and thoughts that the questions trigger. Should you ensure these are caught by your method? Only if your question requires it. If this were a study of refugees or of people with memory loss, those questions would be the core ones for eliciting their accounts of their origins. But your study probably isn't.

So should it be qualitative? The first answer is 'It depends on what you are asking'. Research purpose may require qualitative method. A study of the experience of memory loss would require listening to the varied stories of those who have that condition, and seeking to understand their experience as they talk about what they feel and how they deal with it, the meanings they put on place and time and lost knowledge. Recording fixed answers to predetermined questions about what you see as significant life events would give little of that understanding. You don't just want to know where and when they were born, or even whether they know their date or place of birth; what matters is how they tell not knowing.

The purpose of your present study probably does not so clearly require a qualitative approach. Most don't. So think through your goals and your intended outcome. Suppose this is a study of health advice given to parents: the purpose is to assist the health authority to improve child health delivery, and the goal is to explain why some parents ignore advice. You could approach this by a survey. The health authority may indeed already have the data, from questionnaires given out to clients, about clients' regularity of attendance and their evaluation of advice. Better check if that data exists! Now, why have the authorities not had their answer from their own data? Maybe they just didn't have the time or skills to analyse it – this will be your first task. Perhaps it tells you and them two things – the unsurprising fact that non-attenders don't see available advice as useful, but also the more interesting result that those who most regularly attend are the least likely to tick 'very useful' in the evaluation box. Those survey results provided an outcome – you can now tell the authorities that just upping attendance won't solve the problem. (This will be your first report.) But is that the outcome you were seeking? Check out your statement of goals. *We are investigating for the health authority whether and how parents bypass health authority instructions for their children's health. We expect to provide an explanation of why some parents ignore advice, in terms of parental attitudes, ideologies and beliefs.* To provide this outcome would require you to listen to the parents' own accounts of how they see their children's health, indeed health in general, and their stories of their interactions with the health professionals. Right, you *now* need a qualitative approach.

So the more adequate answer to 'Should it be qualitative?' is yes, if the question requires it, the goals won't be met otherwise, and the outcome will need a qualitative analysis. I've taught hundreds of highly competent quantitative researchers who never intended a qualitative project, but were dragged to it by honest recognition that they could not meet their goals or provide the required outcome by other methods. (This is why qualitative research is now so widely used across epidemiology. If you really want to know why people aren't taking available life-preserving drugs or using the mosquito nets provided by aid organizations, you'd better ask them, and listen to how they see these aid offerings and their health risks.)

There is also a second answer – it should be qualitative if the data demand it. Researchers may happen on data not by design but by good luck or, more often, by the nature of the question. Perhaps you simply asked, 'How often do you attend the clinic?' but the answer took 20 minutes. For this distraught mother the question brought out all her fears about her child's declining health, her ignorance of health issues and her relationship with the child's father, who opposes interference by authorities. If you recorded her story, instead of merely ticking the box for 'less than once a month' (and yes, you should have done so!), you have data that require handling by the methods this book is about.

So, returning to your own project, it's good advice at this stage to revisit why you are proposing a qualitative project. There is nothing morally superior about qualitative work, and it is certainly neither easier nor quicker than quantitative research and certainly more ethically challenging. For many purposes, and to achieve many goals, the outcome required may be a strong conclusion backed by robust statistical analysis of a large sample. So ask early: why are you proposing a qualitative project, and should you? (For more on possible good and bad answers, see *Readme First*, Chapter 2.)

If the answer is yes, please take this seriously. You are making a commitment to designing and conducting a project that is adequate to the task, and then to doing justice to the data you will be creating, and to the experiences people will share with you. You are setting out deliberately to acquire understanding you don't yet have, and to construct a complex account of rich data that deserve rigorous analysis.

DESIGNING THE PROJECT

Setting up a qualitative project need not be daunting if it is designed. In qualitative research, you do not have to be able to specify everything the research task will involve. You are aiming to learn from the data, and this means that you may shift emphasis to a new question, or divert to interview other people who prove significant. So, qualitative enquiry is fluid and flexible. But starting well does require thinking about *where* you are starting and why, and where you, the 'researcher', stand in this scheme.

Setting up a project is a process of getting ready, not a commitment to a conclusion. Qualitative researchers, like surgeons and chefs, set up carefully to be ready for whatever reasonably may be expected. Like the surgeon or chef, you should be able to describe what you aim to do, to say what it is likely to involve and what the expected outcome will be. You should specify how you will go about doing it competently, and be ready with the tools you may need, though you normally will not assume that you can see at this stage exactly how the project will end.

Design is essential for qualitative research. Very often, novices are given the contrary message that qualitative research can start, even finish, without being designed. But this is unacceptable, for ethical and practical reasons. When projects 'just happen', the researchers will rarely have adequately considered the impacts on those they are studying, and the data will rarely offer an adequate answer to the research question.

If you are planning to work with qualitative method, it is probably because you are trying to learn something new, rather than test something that is known.

This may require studying people's accounts, or your observations, of their some-times private thoughts and behaviour. Could you not answer your question with more publicly available data, such as the analysis of documents? Are you han-dling the situation sensitively and the data respectfully? An ethics committee will demand answers to such questions in most research situations. But if they don't, you should.

Practically, you can't start without thinking through where you want to go and what data you will need. Ethically, you must not start without considering the implications of your intentions and proposals for those you intend to talk with and propose to report on.

This early design need not be fixed or rigid. Qualitative designs can and usually should be revisited and reconsidered at each stage of the project, considering what has been done and why, revisiting methods if they prove intrusive or harmful, building on what you are learning, working out what you are asking and what sort of data will be necessary to answer that question. But you need to start with a plan.

This should not be a secret plan! Tell it to everyone who will listen – and listen to their responses. If appropriate, talk it out with the people involved – not just those who are funding the research or expecting a report, but those who will, with you, be creating the data. Think ahead, to when you will be telling the project to an audience: who are you trying to convince, and how would they be convinced? What would you need to apologize for? Adjust the design to cover these risks. In scoping your project and designing the data records, design for a sufficiently broad base to ensure that you would know if you had arrived at a partial picture.

This should also be an honest, open plan. You will not be helped by dodg-ing problems or avoiding discussion of obstacles to entry into the field, or your own uncertain acquisition of skills. With increasing surveillance by research ethics committees, researchers are tempted to evade issues of known or feared challenges and puzzles in what they propose. Better to face these now than meet them when your data are distorted or inadequate.

If you are working in a team, present the ethical challenges, and then each stage of design, for debate. Draw it or write it up, and discuss it with as many colleagues as possible.

The Core Design Questions

The discussion below offers a minimal checklist of things to answer in order to set up the design of your project. Many aspects of your project cannot be designed 'up front', but the following three questions must at least be asked:

(Continued)

(Continued)

1. What are you asking?
2. How would it best be asked?
3. What data will you need to provide a good answer?

Then, always ask, of the answer to each of the above questions: is it ethical?

Each of these questions will be revisited many times during the project.

What Are You Asking?

This is no simple question. Many researchers fail to define what they are asking because they propose the project only at one level, either a very general interest or a very specific topic. Try to embrace both. To do this well, you need to work like an eagle, soaring over the landscape, locating something small that can be captured, diving in to take it and then making sure it's not dropped!

Getting to the Goals

It is often hard to get your grip on something ask-able. If you have this problem, work down through funnelling questions:

1. What is your broad research area?
2. Within that area, what questions in the literature, or the society, are still being asked? What gaps in knowledge can you identify?
3. Within that focus, what is your topic?
4. And within that topic, what is the question being asked?
5. Within that general question, what researchable question could *you* attempt to answer - given your resources and skills?
6. And now consider the relation between you and that question: socially, ethically and practically where do you stand?

Note that these questions are at different levels, and they take you right down into the project. If you are new to this process of refining what you are asking, talk it out, diving down from a broad interest to a specific question that you can research.

In a team project it is especially important to work through these layers of questions, so there is clear understanding of purpose or purposes. Don't try to impose agreement on the same researchable question for everyone. The members of a multidisciplinary or mixed skills team will of course have different questions, and the design may represent these. But if there are differences, they do need to be discussed. If some colleagues really don't know what you are asking, or worse don't think it's worth asking and suspect that your work is subverting theirs, the team will be in trouble.

Working with the questions above, the design will expand.

Down to the Researchable Question

1. Ask: where are you working, and what are you interested in? *Young people's health.*
2. What are the interesting or important questions of that area? What questions are being asked? What others should be? What questions do the practitioners want asked? *We're pouring resources into health programmes, but does anyone know if they are completely wasted? It seems that at least some of the parents bypass them.*
3. Next, what do you want to know? Locate a topic. *Influencing parent perceptions and control over children's diet.* Why do you want to know about this? *Anecdotal evidence suggests this might make programmes more effective.*
4. Now, in discussion with colleagues, or using reading, arrive at a *research question* that needs to be answered. *Why are diet education programmes for parents so varied in effectiveness?* Spend some time checking that it doesn't have an answer yet. (Review literature, search websites, talk about it.) Wonder whether it's worth answering, worth the time and effort and the contributions you are going to be requiring from participants.
5. Now, is it a question *you* are *able* to answer? This is what I call a *researchable* question. Focus on questions that can be asked and answered by you with the resources available to you. *How do parents perceive health programmes, in this town, and how do they portray them to their children?* What sort of a researcher and resources are needed to answer this? Are you that sort of researcher? And are there any ethical as well as practical issues that would stop you doing it well?
6. Where do you stand in relation to this question? Design is particularly important where the researcher is studying a situation they belong to. *You are the health promotion officer whose task is to promote healthy programmes in schools. On your home ground, already accepted as a visitor in the schools, it would seem that your project is already half-completed! Everyone will talk to you; observation is already underway.* Beware! The very ease of making data is a warning of the need for design. Ask in particular: Will your question be adequately answered by interviews conducted by an insider? *What sort of data will result from a health promotion officer talking to parents whose work patterns do not permit supervision of children at home?*

You are ready to proceed with a very careful research design.

How Are You Asking It?

If you haven't done so already, you need to locate your project methodologically.

Studies conducted in an academic context are expected to be appropriately located in one of a variety of qualitative methodologies; that is, ways of reflecting on and studying situations and seeking and interpreting our understanding of social phenomena. There is a substantial literature on each of many qualitative methods and each has its own way of approaching a question, each seeks a specific sort of data, and each carries an armoury of techniques for analysis. An ethnographic study, for example, will ask very different sorts of questions, in very different ways, from a phenomenological study, and of course they will then analyse the data differently and present quite different outcomes. But importantly, in each case, the question, the sort of data, the way of analysing and the outcome will fit together. A strong methodology is coherent. It frames, provides the context for a study, guiding you to the appropriate ways of addressing your question.

Comparison of specific methods is not a task for this book. For a detailed account of what different methods offer, and the ways each provides a fit of question, data and mode of analysis, see *Readme First*.

In an academic context, you need a confident choice of a method that will give you the appropriate fit between question, data and analysis. Locating your project in such a method is a major first step. Think of the method, then, as a vehicle that will carry your study forward in the direction needed to answer the research question well. If, however, you are one of the high proportion of qualitative researchers working outside the methodological literature, can you avoid locating your project in a method? Many researchers see this as irrelevant – they are simply required, by their funders, their supervisors or their own motivation, to get the best possible understanding of a situation, a group or a problem. But if this is your situation, you still need a clear idea of how you will drive this project. *How* are you asking your research question? Is that the appropriate way of asking it and what different results would you gain by asking in other ways? Which combination of data, from which methods of enquiry, will allow you to answer it well? And how will you work with that data?

So whatever your context, and whatever you call it, your study needs a method, and one which offers a *fit* between the question being asked, the sort of data needed to answer, the techniques being used to make and analyse the data, and the outcome you are seeking.

If you use focus groups conducted with the parents, what will you learn and what questions might you answer with such data? How different would your study be if based on a year's work in the district as a health visitor?

The ten projects on the website offer a wide range of research methods, and each method selected is appropriate to the question being asked. For each project, there is a page on setting up. Skim these now to get a feel for the examples provided, and the variety of research designs represented.

——— Finding a Fit Between Question, Data and Method ———

1. How are you asking your question? Is that the only way of asking it and what different results would you gain by asking it in other ways?
2. Read about different qualitative methods, and learn to discriminate between them. Then carefully select the one that fits your study.
3. Reflecting on these differences, and on your own skills, design your own project to gain the sort of understanding its question needs.

Team projects have a special requirement here: if the team already exists, the design should, if possible, consider and plan to use the distribution of members' skills and experience.

4. Whatever the context, keep asking how the project's question and approach will shape the data. Ask often: might there be other ways of doing this, with what likely outcomes? And always ask: is the question pushing me to seeking data in ways that are ethically questionable?

If you are aware that you are asking your question one way, and that other ways would provide different answers, you will be better prepared to organize and interpret your data. This is particularly important if the data you are handling were created or acquired by someone else. Researchers brought into an ongoing project or relegated to a lowly assistant role can acquire data without participating in design. If that's your situation, it is especially important to understand why (and by whom) you have been provided with (only) *these* records of *these* research events or processes.

The literature on qualitative methodologies may seem to have little relevance to large research projects designed to combine qualitative with quantitative data. Rich accounts from field research are very unlike open-ended responses to a survey with large numbers of respondents. But the study still requires a fit of question, data and method. If your intention is to handle the open-ended responses as qualitative data, reflect on the question to be answered, the ways these responses are being elicited and the context required to interpret them well. In such projects, design may be necessarily rigid. The requirement for consistency in a survey, for example, will mean that the researcher will be unable to return to redesign questions. So it is especially important to design and test questions that seek the needed balance of information, from the start.

What Data Will You Need to Provide a Good Answer?

The next questions for research design are about data, and there are always three different sorts of questions. Two are fairly obvious. Firstly, what data are needed to cover your topic area adequately, and secondly, what are the types of data needed to answer your question? Then comes a question that is huge: what is your relationship with this body of 'data'?

In designing data for qualitative research, it helps to think in terms of how well the data will reach across the topic. You will want to be sure that the data have adequate *scope*, rather than that they representatively *sample* a given universe.

And then you need to ask about the *sorts* of data needed to do justice to this topic. This is a different question from 'What data will I need to test this theory?' You are seeking data that will allow you to ask a question, maybe challenge your assumptions, and arrive at a new understanding.

Designing Your Data

1. What is the scope of this project? What variety and scale of data are required by your question?

   o What are all the settings that you need to explore? Qualitative research is rarely restricted to only one.
   o Within the selected setting(s), what types of cases (for example, of people, institutions or places) do you need represented? (And what won't be needed?)
   o If your question contains comparison, or linking of qualitative and quantitative data, pay particular attention to the data scope and the types of cases you seek.

   As you scope the project, sternly ask the relevance and usefulness of each area of data you consider seeking.

2. What is the *nature* of the data required? The next chapters discuss the nature of qualitative data created by different techniques of enquiry. At this stage, you need to address in the most general terms the representations you will be seeking of the situation studied:

   o What *sorts* of data are needed? Does your chosen method require, for example, that you record the words people use to tell their perceptions of their worlds, or that you record your own observations of their behaviour? (Again, what won't be required?)
   o Return to your literature review. What sort of data have other studies used, and can you see ways that those studies were limited by their data? Design to do better!
   o Take particular care that your design attends to ethical considerations. If the question doesn't need intimate accounts of people's experiences, to seek these is inappropriate.

How much data? Noticeably absent from the answers above is 'the sample should be big enough'. That's because size of data records is never, alone, a relevant criterion for a good outcome. Numbers of cases needed for a comparative study may be decided in advance, or numbers of interviews set for a survey. But completion of a qualitative project ideally happens when the question is answered, and projects evolve as researchers come to understand their data and need to ask new questions. Nevertheless you are very likely to be working within a time and money budget, so you have to come up with a satisfactory answer at this design stage.

Perhaps the most common question from novice qualitative researchers is, 'How many [interviews, cases, visits, etc.] should I do?' There is only one situation in which a firm number can be given – when the research question or commission specifies a given number of cases. (And then you will still not know how many times you will need to interview these people.) Otherwise, the only safe answer is, 'I'll know when I have the data needed to answer my research question and all subsequent pertinent questions arising from the data'. You may be required by research grants bodies or committees more familiar with quantitative research to specify in advance a number of visits or interviews. Of course you must do so if required, but it is advisable to explain that the method requires that you revisit your design during the project once informed by the early analysis. Always design a stage of data expansion within the project. Useful in explaining this requirement is the term 'theoretical sampling', which refers to later sampling directed by the discoveries and concepts developed (there is more on this process in Chapter 7). The term, used in grounded theory projects, is now recognized outside that context as a label for this reviewing and revisiting process.

Too much data? Well-designed qualitative research projects are usually small, the data detailed and the techniques designed to discover meaning through fine attention to content of texts or images. These techniques take time and do not need large samples. To confront even a little of such data is challenging. Most researchers go through a period where they feel they have too much data, often very early in a project when they have hardly started. But from there, if the project was designed to make the data which the question needed, they go on to learn to handle those data skilfully and assess accurately how much is needed. There is of course no simple numerical answer to 'how much is too much?' It depends, as has been argued above, on your question. But a qualitative project will normally have relatively few data records, certainly not many hundreds.

In some situations the researcher has little control over the volume of data, or there is a very good reason for there being very large quantities of data. It is no help to these researchers to tell them they should not be in this situation. No qualitative technique assumes projects with bulk data and many simply won't work if they are applied to very large numbers of cases or volumes of text. But some techniques can be adapted to use by the researcher across a bigger project or by carefully partitioning it. Such advice is provided where appropriate throughout the following chapters.

A variety of data? A note on triangulation It is common for qualitative project design to include the use of multiple sources of data or 'views', with the aim of bringing many perspectives to bear on the question.

'Triangulation' is a term widely used for such designs, the most common form being combinations of qualitative and quantitative data. Designing a project to address the same question with a variety of data is challenging. Simply juxtaposing different data sources or types is unlikely to provide comparable data. Such a design must ensure that the same question will be addressed by each of the types of data or approaches. So very careful planning is required for 'triangulation' that is useful. If you are considering such a design, the different sub-projects must be very carefully scoped, and the focus of the data carefully planned. (See suggested readings at the end of this chapter.) And the outcomes of even a well-planned 'triangulated' project require very careful interpretation. If you are proposing this design as a means of confirming or validating your findings, jump now to the discussion of ways of establishing validity of results in Chapter 7.

YOU AND YOUR DATA

Now, return to the big question about your project and data: what is your relationship to this stuff you are calling 'data'?

Whose World Are You Studying?

This enters an area of textbook discussion that often is the main barrier to researchers starting out. There is an ongoing debate about the philosophical basis for qualitative research – in philosophical terms about ontology (what's real) and epistemology (what we know and think we know about it).

The debate is centuries old, but the forms it has taken in social studies in recent decades are new. In the 1980s these issues became dominant in social science academic discourse with often hostile dichotomies claimed. Researchers working with assumptions that social life could be studied by fact-gathering methods were labelled 'positivist' and 'empiricist'. These labels were attached to any quantitative approach and associated with biological and physical sciences. If you are researching in an academic context, you will need to locate your work in these debates. But they also matter if you are researching outside academia, because these issues are the context of your research.

At its simplest, the justification for working qualitatively is that many, perhaps most, social behaviour can't be understood by collecting apparently 'real' facts like date of birth. The census can tell us (if people accurately reported) how many babies were born in each year. But if we wish to understand why the birth rate is falling, we need to know about a different sort of 'reality'; how people see the society they live in, what having children means to them, their perception of their future and their present priorities. This is a socially constructed reality, created collaboratively with others as we live out our lives. And it is that understood version of the social world that will help us understand behaviour.

There is an obvious methodological message in this. If we are trying to understand people's socially constructed understanding of their worlds, we can't know in advance what to ask – or what to expect. We need methods that will access their accounts of their lives, in their words, not ours. And we need to analyse this data using methods that take us *up* from the broad, messy picture to seek linkages, patterns, theories or explanations that make sense of all that variety. This sort of 'bottom-up' research, typical of qualitative work, is termed 'inductive' and is usually contrasted with 'deductive' reasoning, where the researcher starts 'top down' with a theory and tests it on data collected for that purpose.

But pause before you declare your opposition to 'empiricist' research. There will usually be several sorts of data relevant for any social study and any qualitative study will need to seek 'facts' like the attendance at the clinic or birth of the child. When social researchers are tackling topics rather than academic debates, they usually work with many sorts of data. (So, too, by the way, do researchers in biological and physical sciences, who are often greatly puzzled by the hostile dichotomies that social researchers debate!) There are not two types of people, those who are qualitative researchers and those who are not. All good researchers can create data records and analyse them by a range of methods, as appropriate. But all good researchers are also aware of the nature of the reality that they are trying to explore.

It follows that good qualitative researchers are also uncomfortably aware that they are not external to that reality, but part of it.

Where Are You in That Study?

Qualitative researchers find it hard to avoid that question. This is because the data you work with are collaboratively constructed by you and those you are studying. If you are working qualitatively, it is usually because you are seeking understanding of people's situation via their own accounts of their perceptions. These are not normally provided as neat heaps of facts, easily collected and summarized. You attempt to enter the world of those you study (and they more or less allow you to); you watch, ask and listen; they give you one of *many possible accounts* of their experience; you interpret, select and record. You are hardly an innocent bystander in this process of data making.

In many research approaches and reports, this complicated collaborative relationship of researcher and researched is simply not recognized. The methodological approach may not direct attention to the ways we as researchers construct data. Or the relation may seem very clear and be presented as uncomplicated – as when the researcher is handling data created and archived by someone else. But it is important to reflect on the ways in which you enter and affect a situation, and create and use 'data' from that situation. This is so even (perhaps especially) if your relation to your data seems unproblematic.

How to do this? You will find in the next chapter discussion of how you can handle the relationship between you and your data *as* data. Reflecting on this relationship and analysing it is a process that carries the term *reflexivity*, a theme throughout later chapters.

In this context, you can get an early feel for the varieties of projects reported on the 'Methods in Practice' part of the website. For one researcher, himself 'inside' his study of **Inside Companionship**, the research was understood in the context of reflections on the construction of data. Two other ethnographic studies offer accounts of challenges in entering the research field as participant: **Elderly Survivors of the Hanshin Earthquake** and **Youth Offender Program Evaluation**. Compare with projects where the challenges described are those of locating and then being accepted by people to be interviewed: **Mapping Caregiving**, the **Sexuality-Spirituality** project, **Handling Sexual Attraction** and **Wedding Work**. By contrast, the project on **Leading Improvement in Primary Care Practices** was hosted via recognized research channels *and* two projects handled data provided from earlier projects (**REMS** and **Harassment Complaints**).

Designing for Feedback

Are you planning to take your interpretation 'back' to the 'respondents'? This is often a very useful, pleasant and helpful act (so long as that interpretation is not damaging to them and is understandable to laypersons). But note how those terms carry assumptions about data making. Building into your design that 'their' response will be sought for 'validation' of your interpretation is highly problematic.

It may be very important to your purpose (or even required by clients or funders) that those you are studying will be consulted prior to publishing your report, especially when they are also recipients of the outcome of your research. It can be hugely exciting to have enthusiastic feedback. But feedback must be considered as more data, and handled, like all your data, as a collaborative construct. You and 'they' are together making an account of something. So the consultation process takes time and is never uncomplicated. As you plan the stages of your project, plan in any feedback process. Beware of planning for final-moment respondent consultation!

Where the analysis is not addressing a 'lay' audience, for example where the purpose is to inform a theoretical debate, it may still be important to explain to participants what you are doing with their words, but you will be unlikely to seek feedback from them on your analysis.

Different methods use different terms for the feedback process, the most common being 'respondent validation' and 'member checking'. Both those terms warn of issues you must consider if feedback is part of your design. Can (any) respondent *validate* your analysis? Won't they just see another reality? And does it make sense to *check* with a member of your sample what you, as researcher, are seeing? Some of these issues are related to those raised by 'triangulation', discussed above: these are reviewed in Chapter 7.

Declaring the Ideas You Are Taking in

You may have been told that qualitative researchers start with empty minds, no prior theories or concepts. If so, perhaps you wondered what to do with the ideas buzzing in your head about your topic. Now is the time to deal with them.

Start by reflecting on 'bias'. Qualitative researchers recently avoid this term, since it has been given very specific meanings and warnings in the context of quantitative sampling and error estimation. But 'bias' is one of many good English words whose usual, dictionary meanings were distorted by their use in quantitative research. The noun means a diagonal line or stretch across woven cloth. Cut or hung on bias, the cloth will be slanting. A badly cut garment will hang awkwardly, pulled by an unrecognized bias. But *haute couture* uses skilful bias-cut all the time, to achieve a perfect drape. All cloth has bias – you can either control for it by cutting straight, or you can use it well, by careful design. Similarly, all social research has bias, because researchers always take in assumptions and experience. So bias is there in all social research (qualitative or quantitative).The task is to use it honestly and intelligently, as you craft the account of your data.

> Your concern is with the bad nutrition of the poorer kids, and your anger is about the inability of health education to help them. Low-education parents just don't seem to care about healthy diet. If you have that concern, and a hypothesis about cause is hidden there, take it out and examine it. Now, build into your project genuine enquiry into the knot of factors that link education and eating. The study will be different, biased to examining those factors, but it will be stronger for your concerns and for your directly addressing them.

The goal of most qualitative research is to learn from the data. But researchers don't have empty minds, and are likely to have strong values and commitment to their topic. So good research design will always take into account what's known already, and will build into the design the ways this knowledge can and will be used and tested.

Think of the first stage of this process as declaring what is in your baggage, as you do on arrival at an international airport. If you don't declare it, you will take in, surreptitiously, assumptions or expectations that will colour what you see and how you see it. Throughout the research, aim to maximize the usefulness, and ensure the testing, of those ideas.

Declaring Your Ideas

The most constructive way of separating out your prior knowledge and preconceptions is to document them.

- Return now to your literature review. If no review is required by your research context, set yourself the task of assessing the different approaches in books, media, professional groups, etc., to the situation you want to study. Carefully and critically account for the different interpretations of this phenomenon. Why did some writers see a particular aspect? Why were some questions not asked? And where are you in that picture?
- Write a very honest and personal paper about what you *expect* to find when you go to study this situation. How do you expect to *feel* about what you learn? What do you think will be the important factors in the answer to your research question? Revisit that paper during the project.
- After your first 'entry' to the field, the first contacts or first interviews, write out your experiences in detail. Assess your effect on the situation.
- Make a first collection of *ideas about* the topic, listing the categories that have been used in others' accounts, the concepts that seem to matter, and the ideas and hunches you yourself are bringing in.
- *Draw a model* - simply a sketch on paper - of what you think, at this stage, are the main issues or factors involved in your study, and how you think they relate to each other and to the questions you are asking. Keep that model to revisit and develop as the project proceeds. As you get started in software, you might develop the model on computer, linked to your data (more on modelling in Chapter 9).

None of these activities is intended to 'cleanse' your mind of preconceptions, or remove bias. By doing them, you have acknowledged the ideas you bring into this study and set yourself the task of using and testing them. Your method may require you to 'bracket' these prior ideas, and approach the research data not with an empty mind but with a deliberately open one. Or you may set out explicitly to design a project that will address them. But you won't sneak them in.

With this documentation, you have produced data records. Your experience and your views are data, to be explored, reviewed and analysed as the project proceeds. You will find in the next chapters discussion of how to keep these records of your ideas alongside what is more traditionally regarded as the project's data – records you make of your enquiry into other people's ideas and perceptions.

You've started!

To Do

Getting started requires many steps, and these may of course be taken separately over some time. But each of these four major tasks is required for you to move on.

1. The ten projects on the website offer a wide range of research methods selected by the researcher as appropriate to the question being asked. For each project there is a page on setting up. Read one project's story and consider how it would have progressed had a different method been chosen.
2. Outline a literature review for your topic. What is it asking, what literature needs to be explored, what issues will you be raising, what conclusions do you seek?
3. Design your own project, following the steps in this chapter:

   (a) What are your purpose, your goal and your intended outcome?
   (b) What is your researchable question? Follow, and document, the steps:

      o What is your broad research area?
      o Within that area, what is your topic?
      o And within that topic, what is the question being asked?
      o What *researchable* question could you attempt to answer – given your resources and skills?
      o How does it contribute, fill a gap or address a problem?

   (c) *How* are you asking it?

      o Are there several ways it could have been asked?
      o Which have you chosen and why?

   (d) What data will you need to provide a good answer?

      o What is the *scope* of this project?
      o What is the *nature* of the data required? What *sorts* of data are needed?

4. Declare the ideas you are taking in, in a three-part report containing the following:

      o a very brief summary of the *usable* ideas and explanations you found in the literature on your topic area;
      o a very honest account of the values and expectations you are personally taking into your project – 'Me and my topic';
      o a model of what you expect to be finding.

Suggestions for Further Reading

For issues of methodological fit, a sketch map of the choices of methodologies and detail on research design, and the complex issues of ethics in qualitative research, see *Readme First* (Richards and Morse, 2013) Part 1 and Chapter 11. If your work is not already located within the literature of a method, and even if you think this is not necessary in your context, go there for an understanding of the range of methods available and how you can design your project

(Continued)

(Continued)

so question, data and methods fit, and for literature specific to a method. For other recent texts introducing different approaches, see Cresswell (2013), Punch (2014) Chapter 2, Silverman (2011), and Kuckartz (2014).

On ethics in qualitative research, there is now a considerable literature. Start with Chapter 3 of Lichtman (2014). For a range of feminist perspectives on ethics, see Miller and Birch (eds) (2012). On the special ethical issues involved with online data and computer projects, see Paulus et al. (2014).

For advice on literature reviewing, there are chapters in several recent texts, for example Lichtman (2014), and many books, for example Machi and McEvoy (2012) and Ridley (2012).

On qualitative research design, there are several focused texts (see especially Creswell, 2013; Maxwell, 2013; Marshall and Rossman, 1999) and most of the general texts and collections have chapters (for example, Flick, 2014; Lincoln and Guba, 1985; Mason, 2002). Seek reading on design in your discipline or research area, as the criteria for good design vary: for example, in nursing, Morse (1994), in evaluation, Patton (1997), in education, Le Compte et al. (1992). For specific advice on research design for using qualitative software, see Di Gregorio and Davidson (2008) and Bazeley (2013).

FIRST
CHAPTER

THIS
CHAPTER

LATER
CHAPTERS

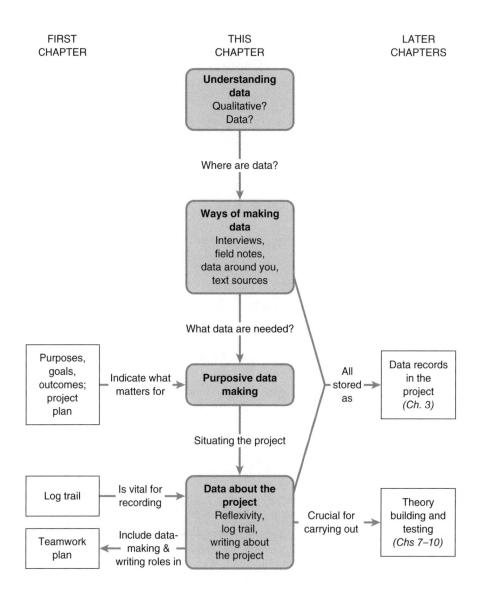

TWO
Making qualitative data

This is a chapter about data: what constitutes data and qualitative data (and when these are useful data). It starts with the assertion that qualitative data are collaboratively *made* by researcher and 'researched' and explains the nature of the data. It offers guidelines to make data in several ways from research events and from reflections about your part in data construction. It suggests ways of preparing to make data, thinking about the ways that data are made interactively, by the researcher and the researched. And it tackles the first tasks of entering the research field, recording what happens and handling that data, including keeping a log trail of your research process that will support your claims for your analysis.

Making qualitative data is ridiculously easy. The challenge is not so much making data but rather making useful, valuable data, relevant to the question being asked, and reflecting usefully on the process of research.

Possibly nobody warned you how easy it is to acquire qualitative data – this is much easier than gathering numerical data. Observation and communication in almost any research (or life) situation will provide huge quantities of information. We turn the information into 'data' when we record it and try to make sense of it. Sometimes, the records precede our enquiry, in memoirs, governmental or journalistic reports, diaries, minutes or letters. This material becomes relevant data, evidence for our arguments, when its relationship to a research question is established. The challenge, then, is to make the data necessary and appropriate to the task of answering the research question. The test is to handle these data well.

The flip-side of how easy it is to make qualitative data is that it is very challenging to design a project in such a way that you make or acquire only the data needed, and handle well what you create. What's required is a body of data from which you can derive an adequate answer to your research question, one sufficiently rich to provide a new understanding of the situation being studied.

This book is not about why you made the data, but about how to make and handle good data, and good reflections on your data.

In all these tasks, I find it helpful to talk about 'making' rather than 'collecting' qualitative data. This is because, as I argued in the Introduction, the data required for a qualitative study are created, usually in conversation, from the complex and contexted accounts people give to the researcher to explain how they see the world. Such data were not there before the research happened, but rather are collaboratively made by you and those you are studying, in interaction. If somebody else did that interview, it would be different.

We return now to a discussion started in the previous chapter – the relation of you and your data. This is your project, and these data are made by you, in a very important sense. They would be different if they were somebody else's. Qualitative research is about *agency*. It helps not to think in terms of collecting data, as though bits of data were lying around waiting for you to sweep them up. Rather, face up to the ways you will make data, in interaction with those you wish to study, and then work with data as you attempt to create accounts and theories from the data that satisfy.

> The data of the cultural student are always 'somebody's', never 'nobody's' data.
>
> (Znaniecki, 1968: 37)

UNDERSTANDING DATA

What are qualitative data like? And when are they good enough?

Neither 'data' nor 'qualitative' is easily (or often) defined. Most texts use the term 'data' as though we all know what data would look like if we had any. Even texts that carefully define other parts of the research process assume we know what *data* are like, and worry only about the terms for a study's end products – theories, models and so on.

It is a short step from the assumption that you would know data if you met them to the assumption that you know what the researcher should do if they did meet or make data. Not knowing what material will make useful data can leave a novice researcher frozen at the start of a study. So this chapter begins there.

Data?

'Data' are the 'stuff' you work with, the records of what you are studying. The researcher identifies events or accounts as data by selecting and using them as evidence in an analysis. *Perhaps you attended a community action group meeting, talked with your neighbour about development issues or photographed a protest rally*. Any of these acts could be performed by any resident, or indeed a passer-by. By recording your observations, the text of the 'interview' or the photographs, and selecting what you record, you made data about those events. Those recorded materials are then available for analysis. Note that already you have put your own shape on the data, since your record is selective. Other aspects of the events are not available, since they were not recorded or reflected on. *You left the meeting before the AGM, since you're not a member. And you had moved on from the rally before the police arrived and scuffles ensued.*

You make something data for your study by focusing on the event or process, recording it or selecting the record to be used, and considering its meanings. This is so in all research, not only qualitative studies. All researchers select what they will treat as data. You are part, in other words, of the process by which information became data – more on this below.

What you treat as data can be very broad. In the previous chapter, it was noted that your literature review is a process of data collection and interpretation. For many projects data may reach far beyond a filing cabinet or a project boxed in qualitative software, to web pages, records in the 'cloud' or ongoing online discussions.

The critical question for any research design is 'What do I need to know in order to answer *this* question?' As you start making data, you will find yourself asking, 'What do I need to hold onto?' If the question requires complexity, I need to hold onto everything that was said – not merely what I scribbled on my notepad – so perhaps I should record. *I need to know not only the participant's account of the community but also how others see her, so I possibly should use participant observation.* But not all questions need complex answers and an understanding of context. So you need also to be asking, 'What aspects of this research event do I need to know, and in how much detail?'

> The reason for protest action wasn't clear, so you talk with participants. The stories you are given are completely inconsistent, even to the detail of what was being protested about. You set up an informal discussion group on these topics.

Selection is always necessary, and by selecting, you impose your interpretation. Making data is thus highly purposive. Any fool with an audio recorder can record what people say about something. But a skilled interviewer makes data *relevant* for the *purposes* of the project. And those purposes will change during the project, as you learn more about what you don't know.

Such flexibility is normally not available to the researcher with large databases. If your data come from the 'write-ins' to a survey, the question asked can't be changed once the survey has commenced. This makes the design of open-ended questions in such projects an up-front requirement. Useful and readable data will be more likely if you ensure that the questions are well-worded and the space adequate for the answers expected.

Qualitative?

Qualitative data are usually messy and fluid records. To pick up my definitions proposed in the Introduction, *qualitative data are records of observation or interaction that are complex and contexted, and they are not easily reduced immediately (or, sometimes, ever) to numbers.*

If you are working qualitatively, it is usually because the question being asked does not clearly indicate what data you need to answer it. This does not mean you don't know what you are doing, rather that you are adopting a flexible approach to a situation to be understood. The situation is likely to be *complex*, and the complexity of the record cannot be reduced until you know if you will lose valuable information because it was simplified. The situation has to be understood in its *context*, so the record must retain that context. Otherwise, you risk losing understanding. Ideally, your data will need to be as rich and complex as is necessary for you to build a new and good understanding of the situation studied. It may be quite hard to predict in advance what data are needed. The researcher with a fixed design, perhaps testing a hypothesis, has a simpler data-gathering task. The prior work to specify the tests has been done, so the researcher can set out to make only the data required by their fixed question. Unexpected results will and should constitute further data to them; indeed many of the greatest scientific discoveries relied on such unanticipated, even unwelcome, data. But it is much easier in a fixed-design study to predict what data are needed and how they should be made.

The researcher in a qualitative project often starts by treating everything around a topic as potentially data. Early on, when it's unclear what will matter, the selection of what will be recorded is very reflective and is typically very generous. This is especially important where only a single mode of formally making data has been selected. For instance, if you have set out to do a study based on interviews, don't assume that there is no data till you do your first interview. Instead, treat the early familiarization as data making, informing the questions you will ask, and providing supplementary context data. And ask yourself what further data would be provided if, as you interview, you also record observations. *You are intending to conduct group discussions outside the formal meetings of the community action group, but have difficulty finding participants willing to talk to an 'outsider'. Do those conversations about your request themselves offer further data?* To turn these experiences into data is easy: you need only to record them and reflect on them.

 Compare the varieties of data used in the website projects. Some recorded more than one sort of data; for example, interviews provided the opportunity to record observations as well as maps in **Mapping Caregiving**.

Thus qualitative data expand, and quickly! The records of research events grow in unpredictable ways, as new sources of data present themselves. They are also often not at all neat. Qualitative data records can be highly varied in origin and style, uneven in detail and unalike in source and reliability. This does not mean that neat data will never provide for good analysis. But if your data are neat, do some hard thinking about whether they will adequately answer your question. A researcher seeking to learn from the data, rather than test a theory already arrived at, will usually be helped by having more than one way of looking at what is being studied. (The term used sometimes for systematic comparisons of different ways of looking is triangulation. More on this technique in Chapter 7.)

Furthermore, a qualitative researcher normally generates still more data by reflecting on the data records. Memos, annotations, background material and reflective essays will happen throughout a project. *You write a memo, reflecting on the term 'outsider' and what it means to be 'inside' an apparently open, democratic group.*

These too are data, since the researcher is themself an active part of the situation being studied. So the data expand further as reflections occur. In almost all contexts it will be important to be able to access and assess memos separately from what is sometimes called the 'original' data: those deriving from the research participants. *How did the participants refer to 'outsiders'? Now what did I record in my memos about 'outsiders'?* As noted in Chapter 3, folders or sets of documents can be sorted separately, and to keep memos separate in this way will allow you rapid access.

Data records that expand are thus highly varied and generate their own 'metadata', which offer another challenge to researchers. But as the project develops, the pace and rate of data expansion will gradually slow down. And that pace is a problem only if the data are not handled skilfully.

Varieties of Qualitative Data

Fluid, rich, complex, 'in depth', naturalistic, holistic – these are words you will find associated with qualitative data. In such projects, the researcher is seen as both a part of the situation studied and an instrument of research, active and deeply embedded in the account being produced. These are portrayed as ideally small-scale enquiries, using many sources of data as the researcher constructs understanding of situations from the perceptions of participants.

For an ethnographic study discussing these goals, go to **Inside Companionship**.

For most researchers with qualitative training, such projects are probably the most exciting and challenging. But it is important to recognize that many, perhaps most, qualitative projects are not like that. Small projects all too often rely on very homogeneous and limited data.

And qualitative projects are not always small. Novice researchers are best advised to start small, since the techniques for handling qualitative data are time-consuming and the focus on detail will be harder to achieve when there is a lot of data. But some research situations or research questions produce massive quantities of data, and qualitative techniques can be adapted for use in these contexts. Policy and evaluation projects quite normally ask questions that are best answered with qualitative data and need to ask them across many sites, national boundaries or time periods.

On the website there are examples of the use of qualitative analysis in two very large governmental projects, with very different goals: in the UK the **REMS** study, for the British Government Qualifications and Curriculum Authority; and in the USA the **Youth Offender Program Evaluation** project for the Department of Labor.

Very large projects may involve creating multi-site or multi-stage bodies of ethnographic or interview data. Or they may rely on sometimes huge bodies of already available data, especially data records available online, amassed by agencies or institutions, without a research design. With advances in archiving techniques, researchers are also increasingly accessing data created by others and stored for later reanalysis. Usually termed 'secondary data', data that was not created by the researcher, to answer their particular research question, presents special challenges.

For an example of research doing secondary analysis of highly limited data, visit the **Harassment Complaints** project on the website. The researchers were constrained not only by the records available as data, but the ways those records had been stored. Compare with the secondary analysis of huge volumes of evaluation data in the **REMS** project, which used qualitative software to develop an evidence database, to store and manage the evidence generated at a national level on educational reform.

In designing your own project and evaluating others', ask always what variety of data would best address the question. Researchers are always restricted to what can be put together, given the resources of time and money available and the data available or accessible, or permissible. But other things being equal, seek variety. This advice has become particularly relevant since qualitative software became available. All such software products in fact will handle a variety of data records, but experts agree that novices tend to retreat to creating homogeneous data sets that fit neatly into the box of the software project.

Qualitative and Quantitative Data – What's the Difference?

There is no simple dichotomy between numerical and non-numerical data. Any qualitative study collects, and most require, some information in numbers. It also collects information, just as most quantitative studies do, and this information is subsequently summarized in categories. (Note that to talk of 'collecting' data is usual in quantitative work.) Numerical and categorical labels are basically expressions of efficient data reductions. If we want to know the income level, and don't need the person's financial life history, we won't make an audio record of their exact words: it will do to record the income figure or allocate them to one of three categories, high, medium or low income. And because quantitative data efficiently reduce, quantitative sample sizes are of course normally bigger.

Very commonly, qualitative projects are associated with, or developed from the results or puzzles of quantitative research. See **Leading Improvement in Primary Care Practices** for an account of the questions that could not be answered by quantitative data.

Qualitative researchers are not antagonistic to numbers, and as Chapter 5 on coding shows, categories are critically important to them. *How many members does this action group have, what are the incomes of the leaders, how many years have elapsed since the dispute over commercial development during which it was formed?* These are important details that will inform the qualitative analysis.

Hence, numerical and categorical data may be critical to your analysis. Often where things can be counted without losing needed meaning, the counts form precious data. Much qualitative research seeks to make sense of the way themes and meanings are patterned by categories, for example, of gender. Reports of such research will and should quite normally cite numbers. *If you know that only three of the twelve founders of a group you are studying are still members, why reduce that information by saying 'very few' remain?* Now that computers offer storage of information about people, sites, etc., qualitative researchers can more easily store and use such information, and the report from such analyses will be more rigorous.

Go to the **Wedding Work** project and read the sections on 'Working with Data and Analysis' for examples of the use of counts and patterns in a small qualitative project.

Thus there is no sharp division between what you may hear referred to as 'qual' and 'quant' research. Nor do these equate with small and large projects. The most important distinction is one of research process and timing. Qualitative researchers are always cautious of *pre-emptively reducing* complex, contexted records to numbers.

If the action group has five paid-up members on the books, this may be all that matters for our study. If we are simply surveying paid-up membership of community groups, our answer to the question about this group is 'five'. No more time and money need to be spent dealing with that question. But if we are seeking an understanding of the role of community groups, and hear others declare they really *belong in this group, we may treat 'membership' as a problematic category until we are confident it is understood.*

The data needed are now much more *complex* – observations, interviews, group discussions. And these data can be understood only in *context* – this person's place in the community, their demographic location, sense of self and history of involvement. Neither approach to understanding membership, the quantitative or the qualitative, is wrong. Nor is either morally or ethically superior. But the processes are different. *The group really did have only five paid-up members, and 'belonging' to it did matter for many others who, we may later discover, saw the requirement to pay as offensive. The researcher now set on understanding the processes of belonging and exclusion in this community will ignore at their peril the interesting fact that only five memberships are paid. So the quantitative data are relevant to either a quantitative or a qualitative study. The difference is that the quantitative study will be done, and the qualitative one only just started. What data are needed now for understanding the meanings of belonging?*

So, qualitative and quantitative data do not inhabit different worlds. They are different ways – sometimes dramatically so – of creating and recording observations of the same world. Most qualitative studies will need both sorts of data and ways of storing both. The majority of the 'Methods in Practice' reports on the website use some quantitative records. But *handling* of quantitative data is rarely regarded as an issue. *Besides the question asking about membership, there are three boxes: 1 (yes), 2 (no), 3 (don't know). Nobody will ask 'What did you* mean *by 2?' That the number was correctly noted will rarely be doubted (though maybe it should!). But when we ask the non-member about the meanings of membership, we get data that need handling.*

The quantitative researcher's task is to work with numbers to find associations, groupings and patterns. It is appropriate in that context to talk about 'collecting' data. They are indeed collecting people into categories, or collecting up items that will be numerically represented. But qualitative researchers often avoid the term. It carries the implication that data are lying around, like autumn leaves, ready to be swept into heaps. When working qualitatively, you need to be aware of your part in *making* these data.

> Compare the '2' in the box with a long interview transcript in which a young migrant woman describes her need to belong in this community and her hurt when her offer to contribute to action group newsletters was rejected, even though she was a paid member.

The interview was conducted by you (not a migrant); the record is wordy, unstructured, amorphous, and full of possibly significant issues that link in apparently different 'belongings' to a lot of other issues in different interviews. You had to think yourself into her position and win her trust, find ways to make it easy for her to tell you how she sees things, frame your questions appropriately.

Doing this sort of research obviously requires quite different preparation from doing, for example, door-to-door surveys. The tasks of creating the appropriate situation for such enquiry, recording the participants' perceptions and experience sensitively and handling such data well, are the stuff of qualitative research.

PREPARING TO 'MAKE' DATA

Given the sort of data the qualitative researcher needs, their methods must be *developed in and responsive to* the situation to be researched. Another way of putting this is that all researchers, whatever methods they adopt for making their data, should first do some field research – and usually should retain a field researcher's awareness of the ways data are made.

Before you set out to 'get' your data, you will need to observe the situation you are about to enter and reflect on the *new* situation to be created by your research, considering how settings and conversations might affect what people see and feel and say. Anthropologists talk of 'entering the research field'. Think in terms of entering your field, and what you need to know before you enter. This is importantly an ethical requirement, to ensure your intrusion is not a problem to those you are studying. But be clear, such preparation is also in your interests, since you aim to explain what is really going on.

Perhaps the worst way to start would be the way most often taken, by creating rigid research 'instruments', like questionnaires or focus group protocols, in advance of understanding the situation being studied. Instead, once design is underway, you need urgently to find and research where this project will take place. If you are seeking to participate in the setting (for example, as a member of a group or a resident of the area studied), there may be many weeks of work to learn about it, find and work with contacts and gain acceptance to your proposal and confidence in your ability to participate without being disruptive. Reading on field research will be essential. So too will time to set up your project in the 'field': that is, the social and physical place you are going to be studying.

> Commenced health visitor rounds and taking only the professional notes needed. Decision to explain project in an open meeting with colleagues next week; meanwhile discussing it informally in casual conversations and keeping checklist of all colleagues on which I record when the discussion took place and response.

Don't assume that a less participatory method releases you from the requirement to understand the research setting and gain acceptance in it – or to observe once you are there. For any qualitative enquiry, there is always a process of 'entering' the field. If you are observing ('field research'), this may be more obvious than if your method involves less contact with the people studied (for example, single interviews). But in either case, beginning well will involve mapping the physical, social and cultural terrain. And observing well will enrich your data.

In **Mapping Caregiving**, the interviewer observed the caregiving context and inter-
actions, as well as conducting an interview and mapping exercise. The researcher notes, for example, how the interview act itself is drawn into one caregiver's role. In an apparently disorganized setting, on a second visit, 'the family caregiver controlled the flow of people, seeing the interview as her time to be important – "I'm being interviewed!".'

The simplest tasks will be physical mapping, but don't underestimate them. You may be greatly hindered later if you can't find your way around in the suburb being studied or the corridors of companies where you are interviewing. And at a more personal level, it may be critical to know your way through the corridors of power in the organization you're studying.

Social and cultural mapping will be far more complicated. Allow a first stage of time for getting knowledge and gaining acceptance, finding proposed research contacts, and becoming familiar with the behaviour and language of those you wish to research.

This preparatory work can be very time-consuming if the situation to be studied is unfamiliar to you. But getting it wrong will be much more time-consuming.

WAYS OF MAKING DATA

Most commonly, the complex records created for qualitative projects come from interviewing – either of individuals or in groups – and, most commonly, these interviews ask prepared questions. This is strange, because in everyday situations, when we want to find out how people understand what's going on in a new place or situation, we would certainly not confront them with prepared lists of questions. We also wouldn't think of herding them into groups to talk in front of our video cameras. So interviews or focus groups are unlikely to be the best or easiest way of making qualitative data. Often they are chosen because such events can be recorded mechanically, so they make a lot of digitally available data rapidly. Sometimes, researchers have just been told this is what they should do, or it's the easiest thing to do, and they have not heard of other ways of acquiring data.

It is also strange that so many projects rely *only* on individual or group interviews. In an everyday situation we would use several ways of finding out and learning, most unobtrusive. Don't assume in research that you should rely on the single most obtrusive method! Even small projects are often strengthened by using multiple methods and viewing the topic several ways. In later chapters, there is discussion of how these different sorts of data may be 'triangulated' to build confidence in conclusions, and large projects will normally use several ways of making data.

 The **Youth Offender Program Evaluation** project used multiple methods; for just one of its rounds, nine different sorts of data were combined in analysis.

Observing and Participating

In the Introduction, I suggested that qualitative methods seek surprises. If you are planning a qualitative project, it is probably because you don't know what you will find. You want to know how people *there* see things – how *they* explain events.

We are all participant observers in all our life situations: that is, we *participate* and we observe. To turn an everyday life situation into qualitative data requires only one more step: to *record* those observations. But the skills of participating appropriately, observing acutely and recording richly what you have observed constitute a craft that takes a lot of learning.

This is the craft usually called ethnography, and practised by anthropologists and field researchers. Records of participant observations are usually referred to as *field notes*. Such methods are used both in very small-scale projects, where detailed understanding of process is required, and in sometimes formidable large-scale projects over time.

Ethnography has a very considerable methodological literature which must be consulted before you embark on a fieldwork project. Start with the references at the end of this chapter for an introduction.

The **Inside Companionship** report gives a detailed account of the preparation and conduct of an ethnographic study, with strong awareness of the researcher's roles, the ethical issues and the sorts of data records analysed.

Whatever means you employ for making data, be aware that you are participating *and* observing. Any research act inserts you into the situation studied, and provides the opportunity to observe, even if the intention is that only quantitative records will be kept. The clipboard-wielding door-to-door interviewer is a non-participant observer of neighbourhood interaction. How different would the study be if the interviewer took time to write a rich description of each street and what was going on there? The medical random control test is conducted in clinical contexts and with explanations: if what goes on there were recorded, you would get field notes. The stimulus and response experiment in a lab is designed for statistical analysis of results, but the records of team meetings show how hunches and insights lead to theories. Any of these situations could provide data for qualitative analysis.

While **Mapping Caregiving**, the researcher observed. Note the significance of observations of the caregiving roles in play and context.

These opportunities may provide the needed familiarization with the research setting before you start more intrusive processes like interviewing. *A chance to join in conversation with a few members of the group in the local pub gives you the background to the conflict: later, write it up in field notes. An offer to talk in private afterwards with one member who was very quiet in that discussion offers another view: write your notes up later from memory.* These may be precious records. Good field notes intrigue with vividness and contradictions, bother and distract with remembered themes and recurrent noises, fascinate even those who hold the view that reliable research cannot be done with qualitative data.

---------------- **Preparing to Do Participant Observation** ----------------

Participant observation presents as one of the most 'natural' ways of making data. But it is one of the hardest ways to make good data records. This is because the two roles – participant and observer – will always conflict. The following exercises will help develop your awareness of these subtle roles.

• Specify a particular half-hour each day for a week when you will be a participant observer - at that time, whatever is going on and whatever the setting. Since you are a *participant*, you should take no recording devices and no notebook.
• Concentrate on training your mind to recall during that time, and write the half-hour up as field notes as soon as possible afterwards. In each observation, try to develop new methods of recalling.
• Compare the length and detail of your seven records of field notes. There will be a steady increase in the volume and (hopefully) quality of your record.
• Now, for your research topic and your question, taking due regard to ethics and courtesy, plan and do some participant observing, and write up the field notes.

---------------- **Observing as a Participant** ----------------

In a class, team or other small-group situation, do the following:

• Start a discussion, and halfway through it, stop and ask everyone to write notes on what has happened so far. You'll get protests. ('We should have been warned!')
• Compare the accounts. Interestingly, some 'participants' can recall far more than others, and it is very useful to discuss why – for example, did they participate less than others, or do they have professional skills or observation experiences, perhaps in clinical settings, requiring recall?
• Now, tell the group that for the remaining time, they *are* being warned: at the end of the session, they'll be asked to write what happened from now till then. The result will be a very boring period, as most people turn to the task of recording rather than participating!
• Now the big discussion – how do you combine participating and observing so you do both well?

Interviewing

An interview is both the most ordinary and the most extraordinary of ways you can explore someone else's experience. It is as ordinary as conversation, and as intrusive as a spy camera. It may offer insights you never expected would come your way and sometimes information the other person would not have considered giving to a stranger. The ordinariness of the method can trap novice researchers unaware of the extraordinary challenges behind creating and ethically conducting an interview and making good interview records.

Many of the projects on the website used interviewing as their principal source of data. Together they show the range of types of interview, from very structured to free-flowing conversations.

It is important to consider the complexity of interviewing as a way of making your data. You ask the questions you want answers to, and record the answers, but is it that simple? How will you know what questions to ask, or what they mean to the person interviewed? How to avoid getting answers coloured by the interview situation, how to encourage the interviewee to offer their *own* understanding of what's going on? And what sort of a record of their views will you have created by such controlled data extraction? Qualitative interviewing requires great sensitivity to the ways in which the interview process shapes the data made.

All of these considerations should apply equally to interviewing individuals and to interviewing in groups. A quick web search will show you that 'focus groups' are now widely treated as a separate method, with sometimes very rigid rules for recruitment, conduct and analysis. In some disciplines, particularly in marketing, focus groups may be the only method considered for making qualitative data. If you choose to use focus groups, assess this literature carefully.

These considerations – and many others – also apply to online interviewing, an increasingly popular approach. If you are considering interviewing or 'observing' online, rather than face to face, go to the specific literature.

Preparation for any form of interviewing is *not* just about deciding how to 'get' people to interview. It requires reflecting on the interview process, on how it will be interpreted and the ways to assist an interviewee in naturally conveying their views and on unobtrusive ways of recording what happens. Don't start 'doing an interview' until you have reflected on what you will be *doing to* the interviewee and the situation, and what you are doing *with* them.

Nor is the first step listing questions to be asked! You might not at any stage have a fixed list and certainly you don't want one before you know the situation. It is rare for a qualitative method to require standardized questionnaires, even in quite large projects. This is because the analysis techniques are seeking emerging ideas, not patterns in responses to a fixed question. Your first interviews will teach you much about the topic, people's experiences and the ways they can be helped to explain and describe what they see and do. Once you have some understanding and feel confident to create guides to your questions, you will need to respond, with agility, to changed understanding of that situation. If the questions you ask at first offend or fail to elicit interesting answers, you'll of course change the questions – or even move away from questioning as a way of finding out.

Most importantly, if you are working qualitatively, you almost certainly wish to ask questions in such a way as to leave open to sorts of responses you can get. The term 'open-ended interview' refers to this goal. An open-ended interview will rarely restrict answers to preconceived categories. (Compare with the survey when the only options are to tick Agree, Don't Know, or Disagree). If you are working qualitatively, you want to know not only why she disagrees, and what she means by 'disagree', but also how she responds to the question – she may see the question itself as raising quite different issues.

Use the following checklist for steps to an interview that will be appropriate, ethical and also provide useful data. You will need to go through each step before you take these proposals to an ethics committee. If ethics clearance is not required by your research institution, don't shirk the steps; be your own ethics checker. There is a serious juggling task as you answer questions about the effect of your intervention on the participants and on the data that result. On the one extreme, unique, sensitive data may be achieved by very intrusive and demanding interviewing; on the other, a pleasant, unchallenging chat could lead to a bland account that tells you nothing new.

Read about qualitative interviewing, using the references at the end of this chapter. You will find a strong message that interviewing creates an interactive relationship. The data are made collaboratively by you and those you interview. Take this seriously! Now use this checklist to prepare for either individual or group interviews.

Preparing for an Interview

- Which participants in the situation you are studying do you wish to interview? Your early ideas will shift, as you recognize the ethical challenges of interviewing a vulnerable group, or the practical problems of reaching others. Whose views should you seek to address your topic? What situation will you create by interviewing them? Each of the following questions should be asked:

  (a) How will these people see you and your study? (How best to present yourself?)
  (b) How will you find and recruit participants? (Will this method skew the study? Will they wish to participate? What assurances or rewards would encourage them?)

 Visit the **Wedding Work** project for an account of challenges in sample selection.

- Now you are in a position to ask: would it be more appropriate and more useful to interview people in groups rather than individually, face to face? There will be many advantages and disadvantages of either choice. If you choose to interview in groups, think about the sort of group that will be most appropriate. Stereotypically, 'focus groups' are made up of unconnected individuals 'recruited' by marketing agencies, rather than social groups of friends or colleagues. Which works for your project?
- For individual *or* group interviews, the next questions are about setting. What would be the most comfortable (and practical) location (place, time, context) for interviews? Consider the comfort of participants and the implications for your data. If you aim to interview groups, compare the setting of a group recruited and gathered in a video room with the ordinary one of an existing social group meeting as usual in their pub.

- Next, what is the appropriate way of seeking information? Conversations can be prompted in many ways other than direct interviewer questions, and most are more natural. Does your research question require that you always ask the same questions, or replicate the same prompts? Consider ways that participants could show you their perceptions of their situation – by drawing their environment, showing photos of their family, sketching timelines of their life transitions, mapping their networks.

Visit the **Mapping Caregiving** project for an example of use of visual tools.

- Now consider the ways you and your interviewees will be collaborating in making data. What will the participants need to know about your project and how will you explain it? (This will usually involve a written statement to be given to participants, and a consent form for them to sign.) What will they expect you to want to hear? How should you avoid skewing their answers by your appearance and comments?
- Only now is it safe to start thinking about specific questions you might ask! This does not mean you should prepare a fixed list and stick to it. On the basis of the first interviews, you may be helped by reordering and rewording questions.

Visit the **Handling Sexual Attraction** project for an example of the adaption of questions to early interview experiences.

- Finally, choose how you will record the interviews. Don't assume you have to be the stereotypical researcher with the clipboard. Is it appropriate to record either audio or video (or convenient, or practical)? Don't assume that to do so will get you better data – the process of recording will significantly impact the social situation and thereby the data. Consider instead, recording in your own notes, or even not recording during the interview, and recording your notes later from memory.

Now that you have planned an approach and thought out its impact and implications, do a trial interview with a colleague or friend, to ensure that your questions are not dominating the flow of conversations, and the flow goes to the topics you want discussed.

A Note on Groups – Focused or Not

Each of the points above applies to any form of group interviewing. Whether you wish to talk with people individually or in groups, you need to read, think about who you want to talk with, ask how and in what setting you should do this. Only then can you start thinking of questions – and you will need to be prepared to change them. You will also have to consider how best to record.

With the increasing popularity of 'focus group interviews' these questions are often not asked. In large areas of social and health sciences, business and marketing, as well as governmental and political research, 'focus groups' have become the dominant (or even the only) mode of non-numerical data collection. Where this is so, the assumption that it's always better to interview in groups (for focused discussion, for researcher convenience or for greatest amount of data) can be so strong that the implications of group pressure and the dynamics of group influence are overlooked. If you are planning to use focus groups, read about the method and critically reflect on its implications for your research.

For an alternative approach, seeking spontaneous discussion by naturally occurring affinity groups in their own setting, read about the work of Hugh MacKay, who argues that the trouble with focus groups is that they are neither focused nor, in any sociological sense, groups: www.ipsos.com.au/publicaffairs.

Data from Unobtrusive Methods

Increasingly, qualitative research uses data from sources other than direct encounters with people. Some studies require only such data and almost all could use some such data. For many projects, the data exist before the project is proposed. Working selectively with archival sources of data is a very different task from selecting what will be recorded in the field. But the researcher is still *selecting* what will be treated as data.

Written or printed words and recorded images most obviously offer access to people's behaviour and its meanings to them. These may be the only or a preferred source of data, as in Discourse Analysis, when the interest is in fine analysis of the words used, or the symbols in images. Researchers studying culture will see these texts not only as containing content to be examined, but in themselves as objects of research. In these methods, there will be interest also in other cultural items. If this is your task, you will need to read about ways of gathering appropriately the needed published or unpublished documents, printed or electronic images and in selecting the relevant passages or items to be your data – and handling them well.

Whatever your method, consider the relevance of all the 'other stuff' researchers have around them. Given good data storage and access, you should not have to waste this. Consider, too, ways of generating data alongside your main method: ask your respondents to keep a diary, for example, or to draw their support network.

New researchers commonly overlook potentially valuable sources of data because they feel 'data' should be more impressive, more substantial or simply tidier than the everyday stuff around them.

This is not a trivial problem. Students who report with concern, months into a dissertation, that they 'don't have any data yet' are probably immersed in data. They have been reading, thinking, revising a research design, discussing the project with stakeholders and observing the setting of their research for months. From all this work they have produced no *designed* data like transcripts of interviews. But they do have a mess of notes, documentary material from government reports, local group minutes, media reports or the written records of relevant people. They may also have their own research proposals, unwritten impressions, even hunches about what they will find if they ever 'get any data' – and data are what that mess is made of! Like Molière's hero who found he had been speaking prose all his life, the new qualitative researcher may have an extraordinary moment of discovery that qualitative data surround them. Some studies, or segments of studies, will have only such data. The researcher has not intervened to create special research events (like interviews) or inserted themselves into naturally-occurring events as an observer. They are instead collecting material that is there already, and making it data by selecting and interpreting.

There are obvious advantages to such methods. With any interventionist method of making data, you risk impacting or altering the situation, and contributing your bias to the data. There are ethical and practical reasons to avoid doing this. On the other hand, some, even most, research questions are not easily answered only with data available. And there are quite different ethical challenges in gathering for study material that was created or prepared by people unaware that it would be analysed in this way.

A good rule is to consider first what documentary research can offer: what questions can it answer, what background data can it provide? If the material is already available in records you can access, go there before you interview. You will approach the interview informed, not waste your participants' time asking questions whose answers are publicly available. And if their interpretation is different from what you read in the newspaper archives, this too is data.

Some research designs combine the gathering and analysis of such documents with later use of more obtrusive methods.

The researcher studying the experiences of **Elderly Survivors of the Hanshin Earthquake** started with media reports, then interviews with officials, before doing observation in communities. Many projects whose design relies on interviews include as data the interviewer's field notes from the experience: see the **Sexuality-Spirituality** project.

So long as they are handled as data from the start, those records of observations, reading, literature notes and draft ideas, offer a firm first step into the unknown, and will properly inform future, more designed, data construction. Handled badly, these records of context can merely confuse.

Data from Online Sources

The explosion of methods of accessing and storing information digitally and communicating online has created suddenly a major new arena of potential qualitative data and with it new versions of old concerns, about ethics and practical problems. Digital data has extraordinary attractions for researchers: online sources can provide uniquely rich and immediate accounts of social events and personal experience, and of new forms of social groupings and communication, themselves exciting research topics. (And for many researchers there is the added advantage that digital records are immediately available, without the chore of transcription of interviews or field notes!) Such data sources will be indispensable in the future, as will be the range of ways of digitally accessing, recording, discussing and exploring data.

If you consider using online sources, there are major opportunities to explore and issues to confront, and an excellent literature emerging to assist you in doing it well (see references at the end of this chapter). Doing it well is far from easy, despite the ease with which we now explore, discover and communicate online. For now, reflect on how very different these research situations will be from traditional methods, and how very different will be the data records they create and the ethical issues they raise. Online data can potentially be acquired – in small or great volumes – from accessible websites, discussion lists or blogs, where the often anonymous 'participants' can be entirely unaware they are participating in a study, or unclear about how their words will be used. Compare such data collection with classic unobtrusive methods such as the analysis of publicly available documents. Or data can be interactively and openly made by the methods described above – interviewing or observation – but the interaction is online, by email or conferencing, for example. The comparison with face-to-face interviews is far from simple. Where anonymity is important to the participant, an online interview may be far richer and more open than in a face-to-face situation and the ethical issues less troubling – but the researcher will also be interacting differently with an online participant and interpretation of the data will be greatly affected by the context. As online relationships rapidly become a greater part of our lives, these challenges will be seen differently – but they won't go away.

DATA ABOUT YOUR PROJECT (AND YOU)

As your data build up, increasingly you will wish to add your own comments, discussion and reflections. These too are data.

To do so informally and directly will assist you in doing it well. Unless it is explicitly banned by your supervisors, always assert your agency. Use the first person and annotate the text. Avoid passive voice ('the data were collected') and mysticism ('the theme emerged'). Admit it, you did it. You constructed and created that interview, you observed. And that in itself is data.

Never lose focus on telling it how you see it, and on making the best possible record for your purpose. But also, reflect constantly on how these data are made and the part you play in them. Remember the warning of the previous chapter: qualitative data are not collected, but *made* collaboratively by the researcher and the researched. The importance of recognizing an individual researcher's part in making data is just as great if you are working in a team. Ensure you agree that each member will initial an annotation, record even their most tentative first hunches and personalize their memos. Experience shows that junior members of teams find the assertion of authorship difficult – so the key is to encourage them to treat their own hunches or insights as of importance to the team process. If you are the junior, negotiate an agreement whereby you can record your early tentative thoughts without feeling they are under scrutiny.

You and Your Project

Qualitative researchers refer to reflection on their own data-making role and their relation to their research as *reflexivity*. Take it seriously! It identifies a crucial feature of social research, namely that a part of the data is the researcher. (A reflexive verb is one that has an identical subject and direct object, as in 'I dressed myself'.)

Reflexivity requires that you are aware of your relationship to what you choose to study, and why you make that choice, where you *are* in that research area (physically, socially, culturally) and what you bring to it, your relationship with the setting and the people and with the social structures and the social knowledge, the assumptions and ideologies, which create those structures and provide the context for the lives of those people.

Thinking about reflexivity alerts you to the need to reflect on the baggage you take in, your biases and interests and areas of ignorance. But it also alerts you to the fact that you yourself are part of what you are studying. This is not something requiring apology and it is certainly not in your power to rectify. It is not bad (or good) for your project, just central to it.

Writing reflexively about these things is so obviously necessary it is extraordinary how often researchers are not advised to do so.

It may, later, be appropriate to take your interpretation back to the people you are studying. If this is done, you don't remove your agency, but add another layer of interpretation: how they perceive what you perceive as their situation. This too will be data.

Reflecting on your part in this research will be necessary from here to the final report. Chapter 7 discusses the implications of reflexive interpretation for validity of the study, Chapter 9 how to handle the different ways you and your respondents see the situation, and Chapter 10 returns to this theme in the context of the final report.

The emphasis on self-reflexion depends greatly on the methodological approach. New on the website is an extraordinary contribution by the researcher reporting on the **Inside Companionship** project. He has recorded in great detail for this site 'the *life story* of my research project, condemned to co-exist with my own life story'. Go to that project, and follow the links to his very detailed reflections on his own website, for an understanding of how reflexivity affects the research and the researcher's later understanding of the research process as data.

Keeping Your Log Trail

You are setting up a project which you want to conclude with claims that you discovered something worthwhile and you should be believed. To make such claims credible, you will need at the end to account for each step and shift in the project, and document where your ideas and theories came from – starting now!

In the forthcoming chapters, there will be advice to record your reflections on your role in the project, the ideas you discover, where they came from, how they seem to work in the data, and the amount of confidence you have in these ideas. These 'logs', like a ship's log, detail the journey taken, and they will help you to validate your analysis. Keeping them carefully will leave a trail that you and your reader can follow to assess where you got to and how you got there.

The advice for keeping such a trail of log records is throughout this book. A note about terminology: I prefer the term 'log' because it suggests, as does a ship's log, keeping a very careful account of the events on a journey. In your field, the term may be 'audit trail', with the implication that consistency is being audited. (Check the requirements against which your work will be assessed.)

Whatever you call it, writing your log, and reflecting on the records you create there and their role in your project, are important research acts.

 The update on the **Inside Companionship** project offers a critique of the way a diary was used in the original project, when the researcher reports he was 'delegating practically all of the conduct of the research into the diary. The diary was my refuge.' If approaching the research task now, he says, 'I would moderate the demand that it assumed as a training ground for phenomenological reduction and I would unburden it of a somewhat neutral theoretical rhetoric that protected me from the conflict of interpretations and from a certain volatility in the production of knowledge. Its influence in the research would therefore be much diminished. It would cease to be a research diary and would become an on-board log.'

And a note about technology: explore all the ways you currently communicate, verbally, in writing and digitally, as ways of keeping your log. The goal is to write reflexively often, easily, rapidly and on impulse. Online records may be your most natural and thus best way of keeping a log, and if you are working with others, online modes such as blogs will undoubtedly be the best way of sharing your thoughts with colleagues. Don't allow your log trail to be hidden from you or them, forgotten and neglected or constrained by data management procedures. Just make sure that you have some way of finding later all these reflexive thoughts.

Logging Purpose, Goal and Outcome

For the life of this project, people around you, including those you are studying, will ask, 'What's your study about?' Like 'What are you going to be when you grow up?', this is an exceedingly annoying question when you are still wondering what the answer is. From the first setting up, aim to be able to answer that question strongly and honestly, and then log your different answers at different stages.

When you have a formal research design document, to submit to a funding body, a graduate or ethics committee or a team, this should be carefully stored. Store with it very thorough reflective notes on how you arrived at this project, the discussions around purpose, your ideas about how (and, perhaps, doubts about whether) the current design meets the goals. Check that the design document adequately covers purpose, goal and outcome. Be sure to write about the aspects of the design that were contentious, and how decisions were made.

Your design document probably will not include hypotheses that you are testing, or expected results. But it will need to include an explanation of why hypothesis testing or quantification approaches are not appropriate – why, in other words, this is a qualitative project. When that answer is satisfying (to you and your audiences) your design is probably adequate.

Logging Changes in the Design

Most qualitative projects share the goal that the researcher learns from the data, adapting enquiry to what is learned. This means your design is going to change. These changes in turn should be logged. Teach yourself, and, in teams, your colleagues to note significant steps in the project, even small ones. At each point where you feel the project has taken a redesign step (in any direction), note it. This note can go in a research diary or a memo, or any other place where it is safely stored. (If you are working in software, link it to the log trail document, noting there that something shifted.)

Logging Changes

Your change log should cover four aspects: What happened? Why it happened? What were the alternatives? And what are the likely results of this shift or step?

1. Note exactly what you did or what happened.

   Changed the research plan: intend to observe for a year as participant observer. No formal interviews will be conducted at this stage. (Ethics permission being applied for.)

2. At each step, record succinctly why this happened (try to record honestly the many levels of explanation). If the reason for change was in your reading or the data, quote or link to that record.

   Well the practical reason was you landed the job as the district health visitor! Why did you apply? Doubts that one-on-one interviewing would give you immersion in the

   (Continued)

(Continued)

experience of long-term patients. (Well, OK, and also you needed an income.) What led you to that conclusion? Reading on participant observation (detail the advantages claimed and counter-arguments and give the references).

3. **Now record, if relevant, what the alternatives were and why they were rejected.**

No other participant role was available on pay and you have to eat. Decision to rely on interviews was rejected after you tried a few and discovered/felt serious discomfort imposing a formal interview on people who had little interaction with outsiders, and the patients, while polite, were responding with very brief, formal answers (link to transcripts of early interviews and your notes). Also realized you simply didn't have enough knowledge of the situation and kept putting your foot in it – ethical and practical problems (references).

4. **Finally, what are the likely results of this shift or step and does it have any implications for the final project?**

Huge implications of this now very different role. (Link to your first field notes.) Expect challenges to your ability to observe and accurately report. (Report reading and consideration re the 'insider' role and its problems as well as advantages.)

In teams, there should always be agreement on areas of responsibility for these logging tasks. Some of the processes that need to be logged may appear quite minor, and many will be the responsibility of junior team members. Ensure that somebody writes about change processes, no matter how senior the team member making the changes. And if possible, always discuss these log entries. It's uncomfortable to confront disagreement late in the project when you are justifying a strategic decision made months ago: *I thought we brought her onto the team* after *she won the district visitor job.*

The log trail can now be seen as a significant source of data. In that trail, you can keep your reflections on your part in the data-making process, as well as accounts of changes and discoveries.

Why Keep That Trail?

Log trails are necessary if you are to make claims for your hunches and fleeting thoughts, theories or conclusions. If you don't start now, you will end the project with an outcome (whether it's a tumble of insights or an over-arching explanation) that frankly can't be justified. As you build up your explanation or account of the data, bit by bit, at each stage you need to log the reasons why you feel it can now be built *upon*. It just doesn't work to invent retrospectively the emergence of a key idea, or try to reconstruct the searches you did and the reason for your increasing confidence. You'll get it wrong, you'll not be believed, and you shouldn't be.

Writing such accounts is at the core of challenges of validity and reliability in qualitative research. Your ability to present your research as believable depends on your ability to answer these challenges. If you log the account of how each step is taken, you will have the records to make claims for your project by the time these challenges are met again in Chapter 7. And when the time for a final report arrives (Chapter 10) there will be a consistent and impressive account of how you got there.

From now to the end of the project, you will be establishing a trail of such logs of important events and decisions.

How Do You Manage a Log Trail?

You may wish to keep one separate account of the project history – in a diary, in memos, in audio or video. On computer, it is easy to link that history to your notes about specific aspects or decisions.

You will also rapidly start generating other documents or notes about specific project processes. There is much to write already in the topics covered above. Most of the steps in this chapter, and in future chapters, require some writing.

At this stage try writing a first reflective memo on yourself and your data. Then make a habit of writing on anything that feels like a step in the project. Once you are working in a software package, start there a 'log trail' or 'project history' document to keep track of these writings, for at the end of the project you will want to find them again. Start with the log of your project design, from the previous chapter. The log trail document summarizes and helps you find again all the pieces of your project's history. This will be of great value in defending the validity of your project outcomes. (Jump to Chapter 10 to see the uses of this trail when you need to do a stocktake of your writings about the project.)

IS WRITING A PROBLEM FOR YOU?

Few people write easily, and for many, it is very difficult.

This is not a diversion. Writing is an analysis tool in qualitative research. Qualitative researchers work with (among other media) words, with text and speech, and they explore – in words – what they find in those words. As you write, you see new possibilities, loopholes, contradictions, surprises. Writing *uncovers* such things. A major contribution for the researcher is seeking to *discover* explanations. Writing is also the way that researchers establish that their conclusions should be believed.

But words may not come easily, especially if you are uncertain what the project will bring, or what the outcome should be. If writing is a problem, now is the time to address it.

Telling Your Project

From the start of your project, get into a habit of 'telling' what's going on, rather than 'writing it up'. Tell it (in diagrams, models, written letters) to yourself, your diary, your supervisor or your friends, in spoken or written words. Tell it to your software project (in memos, annotations and descriptions). Telling is much more purposive than writing - and much easier to do.

- You will always have something to tell, though it will not often look tidy or definitive, not the sort of material you would 'write up'. Today's story may be how hard it is to make sense of your data; it is hard to write up not being able to write it up. Telling will happen more easily and more often. (There's no such thing as 'teller's block'.)
- Telling takes much less time than writing it up and it can be done much more casually. In the following chapters, when you are advised to write about some aspect of the project, never feel a duty to produce a polished, final account. Don't even check your grammar and spelling - just tell it in writing.
- Telling is done interactively - you are telling an audience (it may be you, or a doubting colleague, or perhaps the participants in your research team). Writing it up feels like a lone activity. Use diagrams and models, on paper, whiteboards or software, to draw what is going on and revise it in response to discussion.
- Retelling is much easier than revising a write-up; you will want to revisit and rethink your accounts of events and ideas, so they should never look final.
- If you tell it, you will tell it in the first person - this is your project, you did the interviews, you are wondering about the meanings of a discussion. You don't tell a story in the passive tense ('The nightclub was visited ...').

 The researcher's informal and unedited memos are provided with the **Harassment Complaints** project.

This book ends with a chapter on 'Telling it'. Go there now for advice on all the writing tasks and how to make them work for you.

The ability to 'tell' a project is an important part of team collaboration. You need to work collaboratively with your colleagues to build together the goals and images of the project as well as the details of research design. Throughout this book, there is advice for writing and telling the aspects of project progress relevant to 'logging' the development of an explanation or outcome. If you are working in a team, the processes of debating, agreeing and working a collaborative project need to be told. You may find it useful to run periodic team workshops to develop and maintain processes that everyone can easily use, to troubleshoot problems of diffidence or lack of confidence, and to ensure that there will be, at the end of the project, an authoritative but genuinely collaborative account of the processes that need to be accounted for.

To Do
---

1. If you don't yet have data (or a design for making data), read, reflect and decide on the way you are going to do it, and write a report on the method to be used and how the choice was made. Specifically, discuss how the study would be different if you chose another method of making data.
2. Conduct a 'field note awareness exercise' either individually or in a group, as described above.
3. Plan one research event where you record data, and transcribe a record from it. Study that record and critique it.
4. Start your project log. It's never too early to start. If you are having trouble starting, log your understanding of why it's so difficult!

Go on the website to **Inside Companionship** and follow the links to the author's detailed account of his relation to his data. Writing during and after the project was essential to thinking through his relation to the project. Write a report on his analysis of his relation to his data and its relevance to yours.

5. *Tell* your project to a team, class or other group. Explain to them the fit you are seeking between your question, the data you need and the outcome you are aiming for.

Suggestions for Further Reading

Many texts tackle what qualitative research is, and of course they disagree. For overviews of the debates, see especially Coffey and Atkinson (1996), Flick (2014), Seale et al. (2004), and Silverman (2011). If the terminology of this sort of research is new to you, see the dictionary of terms by Schwandt (1997).

Read some recent texts that discuss a range of methods and explain why there is a range: for example, see *Readme First* (Richards and Morse, 2013), Lichtman (2014), Punch (2014), and Yin (2010). Be careful to find advice pertinent to your area. Collections are a good way to sample variety; for the most recent, see Flick (2013); see also a long line by Denzin and Lincoln (eds) (especially 1994, 2000 and 2011).

To compare techniques for making data, go to the References page of relevant 'Methods in Practice' projects on the website for this book. For introductory information, try Braun and Clarke (2013) and Mason (2002). If you are using interviews, classic texts include Holstein and Gubrium (1995), Kvale (1996), Rubin and Rubin (2005), and Spradley (1979). On secondary analysis of data, see papers and references in the special issue of *Forum: Qualitative Social Research* (2005).

There is a recent literature concerned with online qualitative research; for a full coverage of digital tools, see Paulus et al. (2014). Mann and Stewart (2000), and Davidson and Di Gregorio (2011) tackle possibilities and ethical issues; Flick (2014) gives strong encouragement to explore online resources. See Gibbs et al. (2002) and the special issue they introduce, for a collection of issues in online research, concerns and predications. See also Fielding et al. (eds) (2008). Online interviewing and its practical and ethical issues are covered in Busher and James (2009).

(Continued)

(Continued)

To learn about focus groups, first do a web search and read the approaches taken in commercial and much governmental research. Then go to the literature: Fern (2001), Krueger (1988), Morgan (1997), and Stewart et al. (2006). Harding (2013) compares interviews and focus group data.

On field research, see Agar (1996), Atkinson et al. (2001), Eisner (1998), and Lofland and Lofland (1995). Read about reflexivity in the careful coverage by Seale (1999). For issues around 'the new ethnography', see Delamont and Atkinson (2008) and Goodall (2000).

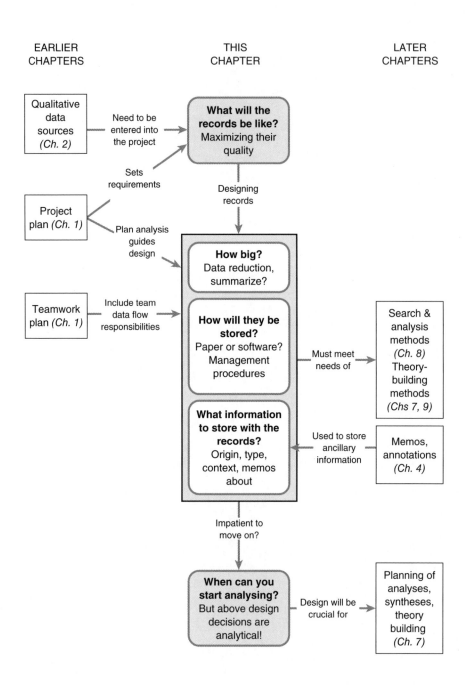

EARLIER
CHAPTERS

THIS
CHAPTER

LATER
CHAPTERS

Qualitative
data
sources
(Ch. 2)

Need to be
entered into
the project

**What will the
records be like?**
Maximizing their
quality

Sets
requirements

Designing
records

Project
plan *(Ch. 1)*

Plan analysis
guides
design

How big?
Data reduction,
summarize?

Teamwork
plan *(Ch. 1)*

Include team
data flow
responsibilities

**How will they be
stored?**
Paper or software?
Management
procedures

Must meet
needs of

Search &
analysis
methods
(Ch. 8)
Theory-
building
methods
(Chs 7, 9)

**What information
to store with the
records?**
Origin, type,
context, memos
about

Used to store
ancillary
information

Memos,
annotations
(Ch. 4)

Impatient to
move on?

**When can you
start analysing?**
But above design
decisions are
analytical!

Design will be
crucial for

Planning of
analyses,
syntheses,
theory
building
(Ch. 7)

THREE

Data records

This chapter has a simple message: think not only about the research acts that make data, but about the ways you are *recording* data. The adequacy of your analysis will be largely determined by the quality of the data records, your access to them and their context. And this is when you face up to one very important and very practical task: you need by now to know what software tools you will use, and to be confident and skilful in using those tools.

The previous chapter began with the assertion that, while making data is easy, making good data requires skill and careful work. This chapter is about the all-important task of making good data *records*.

Not surprisingly, this task too requires skill and careful work. It sounds unexciting, when you are eager to get on with the research, but if you are tempted to delay thinking about records, reflect on what it is that you analyse. That deeply moving or inspiring research interview, or the dramatic encounter with the action group being studied, enters your project as rich data *only* if you record it and its context and your ideas about it – and record them well.

> Field notes from observations in the action group meetings are building up, and it's difficult, though approved, to record them, since people are uncomfortable with my dual roles. How do I record all the complex meanings being put on the protest events?

Qualitative researchers, and textbooks, often focus on making data to the exclusion of concerns about what to do with the data once you have created some. A goal of this book is to overcome this skew, to encourage you to think data *records*. For the rest of a project, what you will work with is the record of your data.

This chapter deals first with the need to be ready for data records and then with ways of handling records as they are made, avoiding wastage and loss of complexity and context. Finally, it discusses storing and using information about your data. And it tackles the topic too often avoided: what software will you use and how will you become skilled enough to use it well? So please don't skip this chapter! If making good records sounds like boring, clerical work, think again. A major cause of failure in qualitative projects is that the researcher did not prioritize recording data well and so was unable to access all their data skilfully. The result will be skewed analysis and partial and unpersuasive reporting. In the absence of good records, you see only the cases you remember vividly, or you overlook the many dimensions in the problem being investigated.

Please also don't underestimate the data management task. In your study area, potentially *everything* is data (at least until you know it's not relevant to your question). All researchers are in difficulty if they cannot select thoughtfully what is recorded, record well and retain the information they will later need to access the record. So you must be prepared to record well and store skilfully a lot of data.

The most ignored requirement of good qualitative research is that the researcher should be ready for data. This does not mean they know what the data will say or even what the records will be like: good qualitative data surprise. Rather, the researcher is ready to *handle* what comes. In this respect (and many others), qualitative researching is like surfing. If you have the right equipment, the ability to use it and the knowledge of what is heading your way – and if you are looking in the right direction – you are less likely to get dumped, and more likely to get somewhere. When the wave is towering over you, this is not the time to realize inadequacies in your equipment or skills. Skilled researchers know well the experience of being overwhelmed by the amazing scale, volume, complexity and colour of their data records. But well equipped and informed, they are more likely to get on top.

The good news is that the use of good software will make this much less of a challenge – so long as you are a good user of that software.

WHAT WILL THE RECORDS BE LIKE?

Before you start making data, it is essential to ask what the data records will be like, and what would make them good records.

 Each of the project reports in 'Methods in Practice' has a section on 'Working with Data'. Go to these sections to learn how data records were made and managed.

Qualitative researchers always record words and sometimes record images, sounds or other ways of portraying a situation. Whatever techniques you choose for making qualitative data, the records will be relatively unstructured, consisting of text with or without illustrations and other multimedia materials. The records will also be surprisingly *large*. They have to be generous enough to show the complexity and context of the stories or accounts of behaviour you are gathering.

If your data records are short and rigidly structured (for example, brief answers to a series of exactly the same questions) you possibly will be planning to reduce these records rapidly to numerical data, keeping only some quotations for illustrative purposes. Such structured records are appropriate when you know what you are asking or testing. But if you wish to keep the detail of the answers, the tools for qualitative data handling, especially tools for coding on computer (Chapter 5), will assist you in data reduction that is very sensitive to the meanings in the records.

Your choice of how and where you made data has already narrowed the choice of type of data record. Your choice of what you want to do with the data will narrow it further. Having considered the required type of data and record, the challenge is to make records and store them in ways that maximize the *quality* of the data records and your *access* to them as you need them.

Quality in Qualitative Data Records

There are many books of advice on conducting good interviews or fieldwork. Less often discussed are the principles of what makes good data records.

Researchers will differ in their standards, since they differ in the methodological purposes to which the records will be put. With experience, you will set your own priorities, but to start, set guidelines for records of qualitative data that are as accurate, as contexted, as 'thick', as useful and as reflective as the project will require. (If you don't know yet what detail will be needed, it is wise to be generous.)

- **Accurate:** Your record should be checked as far as possible against recall and any notes of the event. If a transcription is done by someone other than the researcher whose data event is being transcribed, it is usually essential that the researcher reviews and edits that transcription (and sometimes that it is checked by the interviewee). They (and/or you) will recognize inaccuracies and misinterpretations, and often be able to interpret relatively inaudible passages. (For your project, do you need the exact words spoken? If so, record the digital location of any passages that could not be accurately transcribed.)
- **Contexted:** If you are transcribing interviews or writing up field notes, work to include all context possible (for example, setting, social context, body language, tone). Don't assume you'll remember later. Write up what you observed or felt about the setting of an interview, the context of the respondent, including yourself in that context. Did the research event have several participants, as in an interview or focus group? If so, for your project, does it matter who was speaking? It usually does, so make sure that, where possible, speakers are clearly identified, and information about them is stored. (How do you do this? If you are moderating or observing the group, simply record the initial letter of their name and first word spoken by each speaker in turn. Give this odd record to the transcriptionist, and most speeches will be identified.)
- **'Thick description':** A good record contains detail of recall and imagery, interpretative comment and contextual knowledge, wherever this is appropriate. (The term 'thick description' is from the anthropologist Geertz (1973).) In particular, ensure that what you observed is recorded, and your observations are as detailed as may be useful. Listen to the audio record and review a transcript on the computer, editing in new things you now hear, like laughter or hesitation. (For your project, is it enough to record that the speaker laughed, or should you distinguish between a nervous giggle and a snigger?)

- **Useful:** The record should carry all available pertinent information about the research event, the respondent or the setting, and all the knowledge gained, including your impressions, reflections and interpretations. Never assume you will remember! If you decide for partial rather than complete transcription, always keep a note in the partial document, identifying the passage that was not transcribed.
- **Reflexive:** For any act making qualitative data, you need to consider the ways in which you are part of the study, and write yourself into the account. You made the data, you did the interview or observation. As remarked in the previous chapter, such records are collaborative constructs, between you and the 'subjects' of your study. These are *your* data. Use the first person and accurately record what you did. Pay attention to the situation you created, the context you imposed: by being there, the responses you felt and received. How did you influence ideas or behaviour? Always keep notes on these contexting observations.

HOW BIG SHOULD A DATA RECORD BE?

Qualitative research has a special version of Parkinson's Law: data expand to fill the time available (and indeed very often to exceed those limits).

This is, of course, because if you are working qualitatively, you do not have a clear a priori knowledge of what matters and what doesn't. Since any good researcher will at some stage meet this built-in problem, the practical solution is to confront it up front. These will be big records, generous in the detail they provide and the commentary you add. So you will require skill in selecting the detail you can shed and reducing the bulk of data so you can find and focus on what matters.

Good qualitative research requires an exquisite sense of timing of data reduction.

Reducing Data Records: The Shrink-Wrap Principle

All data require reduction if a story is to be told, an account given of what those data records show. The crucial difference between qualitative and quantitative data is that the researcher with qualitative data usually delays reducing them, and rarely reduces them solely to numbers. This is because the qualitative researcher is usually learning from the data, so does not want to make pre-emptive decisions about what data are important.

Even if you designed the project with this in mind, you may be alarmed by the volume of words and size of transcripts that result from qualitative enquiries. Large records are to be expected. Any normal conversation will, if transcribed, take many pages, but we don't normally transcribe conversations. So skills for informed, timely, designed and appropriate data reduction are crucial.

The critical question is not *whether* you should reduce the data, but *when*. You will want to hold all the complexity and context as long as it is necessary to understand the data – and no longer. At the end of your project, few audiences will find it useful if you give them back the full transcript of all your interviews.

How do you make those early data reduction decisions? My rule of thumb is the shrink-wrap principle. Like the shrunk plastic cladding around an item in a hardware store, your data record should be as large as it needs to be and as small as it can be.

Early in a project, I would transcribe the digression about the health provider. There may be a link here to the community group topic that I don't yet see (perhaps her main interest in group activity is to win clinical care in this community). Perhaps I will write a two-line memo wondering about it. But the discussion about sugar can go; it can't be relevant. Later, if health provision has failed to reappear in my growing body of data, I might revisit that interview, wonder again about the digression, conclude it did not matter and delete that memo.

Transcription or Summary?

If you chose to interview, for example, in a situation where this would be ethically acceptable, you may now have an audio or video record, and fading memories of the situation. These now need to be turned into data for your project, and a series of decisions demand attention.

Transcription Checklist

- Will the digital record be transcribed? If so, by whom, and how confident can you be that the transcriber will accurately and sensitively create a transcript from that complex and difficult interview event?
- Will the whole record be transcribed, and will the record contain not only words spoken but identification of who spoke, and of laughter, or body language, heard or seen? This is particularly significant in group interview records.
- What promises were made during the interview to summarize not transcribe, or to remove sensitive material?
- Will the original record be retained and, if so, where and how? There may be requirements for your ethics clearance that it be kept securely and later deleted.
- Will your remembered observations be added to that transcript, or stored elsewhere, or simply discarded?
- Do you plan to return to the original record? If not, what have you lost? If you are returning, is this merely once, to check the transcript, or again, to remind yourself of the vividly recorded event, or, using software, to coded segments gathered by topic?

Go to the **Wedding Work** project for a discussion of issues in having data transcribed – including the transcription guide the researcher prepared.

> Interviewing members of the group separately now, and recording them. Amazing how they diverge from what I thought was the central issue holding the group together – high-density development in their area.

If you are analysing the nuances of meaning in people's accounts of their experience, you will be likely to want the full transcript. Now consider the detail of that record. You cannot record everything that you saw and heard in every research episode. From the time of creating your first data record, you are making decisions about what is jettisoned. Some are easy. *Why transcribe your respondent's enquiries about whether you wanted sugar in your coffee?* Some decisions are difficult. *The digression to discussing her health provider's advice seems to have nothing to do with the discussion of community groups, but the fact that she wandered into this digression may be significant.* Your decision will largely depend on the method of enquiry and the question being asked.

Perhaps you want only an overview of attitudes, or some rather factual information. Your own summary notes will do, and you can save the time and expense and possibly embarrassment of recording and transcribing, and the challenges of retaining and coding detailed records. (If you are unsure whether you will want the complex account, the safe option is to record and transcribe two or three experimental interviews and assess thoughtfully the data records you have created. What have you learned that you would not have known without that transcript? Does it matter for your project?)

Be aware of budgets of time and money. Transcription is the enemy of both! Transcribing a clearly audible digital record from an interview can take from four to six times the time taken by the original interview. If you do the transcription yourself, you will undoubtedly learn a lot, by re-hearing the voices, and noticing detail you'd misremembered. You will have the great advantage, if you are working in software, of being able to code ideas that occur as you transcribe. But the time is substantial; reflect on whether these particular data records deserve such investment.

Always consider partial transcription, which can be expanded later. And check the abilities of your software to handle audio and visual data, and/or to help you create a partial record that contains your comments and partial transcripts, which can be coded and linked back to the original recording.

Staging Data Reduction

An early task is to plan data reduction, and those decisions must be made thoughtfully and cautiously. It's important to see that data reduction will occur throughout a project. You can't help reducing the data early on - but you shouldn't (and don't need to) do all your data reduction now. A first stage of data reduction occurs in the research event:

- What will you record, then and there, and what will *not* be noted or remembered? Test these decisions with a sample record.
- What supplementary notes or editing will you add to the record after the research event?
- Reflect on the data *not* recorded by your proposed technique. For example, are you writing notes about the setting and interactions you observe during an interview? If you don't, these will be forgotten - and they may be critical for interpretation later.

The second data reduction stage is during the making of the data record:

- What will not be transcribed at all?
- What sorts of material will be summarized rather than fully transcribed?
- How far can each record be reduced without losing potentially important data? The temptation is to save everything, to transcribe every word, to store every image. Make and document your choices about reduction.

The third stage is during analysis - indeed, analysis is all about data reduction:

- As your growing understanding of the data gives you confidence to discard data that are off-topic or irrelevant to the processes studied, you will find you can skilfully reduce complexity, and see more clearly what does matter. (The search processes described in Chapter 8 assist the important checking of these decisions.)
- If this last stage of data reduction is done well, the report retains everything necessary to support the explanation and justify the claims of the report, but *only* what's necessary. Reduction during analysis is rather like the process by which a skilled chef reduces a sauce to just the consistency and richness required to impress. (Jump to Chapter 10 to read about *using* data in a report.)

STORING RECORDS WITH SOFTWARE

How to store these records? Under the bed, in one of the brown filing cabinets, in shoe boxes or 'we'll see' are not adequate answers to this question! To start making data records without knowing what you will do with them is asking for trouble. To store them inefficiently or temporarily while you seek a better answer will multiply your workload. As with babies and rose bushes, it is important to have *prepared* where your qualitative data will go before they arrive.

As I warned in the Preface, this book assumes you will use computer software. This assumption is not just because most researchers now do use software, or even because they save enormous amounts of time by doing so, but because by using software they are better able to do justice to their data. And, significantly, the use of computers has directed researcher attention far more to the quality of the data records. But recall the attendant warning: don't feel constrained to the stable of specialized qualitative computing (CAQDAS) tools. To explore the range of digital tools available, go to Paulus et al. (2014).

When Do You Choose and Learn Computer Tools?

Now! If you were going on a car trip, packed and ready to go, it is unlikely you would have delayed till now the choice and purchase of a vehicle as well as learning to drive it. If you are planning to use qualitative software, choose it and learn it before you begin, not once the data are becoming too much for you.

Start in your software – storing literature reviews, early designs, memos to the supervisor, research diaries. Good qualitative software is not merely about managing data records, but about integrating all aspects of a project – design, reading, field data, analyses and reports. By the time the project data records are being created, you will be skilled in that software.

There are two reasons for urgency.

Firstly, you will not have time later. As soon as your project is underway, data will build up, and if you are still unable to use your software's tools, learning them will distract you, while delaying learning them will mean some data records are handled manually, some with software, and the project is inconsistent from the start.

Secondly, you need the software now. Your software will provide the container for your data and ideas, and the tools for exploring the relationships between data and ideas. From the first ideas, and the first data, you should be able to handle storage and management deftly with software. If you have followed the advice in this chapter, you will have very many project documents already: research design proposals, discussion documents, reflections on the scope of the project and, importantly, literature reviews. These are all qualitative data – complex, contexted material which you need to explore and understand throughout the project. The software can assist you in handling them, and if they are handled in the same project as your data records, you will constantly be reminded of those contexts.

So choose and learn to use the software now.

How Do You Choose and Learn Software?

Go online! The paper literature on computing is necessarily out of date before publication. To find the current packages available, and try them out, go to the website for this book: study.sagepub.com/richards3e. Follow the links to current discussions of the range of packages and to the sites for particular packages and their tutorials. But once you have chosen a software package (or had it chosen for you) go looking for good resources that help you critique what it does, and that teach methods in the context of that package. References are at the end of this chapter.

The 'Qualitative Software' section of this book's website has advice and links to sites offering current descriptions of the packages available. If your project or your institution already has a package, this may pre-empt the choice, but take time to compare it with others discussed. If you are free to choose your software, carefully set out what you want from it, and review software available to you within your resources. A next step is to seek out colleagues who have used the software product you are considering and spend time watching how they work with it.

Now find direct reports of what it is like to work with the software package you are considering! In the 'Methods in Practice' section, compare the reports from the projects using different software products. Five reports offer detailed accounts of working in three packages: Atlasti (**Sexuality-Spirituality** project); MaxQDA (**Wedding Work** project); and QSR NVivo (**REMS, Youth Offender Program Evaluation** and **Harassment Complaints** projects).

Researchers differ in the ways they best learn software. For many, self-teaching is best, but it requires informed materials. In the software section of study.sagepub.com/richards3e you will find detailed advice and links to authoritative sites and tutorials in some of the most used products. Others are helped by seeing someone competently using the software tools; if this is your preference, find a workshop or a consultant near you. Direct learning with an expert may save you months of trial and error.

If you are working in a team, it is highly desirable to have training as a group. Look for a consultant who will come to your site to train you together, responding to the different needs of group members and advising on group processes.

All members of the team must attain competence in the software. A recipe for disaster is the team whose principal investigator (PI) sends a junior assistant off to learn the software and make the project, while the PI and other senior colleagues direct the design and data handling. The assistant is likely to leave; the PI will never trust how the interpretations are stored or be able to contribute directly to them (or even access them!). As the project takes shape, it is effectively conducted and reported by the assistant (so long as they have not left). This is not a team.

Getting Started in Software

If you are to use software as you work through this book, start now.

With what? The tasks of setting up, outlined in this chapter, all produce material you can handle with software. They should all be stored in the qualitative computer program to handle all aspects of your research. Since qualitative data surround the researcher, you can start immediately to record data. You almost certainly will have material to record and consider before your first making of deliberately created data by interview or observation. The software project can start with data such as your literature reviews, early designs, memos to the supervisor, research diaries. These are all qualitative data. Once you are already skilful in your software, you can be ready when the first records of your data-making efforts arrive. The goal is to have a project in which to store them along with any other information that should be kept.

Start immediately! There is no advantage in waiting till data records build up, and there are two important reasons not to do so:

1. Qualitative data appear from unexpected sources in a sometimes tumultuous tumble of events and opportunities. Since your recall is always relevant, the sooner you record data, the better your record will be. And insights from one event can inform how you approach the next. Ensuring a smooth flow of data records into the project from the beginning helps you see and assess the data as they build up, editing and annotating them as they come in.
2. As soon as the data records are in your project on computer, you can use search tools to find out about their content and check their quality. (For example, the search processes described in Chapter 8 can be used to gather all the answers to a question and review whether the question needs rewording, or to find how often a particular word is being used, and how it's interpreted.)

Start aware! When researchers worked without computers, the diversity of records meant they almost inevitably delayed the clerical tasks of data storage and risked losing data and access to records. Of all the advantages computers offered to qualitative researchers, the simplest was that the diverse, messy records of data could be held together, reliably stored and immediately rapidly accessed, without damaging their complexity or losing their context. One of the advantages of computer storage of data is that since access to records later on is easy, they can be stored in any order, and the records and their order can be modified later.

But be aware that this advantage comes at a price. If you have started in a qualitative software package, your project is taking shape – the shape your software provides. All qualitative software programs, in one way or another, help you set up a container for your project. In this you can store the documents and other data you gather, and the ideas and thoughts and categories of analysis that you produce during analysis. But like all containers, this one will tend to constrain. In the chapters to follow, and on the website, you'll find advice on thinking outside the 'box' of your software project.

Getting Documents 'in'

All the tasks in this chapter will create documents and ideas that you want to retain and revisit. These can begin your project.

Setting up Data Documents

Documents already discussed include:

- the research design;
- the logs of your discussions of design issues;
- the proposed stages of entry into the field and observations there;
- notes from books and documents that are building to a literature review.

Each of these can (and should) be stored in your software project, safely and with appropriate comments, where data from your observations or interviews or documents will, later, also be stored.

A useful first document in your software project is a log trail document. You can return to it to note logging events from time to time and, since it is on the computer, you can link it to other documents and memos. Whenever you create memos about 'loggable' matters, you can put hyperlinks to them in the log trail document (see Chapter 4 about memos and links). In this way, you can maintain a trail of important events through your entire project, no matter how or where you recorded them, how big the project is, or how long it goes on for.

Each of these documents can be created or imported into your new project.

Now for Your Ideas and Information

Now consider all the ideas, concepts and questions that you are taking into the project, and ways of storing those alongside the document. Note that to do so does not require that they remain significant, and certainly does not predetermine the ideas you will discover in the data to come. The following are sources of categories, things you are going to think about, identified in the setting-up process. Software packages have different terms for the places these categories are stored, but all will store them, ready for you to code there all the data about those categories (see Chapter 5).

——— Setting up Categories for Thinking about the Data ———

- If the literature, or experience, indicates that certain issues or processes or factors will be significant in this project, make categories for them, with appropriate commentary.
- If you are asking a series of prepared questions (whether or not these are to be asked in structured format), they should be noted (and if they change later, this too needs recording).
- If your entry into the field has identified places, people, roles or tasks that you want to gather material about, put these into the project.

As new data are recorded, and new ideas emerge, the project will grow. If you have decided to use a qualitative software package, it will now enable you to store your work safely and support your exploration of the relationship between your data and ideas. As you build up a body of data, you can use your software to store information about data type, timing and source, and about your interpretations and thoughts.

————————— Storing in Software —————————

There are three ways to record data in your project in a qualitative software package. Check the processes supported by your software, and start making decisions!

(Continued)

(Continued)

1. You can type up a data record in a word processor, and import it into your project on the computer. In some software, you can import non-text records.
2. You can work in your project, and type your record there. (This is strongly preferable if you are transcribing or typing up field notes, as it allows you to work with the record as you type it up, recording ideas that occur to you or links to related data.)
3. You can choose to leave the record elsewhere – in a notebook, a heap of photographs or a video – and put in your project a summary of what's in this external record. (If the event was recorded in image, or not recorded digitally, this option allows you to make the record part of your project without reducing it to text or storing large image or video files on your computer.)

Every time you make some data, there will be a best way of storing the record. The next chapters advise how you can handle your records, store information about them and expand them with your ideas and reflections. For now, start a habit that will last you a researcher's lifetime: as data are made, make a good record, and as the record is made, store it carefully!

Setting up a Data Storage System

Try drawing a flowchart for your data storage procedure:

1. When those observations are made, how will they be recorded?
2. What steps can be taken *before* storing the data record to reduce unnecessary size and remove extraneous material?
3. What are the ethical requirements for 'cleansing' and who will take responsibility for this? How will confidentiality and anonymity be appropriately ensured?
4. Where will the record be placed, and how will it be brought into the project?
5. How and where will back-up copies of the original data be stored?

Such a checklist is useful for sole researchers, but essential if you are working with colleagues in a team. You need to have planned procedures that will ensure the smooth flow of data, and check that no process is left undone because responsibility was not allocated.

 Go to the **Wedding Work** project for a detailed account of data storage procedures.

The Impact and Risks of Computer Storage

Now, take a moment to consider what you have done by starting in software. You are embarking on a journey with your data in a particular sort of vehicle. If you are in a qualitative software package, it will hold your data in particular ways, give you access in particular ways and necessarily nudge you to using those ways.

In my experience, the vast majority of users of qualitative software use it only as a container, usually for documents and coding. Other teachers and evaluators of packages agree (see the website for more on this.) You may not go further, and if you don't, be careful to avoid the temptation to claim the software in some way did the analysis! Compare the website accounts of what the authors achieved through software.

The researcher in the **Inside Companionship** project reports more honestly than many users of software: 'I have to recognize that I used this software as an interactive big folder or a filing cabinet. I ordered texts, subtexts, divisions and sub-divisions. I moved and recovered them according to my new and "floating" criteria. But I could not say that I managed my analysis by this software.'

If you have previously worked on paper, and are now moving to computer storage, the contrast is dramatic. Now you are able to store everything necessary, in as much detail as available. And you can store it very rapidly. For most of us who previously worked with paper records, this is extraordinary progress, whether or not you use specialist qualitative software. Off-computer, all this text and other types of records will take large amounts of space and storage containers, making access difficult, even impossible. When a 30-page interview is deep under others in a storage box, it can be impossible to find a particular passage. Finding all the passages on a theme is likely to be too great a task to attempt. Whether or not you use qualitative software, computer records will be far easier than paper to pack, move around and access.

If you previously worked on paper you may have established processes to identify copies of passages. There is no need now to number pages or lines to access those places in long documents, find coded extracts and figure out where an extract comes so you can go straight to the context. Your software will do all that for you.

On paper, you had to deal with documents one by one. Computers can 'batch' processes, importing 100 files almost as quickly as one. To use this facility obviously saves time, and permits far more bulk of data. It also requires forward planning. Formatting of the document can be used for automating coding or gaining access to particular sections. Consult your software documentation to find what formatting can assist automation. And you need a process in place to ensure that these documents get adequately interpreted.

This freedom of course has its price. Beware the capacity and speed of the computer!

The most obvious challenge is that researchers now need to create their own standards for the number and size of data records. If they previously worked with manual methods, they were saved by the rigid walls of filing cabinets from the temptation to store unreduced data records. Software won't stop you until you have strained the capacity of your hard disk and/or your working computer memory, and with cloud storage possible these may not stop you! No qualitative project should have that much data. Bulk data, especially bulk data that are not yet handled at all, can create a massive barrier to thinking.

And beware the vulnerability of computer files. The obvious risk of any computer storage is that it is much easier to delete 12 large computer files than to burn a book.

_____ Good Housekeeping and Your Computer Files _____

As with any computer process, the storage of data from your research requires good housekeeping:

- As you set up the project and store the incoming data files, establish a routine for storing copies of the original files and ensuring the safety of your growing project.
- If you don't have a back-up routine, now is the time to start one. Whether or not your confidence in computer systems is shaky, you are at risk of damaging or deleting files when you become excited, upset or simply fascinated by your data. (Sadly, qualitative researchers are statistically less likely to be computer competent than statisticians.)
- If your training is in quantitative research, you are at special risk. Working on the census database, you don't back it up, since you are not going to change it. Qualitative research is not like that: you will change your database every time you reflect on an interview or write a memo. So back up frequently.
- Keep all back-up files on a safe medium that is _not_ the hard disk where you have your project. It's the hard disk that is most likely to let you down!

WORKING WITH YOUR DATA RECORDS

The data record is more than the transcript of your recording or notes. It should include appropriate identification of the research event or case, and recording of what has been done with it since. The researcher always has to choose what accompanying materials to store, and this choice takes thought. (Novice researchers often overload their data records, rather as the ancients did their graves, with everything that might possibly be needed in the afterworld.)

Getting Back to the Document

There is no point in keeping records unless you can later find the right record, or the right part of the record, for your purpose. Qualitative research is all about access. As you make data, it is critical to make *accessible* records of those data. The moment you find you are unable to recall or retrieve a part of an interview of significance for your current thinking, stop interviewing! You need to work on access to your records before any more are created.

Mountains of transcripts of interviews will distance you from an understanding of the topic if you have no way of finding the data you need to think about. You can't expect to explore threads of meaning and patterns of responses if you have to rake through those mountains, seeking the documents that sounded different. Stacks of video records will be inaccessible if to explore a crucial issue across all those focus groups you have to replay each to look for it. If the data records are not accessible, the tools to be explored for searching and seeing synthesis or patterns (Chapters 8 and 9) just won't work. The analysis will be skewed to the most recent data or the case most memorable, with the researcher trapped in their inability to overview the occurrences of this issue in all their work.

The sort of access you will want should be obvious from the research design. Most projects need at least two different ways of organizing access to documents:

1. You need access to any document or group of documents. This requires:

- storing different *types or sources of data records* separately, for example, published records and observations, so you can compare them and focus on one or another in questioning. *What did the official record say about the local council discussion of developer applications and what did I find people in the corridors said about it?* Use folders or ways of sorting groups or sets of documents in your software to make this access instant.
- storing *information about the attributes of a site or person* that the record represents: for example, location, industry and type of a site, or gender, age and job of an interviewee. If such data are stored, you can compare the views of women and men on an issue, find if these differ across sites, assess the distribution of income across the people interviewed in an area, and so on. The storage of attributes is a form of coding, and is covered in Chapter 5.

2. And you need access to just the wanted part of any document:

- retrieval of the appropriate surrounding text to make sense of any small or large segment. This requires that the text is segmented by you, using formatting. Use headings in your word processor, just as you do when you are writing a paper, to show the main parts of a record. The word processor or your qualitative software will then be able to fetch for you just the segment wanted.
- access to just the segments about a topic or idea. This requires that you code the data interpretatively. Or to just what one person said, or what all the women said, and so on. This requires you to store information about attributes. These topics are covered in Chapter 5.

Getting Back to the Context

In the early sections of this chapter, the emphasis was on rich records and the requirements of complexity and context. When you come to store the data, an obvious question is: how can you maximize the complexity and context you are storing?

Of course, any data record does violence to the complexity of the event recorded. In choosing events and recording them, you simplify. Why did you choose to interview women only, not their husbands? Why only transcribe their interviews, not describe what you saw? Where possible, you want later to be reminded of these complex other ways of seeing the event.

The act of recording data inevitably strips the data event from its context. So the researcher has an immediate task, to retain the context needed. How do you know what's needed? There are two sorts of context to be retained – the context of the event and the context of the record.

The context of the data event Almost every data record should include its context in the project (what sort of event was it? Which researcher conducted it?) and the social context in which it happened. The importance of this information will depend on the research design.

In most projects, it is worth starting by making three sets of notes with any record:

1. *Project notes*: for example, date, address, who did the interview and when?
2. *Setting notes*: for example, what was the house like, in what sort of area?
3. *Interpretative notes*: for example, your reflections on the biases you think you took to this event or the problems encountered with the questions you had prepared. Or your observation that the respondent was ill at ease and evading questions after their friend dropped in. (See Chapters 7 and 9 on 'member checking'.)

As you write up a research event, develop habits of rereading the transcript or field notes, and writing in a separate document what you feel should be 'between the lines'. Now develop a way of storing those subversive notes, so you will find them again. If transcribing interviews, include all the detail possible (for example, body language, tone, clear identification of speakers). At the least, these notes will assist you in vivid recall. They may also be important contributors to the material you use for claims of validity.

The context of the record You also need to store the context within which you made the record. You will need to keep at least the following context:

- Notes about the recording process (for example, how long between the event and the field notes? who did the transcription and has it been checked?).
- Notes about associated records (for example, have you kept the recording and if so where? are there illustrative records as well?).

Checklist for Access to Data and Context

What information should be stored with each data record? You'll be helped by preparing a checklist to ensure this is consistently done. The following groups of items are usually necessary; adapt them to your project's requirements:

1. Access to documents and document parts:

   - Set up folders for different sorts of data, according to your design.
   - Use formatting of your documents if possible to divide them with headings that identify the parts of the record.

2. Access to context of the event and the record:

   - Record regularly the information about the context of the data event, separately making and storing:

     o project notes;
     o setting notes;
     o interpretative notes.

   - Write about the context of the data record (the recording process and other related records).

Expanding the Record

Each of the processes for useful storage of the record also expands it. They are not to be dismissed as clerical tasks. These are data-enriching processes, by which you can identify shapes in your data and hold your insights and memories. So you need very easy ways of dropping these details and thoughts into your project as they occur, and storing them where you will find them again.

As each record is brought into your project, store that data about the record. Check the features of your software to find the best way to do this.

Ways of Expanding the Record

The processes described above can be done by naming, describing and sorting the document:

1. Name it. The document's name can be used as a brief identifier. Establish a system for naming your documents that will allow you to tell immediately what record this is, within the constraints of confidentiality. Keep names short, so you can view them easily. Names should be meaningful not only to you but to anyone else working in the project, and should be ordered usefully in the project. Ensure that they do not breach anonymity requirements.
2. Describe it. For every document, store a description in a way that is easy to find and edit. On paper this might be a face sheet; in any software, there will be a way to describe a document. Use the description for brief summaries of context.
3. Sort it. Documents can be stored in folders or sets of a kind so you can ask questions just about one kind.

(Continued)

(Continued)

In the following chapters, you will learn to store ideas about the document, link to other data, and store information about the cases represented. Chapter 4 deals with ways of storing ideas about the document:

4. Annotate it. Placing a comment in the text or behind it.
5. Write about it in a memo. Store those memories and reflections on the event or context.
6. Link it to related data. Make a note about the data, or place a hyperlink to a file (the photo of the house, or an audio clip of the voice).

And in Chapter 5 there is a further way of expanding the record:

7. If the document represents a case – a person or a site, for example – you may wish to store information about the attributes of that case (demographics, location, etc.). Now you can access your data by gender, for example, or county.

For your data, review these options and decide how you can use them. Then try to use them consistently. Consistent handling of these ways of storing information will ensure that you retain the context and can reliably access records.

WHEN CAN YOU START ANALYSING?

You've been doing analytical work for most of the tasks of this chapter. If you took the advice in the previous chapters, you have also been logging that analytical work. In doing so, you have been not only considering the data but also building the basis for validating your analysis. Review the processes so far and consider which should be logged. Any decision or process you may later need to explain needs accounting for; for example, the decisions about what was not recorded, or the use of a search tool to gather all answers to a question and the consequent revision of that question. What to keep, what to discard, how to store and what to store with it are all analytical decisions, and the method requires that data be explored and interpreted from the start of the study.

Most qualitative research has no clear beginning and no predetermined schedule. It is in this way that qualitative methods contrast with most quantitative ones – indeed, this might be seen as the critical difference. Survey research, for example, has an expected order of events, sequential stages that can be relatively easily planned and predicted. Usually, and properly, the researcher begins with a research instrument that will remain fixed and a sample design that will be adhered to. Thus armed, the researcher conducts the predicted data collection, codes the data records, then, and only then, embarks on analysis. Quite properly, analysis is delayed until all data are 'in'.

This sequence is not required in qualitative research. Indeed, it is highly dangerous! Many of the processes you have already attempted are analytical. Selecting what are data and what aren't requires analysis of the significance of different topics and processes. Deciding to store some information about relevant context (but not other information) requires consideration of what context will matter. Once you start making records, you have started analysis – and irrevocably affected the quality of the analysis! The processes of reflecting, coding and storing and using ideas build on these early analytical processes. They are the tasks for the next chapters.

To Do

1. Prepare a plan or present one (informally, telling it to an informed audience) showing the methods you will use for:

- creating the records of your data events
- reducing the data records
- storing the data records
- ensuring access to particular documents and parts of documents
- storing notes on the context of the event and the record

2. Assessing software:

Go to the 'Qualitative Software' section on the website and follow links to inform you on ways the different packages assist in storing documents and information about them. Now, choose two projects from the website which used different software. Can you see differences in the project reports that might be explained by the choice of software package?

3. Starting in software:

- Decide which software product or products you are using, and write an account of your reasons for this decision.
- Using links to self-teaching tutorials or a class or workshop, gain an introductory knowledge of how to use your chosen software. You need to become sufficiently skilled to be able to start a project in your software and create and explore documents in the project.
- Set up a starter project on your computer, with the documents and ideas created, as in the exercises above. For each document stored, consider what information should accompany it, and discover how to store that information using your software package.

Suggestions for Further Reading

Most texts have much less to say about the making of data records than about the research experience, and less still about computer storage of records. A thorough discussion of problems of qualitative data is in Miles and Huberman (1994); see also Miles' famous article in 1979.

(Continued)

(Continued)

There is (very different) practical advice in Flick (2014), and Mason (2002), and rich examples in Wolcott (1994). See also the books of papers edited by Denzin and Lincoln (2000) and Morse (1994, 1997). The classic statement of 'thick' descriptions is in Geertz (1973).

Go to the Qualitative Software section of this book's website for advice, fuller references and links to help you into handling qualitative data with software. At the time of writing few texts cover all software that can be used for qualitative research; for a sweeping and thoughtful consideration of the impact and uses of digital tools, not just packages designed for qualitative research, see Paulus et al. (2014) and for a collection Hesse-Biber (2011). There is much more literature on data records in texts on specialist qualitative software (CAQDAS packages). The most recent and most comprehensive review is Lewins and Silver (2014), which also provides a detailed website with tutorials on leading packages. The CAQDAS Networking site, which the authors manage, is an essential place to go for recent developments; go to the website for this book for links to CAQDAS and to other relevant web resources.

For more reflection on the impact and limitation of specialist software, and examples of projects in different packages, see Di Gregorio and Davidson (2008) and Gibbs et al. (2002). From two of the researchers contributing projects to the website for this book, see Humble (2012) and Bong (2002).

For recent books devoted to particular software, see the new edition of Friese's very detailed text on using ATLAS.ti (2012), the text by Kuckhartz (2014), covering software in general but relating particularly to MaxQDA (see also Humble, 2012), and Bazeley and Jackson (2013) on NVivo. Beware a dated and motley literature: the most cited texts are collections from long-ago conferences (Fielding and Lee, 1991; Kelle, 1995). But some books in the past have usefully discussed a range of issues of impact of software on method and include Dey (1995), Tesch (1990), and Weitzman and Miles (1995).

II

Working with the data

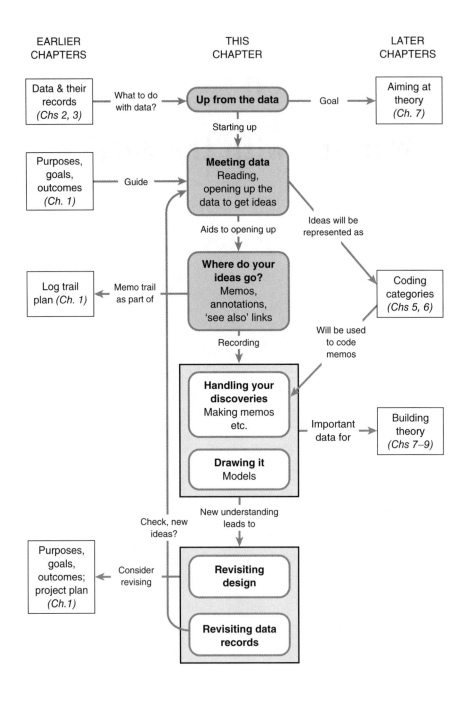

EARLIER CHAPTERS	THIS CHAPTER	LATER CHAPTERS

Data & their records *(Chs 2, 3)* — What to do with data? → **Up from the data** — Goal → Aiming at theory *(Ch. 7)*

Starting up

Purposes, goals, outcomes *(Ch. 1)* — Guide → **Meeting data** Reading, opening up the data to get ideas

Aids to opening up

Ideas will be represented as

Log trail plan *(Ch. 1)* ← Memo trail as part of — **Where do your ideas go?** Memos, annotations, 'see also' links → Coding categories *(Chs 5, 6)*

Recording

Will be used to code memos

Handling your discoveries Making memos etc. — Important data for → Building theory *(Chs 7–9)*

Drawing it Models

New understanding leads to

Check, new ideas?

Purposes, goals, outcomes; project plan *(Ch.1)* ← Consider revising — **Revisiting design**

Revisiting data records

FOUR

Up from the data

The most exciting and challenging processes in qualitative research require discovery and exploration of ideas from the data. This chapter offers ways of generating and recording ideas, handling and using the emerging ideas to develop the project.

> *Data don't speak for themselves. We have to goad them into saying things.* (Barry Turner, unpublished lecture, 1993)

Qualitative research works up from the data. The quality of the analysis is dependent on the quality of your data records and your skills for working up from them to ideas and explanations.

In the chapters so far, the focus has been on making qualitative data records which retain complexity and context. Recall why you were doing this: if the project is qualitative, it is because you don't know in advance what you may learn from the data. If you don't want to learn from the data, but only aim to describe the patterns of people's responses to preconceived questions, you do not need to keep their words or details of their experience. A survey would do. If you do want to learn from the actual accounts in your data, your aim is always to have ideas *emerge* from your working with data.

Go to the 'Working with Data' section of each of the 'Methods in Practice' reports to see the different ways that data records were handled as the projects developed.

You have been commissioned to study the environmental impact of the new 'eco-tourism' industry. You start with a wealth of existing data on the regulations governing operators and the exit surveys of participants in tours. Consistently, they show control of environmental impact and respect for that control. So why is there such suspicion of the eco-tourist operators among environmentalists?

Theory Emerging?

The expression that themes or theories *emerge* from data is frequently heard in qualitative research. The word misleads – theories certainly do not emerge spontaneously, and students who expect them to do so can wait for a very long time.

As Turner put it bluntly at the start of the chapter, we goad data into speaking. It's all in the handling.

If the vague promise of 'emerging' theory has concerned you, think (and read) more about what a theory is. Theory is a human construct, not an underground reservoir of oil waiting to emerge when you drill down to it. The researcher discovers themes, or threads in the data, by good exploration, good enquiry. By handling the data records sensitively, managing them carefully and exploring them skilfully, the researcher 'emerges' ideas, categories, concepts, themes, hunches, and ways of relating them. Out of such processes come bigger ideas, and, by hard work, from these loose threads can be woven something more like a fabric of good explanations and predications.

This process is easier because it always started from some theory. The researcher, in other words, brought in theory from elsewhere – the literature, professional knowledge or on-the-ground assumptions. Theory turns an observation – *environmentalists are being asked to support tourism* – into a research question: *given their ideological differences, can environmentalists accept eco-tourism?* Even in situations where the research seems theory-free – *a simple commission to discover the impact of eco-tourism* – it carries theoretical assumptions of the funders, the research team and indeed those who are being studied. Moreover, as a researcher, you will bring in theories of human interaction, and social structure, which will inform the way you now frame the question. *To understand people's behaviour we need to understand their perception of the situation.*

> Theory, then, should be neither a status symbol nor an optional extra in a research study. Without theory, research is impossibly narrow. Without research, theory is mere armchair contemplation. (Silverman, 2001: 110)

It is on the basis of these theories that you work with your data to produce more theory, up from the data. Reading your data records will lead to growing interpretations.

> The interviews flow well, and the respondents seem very open and cooperative, but you are learning nothing new. Your notes on each of the interviews are similar. The tour operators politely regret and apparently don't understand the hostility to their work, and expect it to disappear as environmentalists get used to such tourism and come to appreciate that it informs a wider public, makes profits that can be directed to PR work and increases commitment to environmental preservation.

As each file of data is imported, or each event typed up, get into the habit of asking the data management questions: how well and how thoroughly was the event recorded? How easily will you be able to access this record? And how confidently can you rely on it when you want to revisit it? Then, really read it. As you do, add your comments and reflect on the record as a whole. This is a first step to the aim of your project – which is not to describe your data records, but to take off from them.

MEETING DATA

Once you have commenced the processes of making data, by interviewing, observing or other research processes, it is often hard to slow down. Contacts multiply, opportunities pile up and it seems risky to pass them by. Especially if a deadline looms, and if you have established a safe storage procedure for your precious records, it is tempting to keep making more.

That momentum is exciting but also dangerous. It became more dangerous when software removed much of the clerical work of building up data. As noted in the previous chapter, bulk data records can be moved swiftly into a project: you can import one or 100 records into your project in one act. The next chapter will cover the ability to allocate information about them or do coding of their content automatically. These processes hugely assist the researcher, but they are clerical, mechanical processes, not analytical ones. They are not a substitute for reading and thinking about your data. Every qualitative method requires that the researcher learns from data, taking into the next research situation what was learned. *Those first interviews teach you something you had not considered: one of the tour operators explicitly claims tourism has an environmental protection role. Next time, frame questions to discover if others think this is so.*

There is no alternative to reading and reflecting on each data record, and the sooner the better. This is purposive reading. Aim to question the record and add to it, to comment on it and to look for ideas that lead you up from the particular text to themes in the project.

Reading and Enriching the Record

When a record is safely stored, read it. Always, while you are reading data, record your thoughts and responses and store safely anything you recorded.

Many processes don't require the computer, and this is one. Nor does it require formality. Sit under a tree with a printout of the data record and scribble in the margin. Or think aloud, record your reflections and type them up. But however tentative your thoughts, record them! Often researchers realize too late how important early reflection would have been. To be safe, store anything that might possibly matter.

Several projects tell how early reflections influenced the process of data making. Go to **Handling Sexual Attraction** and **Inside Companionship**.

However, when it comes to storage, the computer is your friend. It allows you to keep much more flexible records. The ideas can be stored rapidly, ensuring that the results of your thinking get recorded however trivial they may seem. Later, if you are confident that some of those early ideas didn't matter, they can be deleted or amended.

The first meetings with the data are precious, because this is when you are most able to be surprised by the research situation and everything about it. In the record of the early efforts, you notice things you didn't notice at the time and will later take for granted. *There is always an odd tone of contempt when some tour operators talk of environmentalists. It's rather like the way hyper-committed professionals talk of the unemployed – of course we know it's not their fault but ...*

If you are tempted to save the time, reflect on the many reasons why your recall will be imperfect. Yes, you were there, conducting the observation or the interview. But especially early in a project, much of your attention is on your presentation of who you are and what you are asking, as well as on a mix of practical issues (seating, placing a recorder, stopping the dog or the baby from dislodging it, watching the time).

Record and Recall: See the Difference

If you doubt the need to revise and improve your record, try this exercise:

- Conduct an interview, record it and later, without listening to the audio record, write down what you recall.
- When the interview is transcribed, read the transcript carefully and highlight everything that was not recalled.
- Then underline everything that is new to you, broadening your understanding of the situation or problem you are studying.
- The serious discoveries are the passages with both highlighting and underlining – they were not recalled, and they mattered for the next stage.
- Now in your recall notes highlight everything that is not in the transcript. You may find you had two quite different records, and certainly needed both!

Taking off from the Data

This is a particular sort of reading.

With experience, researchers develop their own style of working with data. To begin, it is important to find a style that works for you. If you have no prior training, try these steps.

Taking off from the Data

1. Take a first data document and read it. Skim read, then start again, and read the text very thoroughly, line by line.

2. Record (on paper or on the computer) anything interesting about any of the text.

   He refers to environmentalists always as 'little' or 'small' people.

3. When you find yourself saying something is interesting, ask 'Why is it interesting?' and record your answer.

   Well, it's false - obviously they are all sizes. So why say it?

4. Focus on any passages that are especially interesting and play with them, to open them out and find what they are about. Compare with other situations where this might happen. In a memo attached to the document, write any ideas that come from this game.

   Makes them sound like forest gnomes, not very powerful and sort of cute.

5. Ask 'Why am I interested in that?' and record your answer.

   I'm interested in images of environmentalists - this suggests stereotyping them as trivial, or powerless - or perhaps as little creatures of the forest.

This simple process takes you from the detail of the document ('That's interesting!') to the concept ('Why?') and then to the focused abstraction ('Why will this project benefit from that concept?'). You have moved off the text to the process or perception or event. You're writing conceptually, analytically, not just describing what the original record said.

Opening up the Data

If you have explored the methods literature and discovered the techniques of grounded theory, you will have read of the methods of *open coding*. It is always risky to borrow and adapt some techniques from a wider methodological approach, since they may depend on other techniques. If you find these work for you, you will benefit from reading the detailed accounts of that method. But any researcher can learn from these ways of 'opening' data up, and develop their own. The techniques rely on comparison to assist the researcher to tease out what's going on in the data. If something is interesting, use comparisons to interrogate it.

Here is a very simplified version of that process. The goal is *to get up off* the data and open your enquiry to wider consideration of some aspect of the process being studied. There are no fixed rules, but in grounded theory methods the 'paradigm' used has a series of questions. Note that during the process, a concept is created and named.

Opening up the Data

Focus on a very interesting phrase or statement. Interrogate it, asking questions about the following:

- **Conditions: Firstly**, ask under what conditions you might hear that phrase and what would it mean then. (When did you last hear it? What was going on in that situation?)

  Little people appear in myths and novels. Hobbits, maybe, in pretty, mossy houses. They're not real or politically relevant in real society.

- **Consequences: Then**, ask about the consequences of this idea or attitude. (When someone uses that phrase, what effects will it have?)

  'Belittling' of critics as a group without actually attacking them. Looks magnanimous but does erode their image as real players.

- **Strategies and interactions: Now**, consider what this will mean for their strategies and, finally, for their interactions.

  Belittling will lessen interaction; the belittler will be unlikely to listen to concerns or respect recommendations from those stereotyped.

As each data record is stored, make a routine of taking the steps described to get 'up' from the data record. You will find the texts rapidly expand with your annotations, and the number and interest of your memos are growing daily. You've taken off.

Using team or group sessions Qualitative thinking is often very well done in groups, and the three-step process outlined above works wonderfully as a group process. If you are working with a team, or meeting with other researchers to discuss technique, try taking those three steps into a discussion. It is important to devise ways of raising and using different interpretations, rather than submerging them.

Locating and Discussing Team Differences

A useful exercise early in a team project is to explore the differences and similarities of interpretation:

- Distribute a document for everyone to read. All members should work through it, marking what they find as interesting, asking why and noting why they think this project should be interested in that.
- Each member notes each answer to that last question 'Why am I interested in that?' on a separate piece of paper. This makes a collection of issues or themes that they think the project will be interested in.

> • Compare the answers from different team members.
>
> Some members feel 'little people' indicates affection; others feel that little people have mystical, often feared power. Now in discussion you can build on each group member's work, and debate the interpretations.

WHERE DO YOUR IDEAS GO?

Into the project! The results of these readings and reflections are more data. There are several different sorts of reflections, however, so different ways of storing ideas are needed. Any qualitative software will provide these. To handle the range of ideas discussed so far, you have three different ways of storing reflections:

1. Annotations that belong with the record and refer to its content.
2. Memos, writing about other themes or ideas.
3. Links or pointers to related material within the project or out from it. Link from each relevant passage to the memo, and keep writing. And always link *out* to other material, paper records, or online data that keeps you thinking.

Especially if your first thoughts look unimpressive, take care to store them appropriately. To decide where to put them, simply ask how you will want to meet these ideas again.

Annotations

An idea about a detail in the text should be available whenever you see that particular text. Perhaps the respondent's words assert that they were happy with a situation, but you recall that their expression and body language expressed distress. Place an annotation to record this.

> Each time there is an allusion to the 'little' size or influence of environmentalists, record a comment that reminds you of the many meanings of the terms.

If you recorded scribbled notes in the margin, referring to particular phrases or ideas, take the time to place these as annotations or comments in the document on computer. The scribbled notes on paper might never be found again, but the annotation stays 'behind' the text, always available. It does not interrupt your reading of the account, but whenever you revisit this part of the document, in any context, you will be reminded of that idea (and of course you can edit and develop the annotation).

Memos

Your thinking about the document as a whole, or a theme emerging 'up' from the document, will be best stored as a document in its own right. Usually such documents are called *memos*, and *memo* writing is important in any qualitative method.

Write a memo on 'belittling' and this will remind you to reflect further on this new idea, especially if you find other instances of the process.

Memos are the places where the project grows, as your ideas become more complex and, later, more confident. Writing good memos is a skill to be valued. They need not be tidy or definitive. They should tell the visitor to that place in your project what you were seeing and considering at this point. Memos that are significant in your project history should be recorded in the log trail document, and linked to it so you can find them again.

A Memo on Memos

- Develop a memo-writing routine that encourages quick and easy documentation of the ideas and the ways ideas grow. Treat memos as informal records of thinking aloud, never as finished research productions.
- Memos can be spur-of-the-moment creations. Whatever your routine, the memo is best recorded as a thought occurs, a worry is articulated or a concept emerges. Write a memo whenever you think what you are thinking is something you should be able to find later.
- Develop a very simple and efficient way of storing memos so they are easily found again, when you have more thoughts to add.
- Record especially your thoughts on themes that seem to be dominating the data, or processes by which you are exploring key categories. These records will be essential in later processes of validating your account of the data (see next chapter).
- Identify key aspects of your work and try to gather sets of memos about them. Most likely are these:

  o **Memos about method** (insights into the way you've created these data, how you skewed an answer, etc., that will help you later to interpret these data as yours).
  o **Memos about documents** (one memo for each is a good rule – to keep all observations on this particular record in one place).
  o **Memos about emerging ideas** (for any theme or interesting idea, record what happened when you asked questions of it, what didn't fit, whether you can explain it, and so on).

- Don't wait until an idea is 'memo-worthy', and you can write it up in a properly presented essay; by that time you will have lost the spark of the first hunch or insight.
- Memos are your personal, private record of wild ideas and possible leads. Write them in the first person, and clearly record your feelings about what you are writing and your confidence in it. Avoid the passive voice ('the theme emerged'). Later, when you have built a conclusion from this line of thought you will need the honest record of where it came from and how sure you were then.
- A good memo is vivid, alive, fun to read. It is also, always, linked to the data it relates to, so as you develop that idea you can revisit the data and ground your growing ideas in the data.
- Always date every entry in a memo – and you will find it stores the story of that interpretation or idea. Later this will give legitimacy to your explanation, providing part of the 'log trail' for your account of the data.

Ways of Linking Data

Linking comes naturally to browsers of online social media or internet resources. Linking back to the source of an idea is just one of very many ways your data records build up. Of course your records will be related, since you planned them that way, but you are looking for new relationships. As you find them, record them. Rich data become richer if you can insert pointers elsewhere. When you find something interesting, you may want to place messages that tell you: 'See also the second meeting' or 'That's different from the account from the rival company's director'.

As you work up from the data, these links will help you to move from one data record to another. Especially if you are working on computer, this means that you will be less likely to revisit data records singly than to rethink their relationships. You will then see new themes in the data, and see as significant passages that didn't seem to matter before. A phrase that was just interesting acquires a deeper significance as it recurs in other accounts. If the pointers are placed when you see that recurrence, you will be able to find that phrase again, rethink its context and compare with its other occurrences. A single comment may start building to a theme on its way to a theory.

So you need ways of pointing from one data record to another. If you were working on paper, you would write a reference to the other document in the margin, then (sometimes!) find it again. On computer, you can place a link that will take you straight to the document or part of the document you want to see. Given a live link, you are much more likely to follow it, and consequently, much more likely to see the relationships in the data.

Links are particularly important for memos. Use the ability to link from one place in a document to a memo or from the memo to various records.

> Link from each relevant passage to the 'belittling' memo, and keep writing in that memo about the differences as well as similarities of these comments.

Links are also essential to ensure that you do not lose data records that are not in your project. Perhaps you photographed the group's meeting, or videoed a discussion. If that photo is on the computer, a link to it will remind you, when reading of the meeting, to 'see also' the photo. Or a link to the voice on the record will remind you that the transcript doesn't express the anxiety you heard in the interviewee's tone. You can jump to the extract and listen again, revisiting the memories of the interview and heightening your awareness of the anxiety described.

Linking to records within or without the project on computer will assist you to weave a stronger fabric of data and interpretation. It is no accident that we talk of a 'web' of evidence or the 'fabric' of an argument. Strong understanding is built just like a spider's web, not from individual threads but from their linked nets.

HANDLING YOUR DISCOVERIES

Annotations, memos and links offer different ways of handling the ideas that emerge in 'taking off' from the data. Revisit those steps for taking off, using different ways of recording what happened.

─────── **Taking off and Handling the Ideas that Result** ───────

1. Skim read, then read the text very thoroughly, line by line. (Start writing in the document's memo. Always insert the date and time before you write, and the memo will grow to tell the story of your interpretation.)
2. Record anything interesting about any of the text. (Make an annotation to that text, storing your hunch or insight.)
3. When you find yourself saying something is interesting, ask 'Why is it interesting?' (Go back to the document's memo and record your answer.)
4. Focus on passages, to open them out and compare. (Place a link to remind you to 'see also' another document if your comparison reminds you of other data.)
5. Ask 'Why am I interested in that?' and record your answer. (Where? In a new memo about this newly discovered theme. Place a link so that when you return to the interesting text, it reminds you - see also that memo.)

 The **Handling Sexual Attraction** report tells the story of the emergence of a category and how it was explored, with results for the next stage of the project.

DRAWING IT - THE EARLY USES OF MODELS

Qualitative researchers don't need instructions to draw models of what they see going on in their data. For most, it seems a natural way to express vaguely pictured notions of what goes with what and possibly causes it. This can happen from the start of a project. In Chapter 2, there was a suggestion to use models, on paper, whiteboards or software, to display design ideas and revise in response to discussion.

For many, paper, whiteboards and tablecloths may be preferable. But modelling online has advantages of sophisticated drawing tools and produces images more adaptable to presentations. And modelling within a qualitative software package offers new support for qualitative enquiry. Packages differ in the tools they offer, but expect:

- Items that you place in a model are 'live' to the data - click on the document in your model and it will open on the screen.

  Operator 1 interview gave you the idea of investigation of the 'little' descriptors of environmentalists. Here are the words that were used...

- Relationships that you draw in the model can indicate your confidence in them, the evidence you have for this relationship and, most importantly, the nature of the relationship.

    Once it's drawn up, the importance of 'belittling' appears less impressive, and you realize that the only times you very confidently place that link are in a part of the country where forest clearance for tourist roads is highly controversial.

- Layers can be used to show different aspects of your picture of the data, and help you make new discoveries.

    The 'belittling' relationship occurs always between tour operators and individuals, not groups – they refer to little people, not particular individuals.

Modelling is a way of telling your ideas, and like any telling, it clarifies. It also allows you to display and reflect on different ways of seeing the data.

As an experiment, draw a model of what is going on in your first document, the issues being discussed or the reasons for a response. Save the model, to compare with the picture of what's going on in the next document.

REVISITING DESIGN

Be prepared to have this detailed work with your first data records, show you problems in your research design. This is to be expected and welcomed. The goal is to learn from the data, and anything you learn can now be fed back into your approach. In this way, working up from the data can loop you back to the research design.

> It seems likely that you happened on a particular battle-ground where one tour company achieved National Parks' support for clearing of trees for their huts. This may be a significant case study in hostility, but everyone agrees this is highly unusual. You need data from other areas.

Unlike in variable analysis, there is no imperative for the qualitative researcher that the design or approach should be constant throughout the project. (Indeed, such an imperative would absurdly contradict the goal of 'naturalistic' approaches to the situations you are studying.) You will be providing an overall understanding, not a breakdown of how many people gave a particular response to the same question. So changing the questions asked, or the ways topics are approached, at this stage is possible, though of course it always requires work.

The tools of the qualitative trade are often developed with such feedback loops as the project develops. Adjusting the research approach is entirely proper, and some adjustment is usually required. Qualitative projects quite normally have no 'pilot' stage in which the research 'tools' (questionnaires, tests, etc.) are tested. If you designed a 'pilot' stage to try out an approach, do not feel you have to discard the data from that stage. It's different, certainly, from what the next stage brings, but differences are food for analysis, not a problem for consistency. Indeed, in a method strongly driven by comparison, consistency can be a problem.

Perhaps you designed a cross-case comparative analysis of different tour operators. Now, you find your cases are too alike, there's no contrast to feed the comparison, and the striking comparison is between the ideological world views of operators and environmentalists. Looping back to the research design, consider the scope of data needed to gain adequate understanding of their world views.

What Should Change?

Each time you work with a data record, be alert to things you might change. At the early stages, this will often prove very fruitful. Perhaps some questions you asked won surprising hostility and very short answers? *Apparently, enquiring into the profit margin of eco-tours is out. What to do about this, since the claim that the companies are 'raking it in' is occurring frequently?* Revise those questions, sensitively rewording them to be more appropriate to what you now know matters in this setting. *Perhaps try giving the operators a chance to rebut that claim.*

You started interviewing tour operators but you had no experience of their work. There's a strong message that they are offended that you had not learned more about them first. Well, worse things happen to researchers – a stage of fieldwork is inserted in the research design, and you need new hiking boots. At the early stage, expect feedback loops: your project can cheerfully be regarded as one long pilot. Later, as you become more sure-footed in the research field, and more confident in your assessment of what matters (and what doesn't), studying the data will be less likely to change your approach. A next stage of looping back to design will happen later, as you are pointed by your growing theory to areas that still need data. (See Chapter 7 on theoretical sampling.)

Now assess that first, well-studied data record, and adjust your next excursion into the research field:

- How useful is the information you have acquired, and what's missing?

  A real picture of these businesses at work.

- What else should you have asked?

  About environmentalists in a wider context, not just this area ...

- How much detail does it provide, where was there too much detail, where too little?

  The tour operators talk for hours about how misunderstood they are as principled individuals, but are tight-mouthed about their business roles.

- Are you uncomfortable about any of your approaches or still feeling you are not getting to the issues you need to understand?

  The emphasis from both sides on the heightened personal criticism of operators seems to prevent your talking about the topic you are commissioned to cover - what are the real effects on the environment of these operations?

Write about this assessment, in a memo, and then rephrase your questions or revise your approach appropriately. Log this process in the memo, and note it in your log trail document. Time to move on.

REVISITING AND REVIEWING RECORDS

This was only your first reading of that record. You should aim to visit it, in whole or part, many times during the project, and each time you will see something differently, because you will have a different picture of what's going on.

Reading and reflecting on data should ideally never be a one-pass process. When you first read that first interview, or your first field notes, your knowledge of the situation is limited to what you learned then. After several interviews, you will be interviewing differently, seeing different things, learning from your early efforts. So you need a routine for revisiting records. Without such processes, as the study charges on, you will lose the familiarity with the early records, and forget how different they were.

> On return from the trek, you will have field notes from observations of the trained behaviour of guides, their instructions to trekkers re rubbish, respect for the track environs, provisioning and waste management, etc. Back to what the first tour operator said about all this – does your observation fit his claims?

How do you ensure that you return to this data record for later study, since you know you don't know enough about it now? Almost all of the techniques described in later chapters can, if carefully conducted, take you back to the context of the passage being viewed or the record of the event being discussed. But the most obvious way, if you are working with software, is to use links.

--------------------------------- Revisiting Records ---------------------------------

1. Suppose your next interview offers a very similar account of something interesting. Rather than seeing this as confirmatory, challenge it. Are they really the same? Why should these two people have the same interpretation? Are they both avoiding a less acceptable one? Is there an intervening factor?

   There seems to be a 'party line' in the phrases used to describe environmental protection processes. You could recite them by now. And these are also the items listed in the legislative requirements.

2. Now, as with the other 'taking off' techniques, annotate, write memos or link. You have woven some threads between the two documents, and reflecting on the first will now take you back to the second.

   'Party line' memo linked to both and the summary of the rules.

3. Perhaps the second document contains a theme you previously found in the first. Simply place a link alerting you to the need to 'see also' that other document.

(Continued)

(Continued)

> Field notes link to interview - you've discovered that the young tour guide speaks of the same issues in quite different terms, no party line here. And intriguingly, speaks of the environmentalist 'giants' and how his work supports their efforts.

4. If a theme from the first document was discussed in a memo, and you find the theme again in a second document, you can link to both from that same memo. When you review the memo, or add to it, you'll be beckoned back to that context.

> 'Belittling' memo links the two operators who used this term. It discusses who didn't and the terms they used, linking to those. And a new memo on 'stature' begins the task of building ideas about image and audiences.

Already, the documents are being tied together, so going to one will take you to another. With the discussion of coding in the next chapter you will acquire another way of doing this.

How to Revisit Big Databases?

The problem of moving past data without revisiting is particularly serious in projects where there are very large amounts of data. Such projects tend to work in a mode that is far more appropriate to surveys than to qualitative research (often because the prime purpose is survey research, the qualitative data being an extra). In survey research, quite properly, there is a straight line between design and reporting. Design is followed by data collection, coding, data analysis and then reporting. But qualitative research is, as previously remarked, not a straight line. The researcher aims to learn from the data and to build that learning into the project. How do you do this in a huge project?

Big projects are usually team projects in which revisiting and fully knowing all the data is an impossible goal. Teams wishing (or directed) to 'get' a lot more interviews, or 'move through' more research areas, will be driven on by the task of making data. The sequential survey research tasks can often properly be separated, with efficient division of labour, some team members doing clerical and some analytical work. But qualitative research tasks are interconnected, and division of labour is difficult when all roles contribute to analysis. How do you revisit data in a team project?

 Go to the **Youth Offender Program Evaluation** project to read how case studies were used in the final stage of the huge project.

─────── **Strategies for Revisiting a Large Project's Data** ───────

However desirable, it may not be practical to demand that a project remain small enough for thorough data revisiting. In the large-project situation, it is important to devise strategies that provide some of the experience of returning to data:

- If this is a mixed methods study, go to the literature for advice on the many ways of interweaving the analysis of numerical and qualitative data.

  Using the numerical data from exit surveys of tourists, for example, you might identify clusters of attitudes to the operators, and identify cases that were representative of each cluster. Now revisit just those cases, rereading and coding in more detail the qualitative data.

- In your qualitative project, give a 'slice' of data to each team member for detailed analysis. Use your software to slice the data by theme, by area, by characteristics of respondents, or by event – or any other meaningful divider. These mini-studies may provide new ideas and hunches to pursue.
- If the project's size is because it is multi-site or multi-stage, it may be advisable to take as a first stage just one of these units. Do a thorough exploration and revisiting of the qualitative records and take the analysis through to an interim report. Now return to the other units with ideas, hunches, themes to be sought, developed in comparison or disconfirmed by the new data. Ensure that the data from the different units are clearly identified by keeping documents in folders or sets (Chapter 3) or by coding (Chapter 5).

  You will be aiming for pattern displays and analyses that will require such differentiation (to be discussed in Chapter 8).

Any such strategy must of course be carefully used and evaluated in the context of the whole programme. If a 'slice' or unit is to become a smaller qualitative study in its own right, loop back to the guidelines for research design in Chapter 1 – and design it! You will also need to design rigorous testing of the ideas that emerge from one unit through the data provided in others. This can be especially challenging and, if well done, rewarding in longitudinal studies.

WRITING IT

Are you logging each step in your project? If this reminder is getting boring, you have the habit of a lifetime. The log you have built up since the beginning of the project should be easily recording each step and the context, and reflexively considering your relationship to the ongoing work.

Ensure that the memos you have written are logging the answers needed for each of the following issues:

- Identify each step.

  This is interesting and I will write about it.

- Why was it taken?

  This idea is different – needs separate exploration.

- What were the alternatives and why rejected?

  Treat it as much the same thing as the previous memo.

- What did you then see as the likely results for the final project.

  Shifting emphasis to a less unitary interpretation of eco-tourism with separate analysis of businesses and their individual operators, tour guides and tourists and their very different interpretations of the purposes of such tourism.

If visual display of your ideas assists you, models may now have become part of the logging process. Store or archive past models, as they will show what you have been doing. (For a dramatic presentation of the project history, layer the stages of development in a model and project it on a screen for discussion.)

UP TO THE CATEGORY

The result of each of the processes in this chapter is data expansion. When you read and annotate, write a memo, reflect on comparisons and place a link, you are adding further data. These are ideas data, not records of your 'original' observations or enquiries. Treat ideas and reflections as more data. Just like your 'original' data records, reflective memos can be read and revisited and linked and written about.

In most projects, in most methods, at this stage the researcher will want to see the data in a different way. So far the view has been from the original event, via your record of observation or interview. Looked at this way, you see the project by cases, focusing on how issues and processes played out for each person or site.

Now you are likely to want to focus on a category to think about – an issue or topic – and see it across all the cases. *Does 'business' have the same meaning(s) across these different settings?* This leads to a quite different requirement for handling your data records. When you read and reflect on each record, the result will be a series of thoughtful summaries of cases or events.

How do you move up to asking about a process or an experience, past how each person sees it, to discover and explore themes that emerge from everything anyone contributes about it? To build theory, you need to shift focus, and for this you need to access the data differently – by category instead of by document.

To do this, you need to code your data. This is the subject of the next chapter.

--- **To Do** ---

For these exercises, choose just one document in your project. Work with it on paper or computer:

1. Read the record, adding to it from your recall of the event. Conduct the 'Record and recall' exercise.
2. Go back to the beginning and this time read the text very thoroughly, line by line. As you find material that is interesting, conduct the exercise above on 'Taking off from the data'.

3. Focus on an interesting phrase or sentence and conduct the exercise above on 'Opening up the data'. Write a memo on what you learn.
4. Ensure that you use each of the ways of storing ideas about the document:
5. Annotate it.
6. Write about it in a memo.
7. Link it to related data.
8. If you are working in a team, conduct the exercise on 'Locating and discussing team differences' and record the results.
9. Draw a first model of the ideas you have brought into the project and the ideas coming from the data.

Suggestions for Further Reading

To follow up the quotations in this chapter go to Strauss (1987) and Turner (1981). The processes of getting 'up' from data are covered in *Readme First* (Richards and Morse, 2013), Part 2.

These processes are handled very differently in different methods. Practical advice is in some of the collections, especially Denzin and Lincoln (1994, 2000) and Seale (2001). Among the few books to discuss the detail of methods of memoing and annotation are Lofland and Lofland (1995), and Miles and Huberman (1994).

To read more about the differences between grounded theory techniques and those of other methods, go to Lichtman (2014), Silverman (2001) and *Readme First*. To explore the particular techniques of open coding, the most vivid account is in transcripts of discussions between Strauss and his students, in Strauss (1987: Chapters 2-3) and in the second edition of Strauss and Corbin (1998). See also Charmaz (2006). On the goals of grounded theory, see the original text, Glaser and Strauss (1967) and Glaser (1978). See also Dey (1999). Recent works on grounded theory are brought together in Bryant and Charmaz (2007).

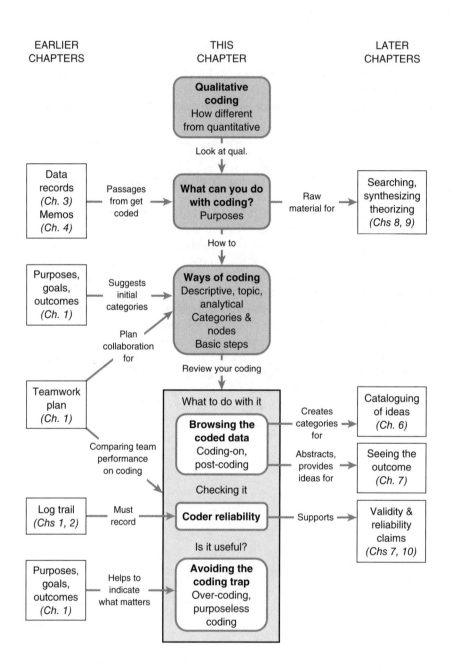

EARLIER
CHAPTERS

THIS
CHAPTER

LATER
CHAPTERS

Qualitative coding
How different
from quantitative

Look at qual.

Data records
(Ch. 3)
Memos
(Ch. 4)

Passages
from get
coded

What can you do with coding?
Purposes

Raw
material for

Searching,
synthesizing
theorizing
(Chs 8, 9)

How to

Purposes,
goals,
outcomes
(Ch. 1)

Suggests
initial
categories

Ways of coding
Descriptive, topic,
analytical
Categories &
nodes
Basic steps

Plan
collaboration
for

Review your coding

Teamwork
plan
(Ch. 1)

What to do with it

Cataloguing
of ideas
(Ch. 6)

Comparing team
performance
on coding

Browsing the coded data
Coding-on,
post-coding

Creates
categories
for

Checking it

Abstracts,
provides
ideas for

Seeing the
outcome
(Ch. 7)

Log trail
(Chs 1, 2)

Must
record

Coder reliability

Supports

Validity &
reliability
claims
(Chs 7, 10)

Is it useful?

Purposes,
goals,
outcomes
(Ch. 1)

Helps to
indicate
what matters

Avoiding the coding trap
Over-coding,
purposeless
coding

FIVE

Coding

Most qualitative researchers code. Coding generates new ideas and gathers material by topic. This chapter tackles the coding task, the different sorts of coding and how to ensure that coding does not become dominating and unproductive. The emphasis is on purposive coding, using the results of your coding to develop ideas, to take off from the data and drive enquiry further.

Reading and reflecting on data records, you see your project document by document. But your project requires you to see *across* the data, and *above* the individual documents, to themes and ideas. Usually it also requires you to gather all the data on a topic, to think about it and rethink it. To gather everything on a topic, you need to *code*.

> In a study of isolated housing estates, you may have noticed that the theme of 'privacy' seems to occur in several data records, even when people are deeply committed to community. Move up from the data to the concept. You want to consider the concept, privacy; not the individual reports, but the varieties and patterns in all the discussions of privacy. This will help you reflect on the values and experiences of privacy and how they co-exist with the apparently contradictory values of community.

To shift focus to the topic or concept, you need to access the data differently. You want to read and reflect on all extracts, from any of your records (or from just some selected ones), where the theme of privacy occurs. *Bringing those parts of the accounts together, you will be able to learn about the variety of responses or experiences, and reflect on how the emphasis on privacy impacts on goals of community and family.*

Almost all qualitative research involves some sort of coding (though different methods do it very differently). But that does not mean you need to spend your life coding. It's a first step to somewhere else.

QUALITATIVE AND QUANTITATIVE CODING

Most qualitative researchers code, but no qualitative research is only about coding.

The term itself confuses. In common use, 'coding' refers to data reduction either by a system of symbols (as in Morse code, which reduces everything to dots and dashes) or by numbers (as in the coded boxes to tick on a questionnaire). Most researchers have done quantitative coding before they try qualitative coding, so it is worth starting out by clearing this confusion.

In qualitative research you do usually have to do some of this sort of data reduction, to store information describing the attributes of an interviewee, for example (gender, age, ethnicity, etc.).

But while quantitative coding *reduces* data, qualitative coding is about data *retention* (see Table 5.1). The goal is to learn from the data, to keep revisiting data extracts until you see and understand patterns and explanations. So you need to *retain* the data records, or the relevant parts of them, until they are fully understood. Coding is not merely to label all the parts of documents about a topic, but rather to bring them together so they can be reviewed, and your thinking about the topic developed.

This sort of coding is more like the filing techniques by which we sort everyday information and ensure access to everything about a topic. Recipe clippings are most usefully gathered by food type. Go to 'cakes' and then 'chocolate cakes' and all the recipes will be there to review. In sophisticated (usually computer) systems

Table 5.1 Two very different modes of coding

	Quantitative	Qualitative
Place in research process	Normally a single stage between data collection and analysis	Occurs throughout project
Relation to categories	Applies predetermined categories	Generates categories
Relation to original data	Code applied summarizes or represents - and replaces - original data	Code retains copy of or pointer to original data, ensuring access
Flexible or inflexible?	Revisiting is often not possible, since original data not retained	Revisiting of coding to check development of categories
Changing coding categories during project?	Normally after piloting, no new categories will be added	New categories are generated until last stages of project
Reshaping categories?	Collapsing of codes to obtain a simpler picture	'Coding on' from coded material can create new categories/dimensions. Merging of categories takes place as common meanings emerge
Team processes	Coding is a clerical task that can be severed from analysis	Coders are doing analytical work, involved in project interpretation

they may be filed by more than one dimension. Ask for anything coded 'cakes' and 'chocolate' and you should get all the recipes for chocolate cakes. But however you got there, you want the recipes, not merely the information that there are six. The point of this sort of coding is to *find again* the material coded. Coding allows you to return to the data you want to inspect, interrogate and interpret.

WHAT CAN YOU DO WITH CODING?

This chapter has a message: coding should always be for a purpose. It is never an end in itself.

Qualitative researchers code in order to get past the data record, to a category, and to work with all the data segments about the category. Coding aggregates these, so you can then work with them together, gaining a new view on the data. It's a first step to rethinking the data. When you make a final report on this project, you are aiming to do more than describe all the text coded at a category. That report will give the results of analysis deriving partly from your *work* with the coded data.

Why would you want to work with that category? There are many ways that a researcher can use coding: that is, for all the purposes where it matters to have all the data about a category.

Each of the 'Methods in Practice' projects used coding. Go to the 'Working with Data' sections to compare how it was done and used.

─────────────── **Purposes of Qualitative Coding** ───────────────

There are very many purposes for qualitative coding, and most researchers use it for at least several of the following:

- To reflect on what the coded segments tell you about the category, and its meanings in the project;
- To ask questions about how the category relates to other ideas from the data, and construct theories about those relations;
- To gather all material about a case, from different sources, so you can apply the information about that person or site to everything from there, and compare cases on their attitudes, experiences, etc.;
- To make further, finer categories, from finding different dimensions in the data gathered by the first coding;
- To search for blends or combinations of categories, to find patterns in attitudes on this subject, for example by gender, or to compare text at different categories, seeing the category from a different viewpoint; and
- To compare how different researchers interpret data.

Some, or even all, of these processes may matter in your project. If so, as you start coding, reflect on what you want coding to do for you.

The purposes to which coding is to be put strongly influence the standards of coding and the style you will use. So ask what you want coding to do. Especially when you are working with software, searches of patterns of coding can be very rigorous, and their results will vary according to the amount of context coded. *When people talk about 'business', are values of altruism or social good ever mentioned?* If I always code the whole passage when these themes come up, a search for where they intersect will answer my question. But if I have merely coded the word 'business', it probably will find nothing.

WAYS OF CODING IN A QUALITATIVE PROJECT

I find it useful to distinguish three sorts of coding in qualitative research, since they require very different processes. The terms I use are 'descriptive', 'topic' and 'analytical' coding. (See *Readme First*, Chapter 6, for a fuller account of these and their place in different methods.)

Most studies use all three, and two are qualitative tools in the sense that they interpret, rather than only describe, data. Researchers are much helped by seeing them as very different tasks, using different tools and for different purposes.

The first, descriptive coding, is more like quantitative coding (see Table 5.1 above). It is often used the same way. It involves storing information about the cases being studied. Information usually applies to a document or a case, so there is not a process of selecting just the text to be interpreted – simply, the appropriate values of variables (e.g. gender = female) are stored at that case.

Then there are (roughly) two very different types of qualitative coding which we use to gather all the text about a category. Topic coding is the hack work of the qualitative researcher, labelling text according to its subject. This labelling can often be automated with software.

Analytical coding, not surprisingly, is central to qualitative enquiry. This is the coding that leads to theory 'emergence' and theory affirmation. Don't think of automating it! But although the computer won't automate interpretation, it does give far more flexibility to this central interpretative task, helping you to read and think about the coded data, and keep coding.

A passage of text will quite normally require all three types of coding. *A man interviewed is discussing the need for community action in the local council elections, in which a schoolteacher is a candidate. This man says that he never listens to gossip about the schoolteacher; it's women's stuff. But he does worry that she is standing for the local council, when she is obviously not a responsible person.*

- Descriptive coding: Firstly, store the information about the speaker, perhaps about three attributes: gender, age and job *(male, 45 yrs and tradesman)*.
- Topic coding: Now, what topics are being discussed in this passage?

  The need for community action and the schoolteacher; perhaps too we need to code for her multiple roles.

In two ways, the coding has described the passage: what sort of person offered these ideas, and what they were about.

- Analytical coding: Now, what's going on in the statement about the schoolteacher?

  Several themes there that need noting, about patriarchal assumptions, the credibility of 'gossip', the informal networks of women, the authority of the schoolteacher and the interplay of interpersonal and political relations.

The one passage may now be coded 11 times, because it's about 11 different aspects of the project. This is not a problem if you are working in a computer rather than a filing cabinet. In the computer, these codings will be stored differently (descriptive codes are stored as attributes, in spreadsheet-like displays). As such coding progresses, we are able to ask useful questions – Did men always deny they gossiped? Are the negative attitudes to the schoolteacher coming mainly from the over-40s? And how do they relate to attitudes to community action?

Qualitative Coding and Computers

Qualitative records, in the days before computers, were coded much as the records in a home filing cabinet are coded.

Descriptive coding was done by storing face sheets of data about the respondent or the institution being studied. (Or worse, it was done by punching holes in cards and sorting descriptive categories with knitting needles!) This meant that information was often inaccessible when you wanted to ask a question like 'What do the *women* say about privacy?' Computers changed the use of such coding totally since they can store data about a case very efficiently and give access to it at all stages in a project. Descriptive coding can usually be done by importing the data in tables, rather than selecting and coding text, or by working in a table of cases and attributes, selecting the value for a cell, as you would work in a spreadsheet.

Before computers, both types of qualitative coding (topic coding and analytical coding) were clerical challenges. Since the goal was that the researcher should be able to retain a copy of or pointer to original data, a lot of paper was required to ensure access to all the data about the topic or concept! If a passage was about privacy, you made a file for 'Privacy', copied the data and placed the relevant segments in that file. If it was also about community, you would copy those segments again and place them in a file titled 'Community'. Then, when you wanted to write about privacy, you took out that file and spread the cuttings over the floor. The task was boring, time-consuming, and not very rigorous, since dogs and babies were likely to mix with the precious paper segments. But most importantly, it worked only when you restricted your goal to getting back everything about one topic. It failed when you wanted to ask just the sorts of questions that qualitative research is about. *When people talk about privacy, how do they reconcile it with values of community?*

Even from that simple example, it is evident you will be able to do more with the coding stored in your computer project than you could with any number of cardboard folders. The computer stores information, not paper. Each abstract idea you have – the category – is accessible at any time. The computer can go to all these places or combinations of them, for information and exploration of patterns.

Categories and where you put them When coding on paper, most researchers talked about the *categories* or *codes* they were creating and they filed in folders all the material *coded* at these categories. On a computer, you can much more easily treat these categories as objects, move and arrange them and explore the relationships of the data coded in more than one of them. You can also manage categories much more flexibly than in a filing cabinet, because software can store their positions in an index system (see next chapter).

In information systems the term for a place in an index or a network is a *node*. The term is used across a wide range of areas (botany, engineering, geology) to represent places that are related. The orchardist prunes fruit trees above the node. New growth comes from the node. (So too in qualitative research.)

The term 'node' is used here to refer to the place where the software stores a category. There is more about nodes and node systems in the next chapter. You create them to hold categories and store coding, and you can handle them flexibly and ask questions about them, since the software will be able to check at any time where they are and what coding you have done at them. They need not hold coding; for example, you might store anticipated categories at nodes in your system, ones that you think might be important later. Or you might create them to store ideas and memos about the goals of the project (Chapter 1) or the quality of the data (Chapter 2), or topics to be considered in another stage of the project (Chapter 3).

You will find that terms associated with coding and with coding processes differ among qualitative software packages. It is important to check that you understand how coding is stored in your software, and what can be done with the coded material and the categories.

For very different detailed accounts of the processes of coding on computer software, compare the **Wedding Work** and the **Harassment Complaints** projects.

---------------- **Basic Steps of Qualitative Coding** ----------------

There is no mystery in doing qualitative coding:

- To store descriptive coding (information about characteristics or attributes) is simple; either one at a time, or by table import, you allocate to each case the appropriate value of each attribute.
- To code something qualitatively, *retaining* the relevant data, you do three things:

    1. Select the material of interest and decide what it is *about*.
    2. Create or find the appropriate *category*. In a manual system the category went into a cardboard folder labelled with its name. In your computer project the category, its description and any coding will be stored at a node.
    3. Now, code! Working on paper, you put the relevant material or a copy of it in the folder, or mark it in some way on the paper. Working on computer, depending on the software you are using, you copy the extract to the code, or place at the code a pointer to the relevant material.

Now, consider what coding your project needs.

Descriptive Coding

Descriptive coding is the sort of coding occurring in quantitative studies – storage of information that *describes* a case.

Every qualitative project requires this sort of information. Where cases are being studied – cases of interviewees, cases of schools or businesses, for example – there will be information about the *attributes* of these cases (the person's gender, the school's size, and so on).

If you were working on paper, you would probably save a face sheet of information about each case, or a table summarizing them all. In software, similarly, storing information about a case's attributes is handled in a separate system from coding text. Storing and using these data is both easy and highly productive given computer software. If you have a table of data about your cases from a spreadsheet or statistics package, it can be imported directly to your qualitative software, creating the attributes of your cases, such as their gender and marital status. Now you can ask questions about the sample using that information, and split or sort the data by its attributes.

The challenge is usually not whether to store such information, but how much to store. The amount of such information available may be overwhelming. For example, in a mixed methods study, cases of interviewees from a survey may be selected for in-depth interviewing. From the survey, you have data on perhaps 50 variables, but it is highly unlikely that all these are relevant to your qualitative questions. As in many areas, software compounds the challenge because it removes barriers.

If you are working in a team, you will find that descriptive coding is the only sort of coding easily handled without collaboration and communication. The task is basically storing information that is (presumably) reliably recorded. For topic or analytical coding, collaboration is essential.

Storing Attributes

- Plan to collect all information about cases that you'll need to ask the project's questions. To know what you'll need, reflect on what you want to ask. Your research design should indicate what information is required.
- Keep this information systematically, preferably in table form. This will remind you of all the data needed for each case, and as you fill in each row of the table, you'll notice the patterns of characteristics your sample is building up.
- Don't import attributes you don't want. Excess information makes it hard to see the data clearly. It can always be imported later (so long as you heed the next point!).
- Don't discard information that you may want. Find a way to store it so it doesn't confuse and clutter the data you are working with. Information about attributes that may be needed later can be stored in a separate spreadsheet or table, and imported later if relevant.
- Storing information can be boring work, so aim to automate it. If you are using software, you can do this by preparing and importing tables. Be sure to check before you type it up, how to prepare your data so your software can import it.

Topic Coding

Topic coding is my term for coding that merely allocates passages to topics. It usually involves little interpretation. You are putting the data 'where they belong' – a sort of data disposal. *'This is about the local schoolteacher', 'This is about neighbouring',* and so on. This sort of coding is almost always easy to do and almost always boring. It is, of course, also necessary. *If the role of the local schoolteacher is relevant to your community study, it is obviously important to get in one place everything said about the role and its occupant. Only then will you be able to get an overview of the range of interpretations of her role, and write about the ways her authority was challenged. Moreover, coding everything about the schoolteacher in one place is necessary if you wish to ask whether, when there was gossip about the schoolteacher, it came from her neighbours, the parent group or her colleagues.*

Often, topic coding dominates early in a project, because it requires relatively little understanding of the situation. You may be very puzzled to understand the complex relations of privacy and community, but you do know if they are talking about the schoolteacher. The topic coding may also be a first step to more interpretative work. Having coded everything that is about the schoolteacher, you can review that material and from it develop the analytical categories.

Such coding is relatively unchallenging, and this may be a problem. The 'coding trap' (see below) is almost always about topic coding.

Topic Coding

1. Plan what topics you need to gather data on in order to ask the project's questions. Just as for attributes, to find out what you'll need, reflect on what you want to ask:

   - Your research design should indicate what information is required. A great way to start is to put your research design into your project on computer and code it, making the nodes as they are indicated in the design.

2. Record these as a starter list of categories, or better still, create them in your project. If they can be organized, in category/subcategory trees, do it. Critique this starter list, checking for relevance and overlap of categories.
3. As you read, ask always 'What is this about?'

   - If the answer is a topic for your project, select the text about it.
   - If you have that topic already as a category, select it and code.
   - If the topic has not been recorded as a category, create the category, and code. As a new topic appears, consider whether it deserves a place in your project. Why will you want all the data about this topic coded at one place?

4. Automate topic coding either by section coding (if topics have been set out as sections in the document), or by text search (if a word or phrase identifies this topic).
5. If you can't automate it, protect your project against boredom:

   - The topic coding task can be given to a competent assistant (it's a good training ground for software competence). Better, combine it with analytical coding. Keep visiting the topic. This is getting analytic!

   Now you have a lot of material about the schoolteacher: browse it and you will be struck by the very different ways she is seen and the different responses to her efforts for the community.

A note on autocoding Using many sorts of software (not necessarily qualitative software) it is possible to do rapid coding to identify the key topics or issues in the record immediately. This is done either by identifying the section of the document about the topic, or by finding specific words in the text. (Recall the warning in Chapter 3 that to do autocoding you need to know how to format a document so the relevant text will be found and the relevant context can be coded.)

It's important to be clear that such 'autocoding' is no substitute for your interpretation!

- The software is not reflecting on the meaning of your text. It is searching mechanically for words that occur, and coding mechanically the slab of text you specify. Never assume that a 'find' implies meaning: it indicates merely the presence of specified characters.

- It will miss anything you don't tell it to look for.

  'Schoolteacher' will not find references to the teacher by her name. You can of course nominate alternative strings to search for, but did you remember to search for 'that bitch'?

- Autocoding will inevitably make some weird errors, so you must always check the results. If in doubt, check back to the context. And always keep a note that this coding was done mechanically.
- You have a choice of ways to clean up the errors: review each find as it is made or (usually better) browse all the finds, in their context, and think about them. Always do one, and sometimes both. Never leave autocoding without reviewing – later you will be tempted to think the coding was reliable.
- Autocoding will always save huge amounts of time, so it is tempting to over-code, and the resulting topics may be far too numerous and confusing. If you can't think why you would want to ask a question about this topic, don't code for it. So long as you prepared the document appropriately, you can always ask your software to autocode later.
- One very helpful role for autocoding is to get everything about a topic in one place in order to explore and establish the more subtle categories you should code at. In other words, autocoding can be used as a first step to analytical coding. (See below for a discussion of coding on from the first coding.)

 Examples of the use of autocoding with computer software are in the **Harassment Complaints** project.

Analytical Coding

The three sorts of coding are not always clearly different, and to some degree analysis, of course, is involved in all three. But it is worth distinguishing coding that requires interpretation from descriptive and topic coding (both of which are fairly matter-of-fact processes, even to researchers who dispute the existence of facts!). I use the term 'analytical coding' here to refer to coding that comes from interpretation and reflection on meaning.

Of the three sorts of coding, it is the hardest and also the most rewarding. Rather than just store information or name the topic of the text, you are considering the meanings in context, and creating categories that express new ideas about the data, coding to gather and reflect on all the data related to them. This is qualitative research!

Qualitative research is not a task to be hurried. The goal is careful interrogation of the data. What is a particular passage about? What category or categories will properly represent that passage? What context should be coded there? Well-handled, analytical coding is a prime way of creating conceptual categories and gathering the data needed to explore them. Coding is a first step to opening up meaning.

What meaning is sought, of course, will depend on the project's question and method. In some approaches to text, coding may be used to mark and return to features in the language (for example, ideological assumptions) or points in the narrative or conversational structure of the text (contradictions, omissions, turning points). In others, it will be a way of creating concepts. In any of these cases, the act of coding has gathered the material that brought the idea and put a pointer to it, so the researcher can return there to think some more.

Analytical coding follows most easily from the quick steps to 'taking off' from the data suggested in the previous chapter. Revisit those suggested steps now. In a series of questions, you moved from some detail of the document ('That's interesting') to comment about it ('Why is it interesting?') and then to the abstraction ('Why am I interested in that?'). The answer to that latest question was an analytical category. Annotations and memos were used to record the insights. Now, replay those steps for one more time, this time thinking coding.

Analytical Coding – Taking off and Coding It

1. As you read, if a passage is interesting, select it ('*That's interesting*').

   Perhaps a hostile comment was made about the nosiness of neighbours. Ask 'Why is it interesting?' It seems odd in context, as the interviewee had been very positive about the community. Make a note.

2. Now, you have a passage selected: where do you code? Step up to the abstraction: '*Why am I interested in* that?' This is a very different question. The answer is a category, and a place you will want to code data. Make the category, and carefully name it. (Naming is an analytical process in itself. You may also want to describe the category you have created.)

   New category for 'tension between ideals and reality', and another, since it seems also necessary, for 'ambivalence re neighbouring'.

3. Code the selected text at the category. (Software will place at the node a reference to just that text.) Before you move on, you might use the techniques described in Chapter 4 to reflect 'up' from the text. If these take flight, write a memo about that category.

4. Now later in that document, or in another, when you again hear the ambivalent messages about nosy neighbours but how needed neighbour help is, you know you are interested in that. Select the text, find the category you created, and code.

Analytical coding rapidly becomes a very smooth and exciting process of identifying text to be coded, creating categories or finding the categories already created and coding at them. The main challenges are to keep your thinking 'up' at this abstract level, and to keep generating ideas and questions. Especially if you are tired, it's easy to drop back down into topic coding, merely saying what the data are about. Be aware of this pattern – time to walk the dog.

A note about *in vivo* coding One valuable technique is to look for '*in vivo*' categories. This term (from grounded theory) refers to categories named by words occurring 'live' in the data, when people studied themselves using those words.

Several software products allow you to select words and code *in vivo*, naming the category with the selection.

Often, by focusing on a phrase or expression that is surprising or recurring, you will find you are helped in taking off from the data again, thinking about themes, rather than merely noting the topic discussed. Understanding grows as you bring together instances of a 'sound' in the data.

An example from my real project on community and privacy was an *in vivo* category 'not in your pocket'. Definitions of good neighbours, in the setting I was studying, often contained that phrase, or other phrases asserting what good neighbours should *not* be in (your lap, your house, your kitchen or your hair)! As these *in vivo* categories built up, they helped me reflect on the sense of physical invasion and danger that was associated with neighbouring (Richards, 1990).

REVISITING THE CODED DATA

Coding in qualitative research is never merely a way of getting everything about a topic in one place so you can count it or summarize it. Of course you may wish to do that, but if that is all you want to do, why have you gone to the trouble to retain the detail of the data until now? Sufficient information to support the count or the summary would have come from ticked boxes in a questionnaire. If you have coded qualitatively, retaining the text, it must mean you thought there was more to be learned from reviewing it in this new context.

Whether coding has been only according to topic, or more analytical, there will always be surprises in reviewing coded data. Often the most extraordinary discoveries come from browsing together all of the segments you coded at a category.

Don't wait to review the coded data. From the start of coding, visit the categories and think about the data coded there. You literally see the segments anew. At any time when you want to think about the theme, go to the category and read, think, reflect. Coding has given you an opportunity to review the data, getting closer to the words of the text and revisiting their context.

——————————— **Working with the Coded Data** ———————————

Find how to see together all the passages coded at a category. Read them as though they are a different sort of document - about the category:

1. Look for differences, especially differences that surprise you. Can you explain why two people you had seen as similar have such different views on this topic?
2. Now look for similarities that surprise.
3. Scan the material. Are you happy with your coding? Anything here that seems not to belong? If so, find how you can 'uncode' that passage from the category.

Assess context. Perhaps a segment doesn't make sense because you coded only a narrow context? Go back to find the context and read it in the original, or expand the coding to give the appropriate context.

> The words spoken about the schoolteacher sound very angry – but was the anger in response to an earlier question?

4. On the basis of the data coded here, reflect on the category – what have you learned about it? (Record these thoughts in a memo.)

Seeing together everything about the same topic may be the critical step to understanding it. You can of course do this with paper files which store all the copied segments about a category, but the ability to do it on computer brought an extraordinary change in method. Because those segments are not cut out from context, you can work 'live' with the data about a category. Software can take you back to that extract in context, so you can code the record differently, as your ideas develop.

If you have previously coded on paper, there are two very significant differences in this way of browsing the coded text. Both will support new ways of working:

- Coding on computer can be very flexible. One major advantage for novices is that they can shed the fear of not immediately 'getting it right'. Do first-pass coding, into very general, broad-brush categories: *'privacy stuff'* or *'community stuff'*. (My personal indicator of a broad-brush category is that its name includes 'stuff'!) As you become more confident of the meanings in the data, return to browse the broad-brush categories and recode the data to finer categories with more definitive names.
- Coding on computer need not decontextualize. For some purposes, you want to have just exactly the text coded at a category (for example, if you are searching for anything coded at 'privacy' and also at 'loneliness'; see Chapter 8 for such processes). But for other purposes, you want generous context, to see what was said before, or what another group member had said about this. The browsing process can go out to the wider context as needed. (Note that this means you don't have to make your coding over-generous of context; code just the text you want to retrieve in the knowledge that you can always go back to where it came from.)

Coding On to Develop Your Ideas

For any sort of coding, but particularly analytical coding, you will want to reconsider the category as the material builds up. This reconsideration may lead you to revisit or extend your coding. I term this coding *on*.

Revisiting may be simply for housework. The main reason for revisiting descriptive coding is if you decide your early categories were too coarse or too fine (we needed age in months, not in decade age groups because these were too coarse). Topic coding can also be adjusted similarly. *You may need to separate out the material on the schoolteacher's work and her personality, or correct your coding – the 'bitch' referred to was the postmistress.*

But revisiting text coded at a category, and reviewing coding, can be highly analytical. Your understanding of the categories and concepts emerging as you code will develop and change as you review the data. (It was for that purpose that you retained the data.) Analytical coding gathers material that should be rethought and reviewed during the project. *Data coded at 'privacy' will need recoding when you discover there are several different meanings of privacy in this community.* Now you will need to code *on* from the first coding, to create and reflect on new categories.

--- **Coding On** ---

- Browse all the data coded at a category, and reflect rather as you would on the text of a document. What new meanings can you see?
- When a new category occurs to you, create it in your coding system and code the text, just as you would if you were in the document.
- Now back to the originally coded data – should these segments all be in the same category? Are you discovering new dimensions of that category? If so, record these as new subcategories, coding the material that belongs in them *on* from the original coding.

This process of revising coding, and *coding on* to newly discovered categories, makes coding a process of discovery rather than merely description. Work this way, and coding is never an end in itself, just a first step to thinking through the material.

If you are working with software, the ability to code on from a first stage of coding may radically change the way you code. There is no need to 'get it right' first time. Coding with a broad brush, you can gather everything about a general topic in one place. Then, as the subtler meanings of your data emerge, revisit and code on from that broad category to codes reflecting finer dimensions.

 The use of coding on in revisiting a previously coded data set is described in the **Harassment Complaints** project.

Post-coding for Data Reduction

In most qualitative projects, the goal of coding is to gather together everything about a topic or an analytical concept, in order to review and refine thinking about this category. You go on from the category to finer dimensions. *There are several different meanings of privacy in this community; some of this text is about what, for now, I'll term 'haven home', some about 'personal life privacy' and some about 'anonymity'. Not all will conflict with ideals of community cooperation.* In browsing and working with the coded data, the researcher will expand their ideas and create new categories.

But the same tools, for coding and 'live' browsing of coded data, can be used in large projects for data reduction. If your challenge is a very large number of open-ended responses to a survey, the goal may be 'post-coding' them. This involves deriving from the answers a group of categories that sufficiently represent the range, then reviewing each answer and coding to the appropriate category. The results of this post-coding exercise can be simple counts, or information about the coding of cases, exported to your statistics package if appropriate.

> Question 6 in a survey of this community asks each respondent, 'What does privacy mean to you?' Answers are typed up and coded automatically, descriptively and by topic. (Characteristics of the respondent are imported from the statistics package, and the topics are identified by question headings, so they can be section coded.) Now go to the new category, 'Q. 6. Privacy', and browse all the answers to that question. Make a new category each time you see a new meaning of privacy. Rapidly, you will arrive at a satisfactory group of new nodes. Importantly, the text for each of the newly discovered meanings of privacy is available, to inform debate about the category or illustrate it with quotations.

CODER RELIABILITY IN QUALITATIVE RESEARCH

Reliability in qualitative research is a contentious topic, discussed in more detail in Chapter 7. Qualitative methods are all about interpretation and individual agency. Field researchers claim credibility for research in very different ways and with different standards from those used in a randomized control trial.

But being reliable (to use the adjective) beats being unreliable. If a category is used in different ways, you will be unable to *rely* on it to bring you all the relevant data. Hence, you may wish to ensure that you yourself are reliably interpreting a code the same way across time, or that you can *rely* on your colleagues to use it the same way.

The need to check consistency is of course greater in larger projects, for many reasons. When data records are bulky, and project timelines longer, researchers lose recall of earlier coding or ability to review colleagues' coding. And there is more emphasis on consistency for two reasons. Practically, the coding is more likely to be output directly to another stage of analysis (for example, statistical) rather than used to revisit and review coded material. Such projects are likely to spend less time browsing coded material (and thereby confronting inconsistencies). And politically, these projects are likely to be in research contexts where the standards of quantitative research prevail and suspicion is cast on qualitative processes that cannot show reliability checks. (Don't get aggressive about it: qualitative researchers can do this!)

Warning! Do the tests but interpret them carefully. You would not expect consistency of qualitative coding, over time or between colleagues, and you may not desire it! Your understanding of the categories has of course changed over time – that's built into the method. (Your coding categories are emerging as you learn from the data.) And your colleagues probably see the project and data differently from you. The research design may even specify that two researchers will come from different disciplines to give (*reliably!*) different views. So we will not be concerned when we find inconsistency. We do, however, need to know about it, discuss it, to place any coding-dependent analysis in that context, and document differences.

Coder consistency tests usually apply to combinations of topic and analytical coding. Descriptive coding is not interpretative, but requires only accurate entry of information about a case.

Doing Coder Consistency Tests

In this context, reliability means consistency, and it is easy to discover inconsistencies in coding over time or between colleagues. The best method is to compare two codings of the same document:

- For consistency over time, code a clean version of a document you coded earlier. Don't cheat and check the earlier coding! It is important that you discover how different your coding will be now.
- For consistency between colleagues, each colleague codes a duplicate of the same document.

Now for either purpose, print out the display of that coding and compare. (Or use your software to make a report on the differences.) You are interested in the following differences:

- What categories are used by one but not by the other?
- What differences are there in the segments selected for coding at each category?
- Are the styles of coding different? In particular, is one version of the document more richly coded (at more categories) and does one coder select substantially larger passages for coding?

Coding consistency is a different challenge if you are working in a team. If you and your colleague are coding at the same category, you do need to know that you are using it similarly.

 Visit the **Youth Offender Program Evaluation** project for the saga of a project with very many coders in many sites – and many ways of working towards consistency in coding.

AVOIDING THE CODING TRAP

Coding, especially on computers, is terribly easy! It is easy to do ever-increasing coding – especially descriptive or topic coding – if you are unsure what else you can do and the theory does not seem to be emerging from your data. Sadly, this is the best way of stopping emerging ideas.

Coding was always a trap to researchers, but its danger is far greater with software. This is, ironically, because of one of the great achievements of qualitative computing: that at last, as the method demands, there are effectively no restrictions to the number of categories you can code data at, or the number of times you can code very rich data. So coding can be a way of never finishing your project. The problems are worst when researchers become over-zealous about coding everything, and making as many categories as possible. This sort of coding fetishism can delay or even destroy a project.

Therein lies one of the most common concerns about qualitative computing packages. A second concern, and a less obvious one, is that the ease of coding in these packages and the powerful tools for using coding, encourage researchers to contain their projects within the 'box' the software provides. Anything in the project can be coded, coding becomes dominant. And thus they too are encouraged towards making data that is easily coded (and likely to be more homogeneous) and using analysis methods based on coding.

There is a particular version of the coding trap for teams: in order to keep workload steady and output guaranteed, topic coding takes over. When collaborative construction of the meanings of codes becomes a challenge, it is easy to keep topic coding. *It's about the schoolteacher, and we'll worry later about the more subtle meanings.* Teams need discussions about what they are coding for and what the codes mean. Meet often, especially when coding has become routine.

To avoid the trap, insist that all coding must have a purpose. If it has a purpose, it will be interesting. If it's boring, stop and do something else.

Avoiding the Coding Trap

Practical routines that work to avoid the coding trap are the following:

- Do all descriptive coding (storing information about attributes) efficiently and, where possible, automatically.
- Watch the balance between topic and analytical coding. The first will dominate when you are uncertain about what is to be done, or prevented from progressing. Keep asking not just 'Where does this text go?' but 'Why am I interested in that?' If your project has no interest in it, don't code it.
- Especially early in a project, during coding, be generous with your categories. It is very easy with software to revise and remove categories that prove extraneous, so don't spend time worrying if a new meaning deserves a new category; just do it. (If it is node-worthy, make a node for it.)
- Periodically monitor what you are coding, where and why. Review and be stern about proliferating categories. On review, any new category has to promise something.

(Continued)

(Continued)

(What might you use it for?) There is no point in coding a category if you are not going to use it for discovery that's relevant to your project.

- Always combine coding with thinking about the categories you are creating. Frequently drop out of the document you are coding to visit a category you coded it at. What else is coded there? Does it now seem to have several dimensions? Reflect on the different meanings in the coded material.
- If it's boring, stop! Take time out, do something entirely different. An excellent step aside from coding is to assess the categories being created and do some thinking about them.

ESTABLISHING YOUR PERSONAL DATA PROCESSING STYLE

Qualitative research is intensely personal; agency and ownership of the data are critical factors in the project. Establishing a data processing style that you like is essential – as is reworking it so new ways of relating to data keep it alive.

Celebrate variety in coding styles within your team. Swap tricks and techniques and write a paper about the different ways you code, and the different sorts of insights and discoveries achieved by different approaches. This will assist you to write the coder reliability paper in the proper context!

Setting a Style that Is Yours

1. Start coding data records as they come in and keep coding – never allow them to build up unprocessed. This is a hard job, so treat it as a challenge, a crucial step in your project. Carefully assess your access paths to all data that may matter.
2. Don't delay because you are uncertain of the coding needed: as a first pass through the data, make broad categories and do 'broad-brush' coding, especially early in the project, to indicate areas of text you wish to revisit. Remember, you can go back for coding on.
3. Browse categories frequently, to explore the variety or similarities of the material being gathered, and reflect on the idea or concept the category represents – and write about it.
4. Watch the categories you are making, seeing them as a continually changing representation of what you are finding in your material.
5. Aim for a system that is yours. If you're convinced some 'expert' has a perfect system, deliberately critique that method. Don't be afraid of trying new ways of seeing new meanings in your data. Design and celebrate tricks and gimmicks of your own that work to alert you to interesting things and spark new views on previous data.

6. Get quick and efficient at data disposal tasks - descriptive and topic coding - so they don't become onerous. If it can be properly automated, automate it.
7. Find a qualitative colleague or group of colleagues: if there isn't one, start one. Coding discussions in groups are highly productive of ideas and exploratory concepts; you will never see your data the same way after sharing a transcript with a group and discussing it. If you have no real group, find a virtual one, a supportive list serve or discussion group.

WRITING ABOUT CODING

Log changes in your coding method and codes as part of your continuing report on the story of the project.

- A new category that has any analytical momentum requires a memo.
- A shift in the meaning of the category requires thought, and noting, especially in teams.
- The building up of data at some but not other categories requires reflection.

As with previous advice about project logging, the basic requirements are that you note a new step and why it was taken, what were the alternatives and what are the implications for the growing project. Don't shirk this logging. You will find that when coding gets underway, in any method, it has a momentum of its own. (Strauss remarked to me in 1992: 'We create categories like God creates raindrops!')

 To Do

For these exercises, choose just one document in your project. Work with it on paper or follow the tutorial for this chapter on the website study.sagepub.com/richards3e to conduct the following exercises on computer:

1. Do some of each sort of coding (descriptive, topic and analytical coding) for the data you have so far in your project:

   - Descriptive coding: Enter attributes and assign the relevant values to the cases you are currently considering.
   - Topic coding: List what you expect will be your main topics and code the relevant data at them.
   - Analytical coding: Make categories for the new ideas or concepts that you find in the data. For each new category you create, write a description and a memo.

2. If you are working on computer, find how to automate some non-analytical coding:

   - Do descriptive coding by table import.
   - Do automatic coding of questions in your interviews.
   - Use text search to gather material on a topic.

(Continued)

(Continued)

3. Compare your coding with a colleague's coding of the same document. Discuss categories you have used differently, and the differences between your styles of coding.

If you are working in a team, extend this exercise to a discussion of ways to maximize benefit from coding different styles and manage the differences.

4. Choose one analytical category, at which you have done some coding. Browse the data you have coded at this category:

    *   remove inappropriate coding;
    *   revisit the context of coded passages; and
    *   code on to make new categories.

Suggestions for Further Reading

The processes of coding are covered in *Readme First* (Richards and Morse, 2013), Part 2.

For a wide-ranging and widely referenced discussion of what we do when we code see Chapter 4 in Ely et al. (1997). For introductory accounts, see Harding (2013), Braun and Clarke (2013), and Lichtman (2014).

Few texts explain how to code using manual methods, the notable exceptions being Coffey and Atkinson (1996), Miles and Huberman (1994) and the texts of grounded theory, where coding has very specific procedures (see references to the previous chapter).

Coding is discussed by Flick (2014), Mason (2002) and Seale (1999). For a very thorough account with detailed examples and comparison of coding in 32 different qualitative methods, see Saldaña (2013).

Detailed discussion of coding on computer is in Lewins and Silver (2014), Di Gregorio and Davidson (2008), Bazeley and Jackson (2013), and Kuckhartz (2014). See also Auerbach and Silverstein (2003). And go to the website for more information.

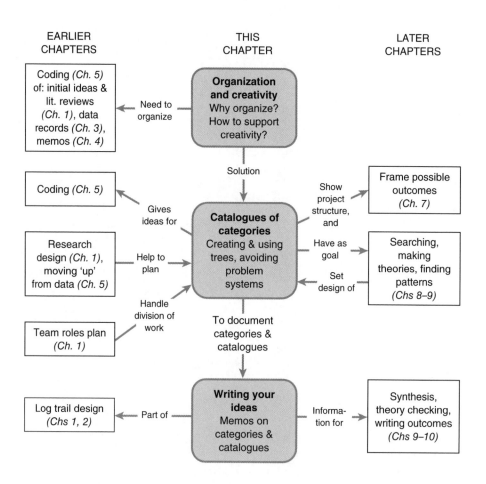

EARLIER
CHAPTERS

THIS
CHAPTER

LATER
CHAPTERS

Coding *(Ch. 5)*
of: initial ideas &
lit. reviews
(Ch. 1), data
records *(Ch. 3)*,
memos *(Ch. 4)*

← Need to
organize

**Organization
and creativity**
Why organize?
How to support
creativity?

Solution

Coding *(Ch. 5)*

Gives
ideas for

**Catalogues of
categories**
Creating & using
trees, avoiding
problem
systems

Show
project
structure,
and

Frame possible
outcomes
(Ch. 7)

Research
design *(Ch. 1)*,
moving 'up'
from data *(Ch. 5)*

Help to
plan

Have as
goal

Set
design of

Searching,
making
theories, finding
patterns
(Chs 8–9)

Handle
division of
work

Team roles plan
(Ch. 1)

To document
categories &
catalogues

Log trail design
(Chs 1, 2)

← Part of

**Writing your
ideas**
Memos on
categories &
catalogues

Informa-
tion for

Synthesis,
theory checking,
writing outcomes
(Chs 9–10)

SIX
Handling ideas

This is a chapter about what to do with the ideas generated by your design, your data and your coding. The message is that organizing is necessary for creativity, not its enemy. If your ideas are accessible and well managed, you will be able to reflect on the big picture, find and develop each category, and start linking concepts. Here you are advised on how to catalogue the categories created, manage this catalogue flexibly and creatively, and reflect on these processes as the project grows.

Working qualitatively expands data – rapidly. The new researcher may feel like the sorcerer's apprentice, facing apparently unstoppable processes beyond their control. This chapter is about knowledge management, organizing those processes, and the ways of balancing organization with flexibility.

It seems obviously helpful to manage data expansion by reducing records and organizing them, as in Chapter 3. But record management is not even half of the problem. Working qualitatively also creates and expands *ideas*. You started with a few concepts and topics to be explored (Chapter 1) and some data records. Your data generate more interpretative data in memos and annotations (Chapter 4), and by coding (Chapter 5) you create categories. Now the ideas, and their relation to the documents, are expanding by the hour, and this is what the method requires. But it also requires that you work with those ideas to analyse their relationships to each other, to categories that have not yet occurred in the data and to the data records themselves.

Software makes the expansion of qualitative data records far less alarming than it was with manual methods. Coding required that you mark up and duplicate paper records and file any copied segment under all the categories it was about. There is no duplication when you work with software; instead, you place at each of these categories a reference, or pointer, to the data segment you wish to code.

But expansion of *ideas* is more alarming with software. Software allows you to create many more categories and do much more with them than a manual system could possibly hope to handle. With any software, you can create rapidly very large numbers of new categories, and (at least sometimes) so you should. To do so does justice to the multiple meanings in your data.

The good news is that computers handle categories much more flexibly and efficiently than filing cabinets. The challenge, of course, is to manage ideas efficiently without killing creativity.

ORGANIZATION AND CREATIVITY

Qualitative research is full of apparent conflicts between efficiency and creativity, and these are most evidently faced when you begin creating ideas. If you don't organize and manage ideas, you will almost certainly lose them. Or worse, you will lose them sometimes.

As in most areas of the method, it turns out that efficiency is necessary for creativity. Creativity in qualitative methods requires the building of early ideas in ways that ensure that they provide a firm base for later, larger ones. Thus scaffoldings of explanation or theory are built up as you create, explore, test and link ideas. Firm constructs will result when the ideas are consistently accessed and interrogated, reliably followed and developed and carefully related to the evidence. The unintentional loss of an idea, even if at present it does not seem useful, puts these processes at risk. Accessing ideas inconsistently threatens the reliability of your coding. So managing ideas efficiently is necessary for confident creation of theory.

With or Without Computers?

The tension between efficiency and creativity is regularly raised in the context of computers. Researchers who prefer to work with paper records often see computers as number-crunching or database-storing machines, enemies of creativity. Of course, computers (and indeed any qualitative software) will handle numbers and store databases. But researchers working with paper records may see ideas handling on computer as a sign that the computer is 'taking over'.

Working with paper records, in the past, we managed the expansion and use of ideas just as we managed any other task requiring access by topic. Files and folders in filing cabinets were catalogued, using hierarchical index systems (category/ subcategory) so that categories were accessible and reliably accessed. Sometimes, index cards were used, hierarchically organized.

Hierarchical cataloguing of ideas existed long before Aristotle wrote the *Categories*, and such catalogues are as familiar as your local library. The methods described here for handling ideas derived from the ones that worked for me when I used and taught manual methods. Later, cataloguing methods were supported in qualitative software, and in developing software I learned more about cataloguing. But all the strategies discussed in this chapter can be tried on paper. The advice given does not require that you are using software.

The **Handling Sexual Attraction** project did not use qualitative software, but the report of ways of 'Working with the Data' stresses the importance of ordering of coding categories and reworking the catalogue of categories as theory developed.

However, if you are working without software, it is even more important to organize your ideas for easy finding, since you don't have a computer to find them for you. Without the computer, much time can be spent on producing even a limited and relatively inflexible system for managing ideas. So you will need to keep your system of ideas as simple as possible, and change it as seldom and as little as possible.

The Need for Organization

Reduction of ideas is as difficult as reduction of data records, and for much the same reason: you don't know yet what will matter. As coding gains momentum, the new categories created are exciting, confusing, promising and threatening. If the new idea coming 'up' from the data might prove significant, you need to hold on to it. And later, you need to know where you put it. As you make more categories for thinking about, and asking questions of, your data, you need to ensure that organizing them does not get in the way of thinking and asking. So by organizing ideas as they come in, you gain in three ways:

- **Speed:** When a theme recurs, you will want to code it where you coded last time. You need to find the category – fast! If you can't find it, the coding process intrudes on or distracts and detracts from your thinking.
- **Reliability:** If you don't find that category, or find it just sometimes, you will code at it inconsistently, and will be unable to rely on having all the material on that theme to retrieve, review and use to develop your understanding of the theme. The delicate task of establishing reliability of coding without reducing its sensitivity to meaning becomes much harder if the categories are inconsistently found.
- **Efficiency:** You need to develop many ideas and think about their relations without losing or confusing them. Think from the start not just about a particular category for your project, but about how you can handle all the many, perhaps hundreds of categories that will be needed to gather material and ask research questions.

Of course, no amount of organization will guarantee that you achieve these goals. But being organized is a necessary precondition to achieving them.

CATALOGUES OF CATEGORIES

Most commonly, the system used (in a filing cabinet or on computer) is a simple hierarchical one – usually referred to as a 'tree' of category and subcategory. As you work with the categories you are creating, if they have a logical place, they are placed there – below more general categories and alongside ones that are the same sort of thing. The simple question to place them is, 'What's this a *sort* of?'

Most qualitative researchers use tree-structured catalogues to manage their categories. As noted in Chapter 5, qualitative coding is like the filing techniques by which we sort everyday information and ensure access to everything about a topic. We do that in trees: 'chocolate cakes' are a sort of 'cakes'. It works just as well for categories of thinking about your data.

> Suppose you were doing a comparative study of businesses. This would include categories for the roles, and these would logically be under a parent category like 'company positions'. You would go to that tree to look for 'CEO', and if you had coded data where people are talking about CEOs, you would find references to that data.

As explained in Chapter 5, the place on a computer where you put a category is sometimes called a 'node'. In the terminology of systems and networks – and gardening – a node is a terminal of a branch or an interconnection of two or more branches. This term is used in several software packages for the place where you put a category and coding. At a node you can store not only the category but also, if you wish, thoughts about it or coding references to data about it. By placing the node in a hierarchy, you denote and store information about its relation to other nodes.

Of course, you don't have to store coding there. Some researchers don't code and most have a lot of ideas that they wish to store, but not to use as codes.

What Can You Do with a Catalogue?

The cataloguing of paper records has a simple purpose: to allow you to find them again. That beats not finding them. When you find the right cardboard folder, you can retrieve all the segments of text about that topic. But qualitative coding is not simply to get back everything coded at a topic. Its purposes include developing the ideas and exploring their relationships. This is where cardboard folders frustrate. Combining and then re-sorting folders is possible, but recoding their contents is very difficult. And you can't ask a data segment in a cardboard folder what other folders it is in or what the participant said before that segment, or whether any other women with the same characteristics saw this problem.

Nodes catalogued on computer, unlike folders for segments of data, are items you can easily move, combine and re-sort, recoding the data coded at them, as you explore ideas. Ask, 'What data segments are coded at this node?' and browse the results. Then work live with those segments, rethinking and recoding.

Why Catalogue in Trees?

A simple logical ordering by category and subcategory clarifies not only the ideas you are producing but also the growing structure of the project:

- **Showing and exploring the relations of categories:** Seeing them hierarchically stimulates thinking beyond the immediate category. *What are the nearby categories, and might they be useful here?*
- **Reviewing and strengthening the ideas:** What's missing? Coding up from the data, the discussion of how people learn about things in this company has produced categories for two official sources of information and one widely regarded as mischievous – gossip. Does nobody learn by consultation or discussion?
- **Monitoring the big picture:** A well-designed system of categories will tell you, your colleagues or supervisor what are the major dimensions of this project (and what isn't being covered).
- **Searching:** On computer, you can ask of any node what its relationship is to other nodes, either in the catalogue or in the coding it holds – and then keep asking about relationships until you have satisfied the line of enquiry. Cataloguing the nodes in trees makes it far easier to see clearly how you are constructing such searches. Searching the coding at nodes stored on computer provides ways of interrogating data that simply were not possible with filing cabinets, and you will be much helped by easy access to the nodes you are searching.

Most data will be coded many times (that is, at many nodes), since most qualitative records are about many things. In a hierarchical catalogue, the trees will represent the major dimensions of your project. Exploring how these dimensions relate will require searches for relationships of categories in different trees. *If you have coded at a node the text about 'positives re working environment' you might wish to ask a question like, 'When people are talking positively about the work environment, are they ever talking about the CEO?'* The question to your software is simply, 'What text is coded at both these nodes?' *It seems the CEO is indeed mentioned in this context, but is this only by managers?* You can now ask what is coded at the new node *if it comes from any of the cases of interviewees where the job is below management level.* In Chapter 8 we return to such questioning.

Goals for a Useful System

Most researchers have some favoured procrastination tasks to which they retreat when the project is too challenging. Yours may be gardening, fixing the car or rearranging the furniture. You have now acquired another way of putting off working with your data – reorganizing categories! Organizing the nodes in your project is both hugely rewarding and potentially unending. So approach this section with caution – the tasks of organizing must not be allowed to overtake the tasks of analysis.

Aim for a system of categories that works for you. A minimalist system may work, depending on your research goals. There are three rules of thumb:

1. If you want to ask a question about coded data, you need the nodes to represent the things referred to in the question.
2. If you don't want to ask about it, you don't need a node for it.
3. The catalogue of nodes should be clear and logical, so that you can always find the category you want. It will alert you to missing categories, inform you of duplications, and show the directions in which the project is progressing.

More about logic later; the first question is usually 'How do I start?'

Getting Started

As soon as the ideas are building up, try shaping them into a catalogue. This may happen before any data records exist. The exercises in Chapter 1 might produce a beginning catalogue, or the early stages of working 'up from the data' might have encouraged you to sort the products of those exercises. As soon as ideas are happening, try shaping them in trees.

─────────────── **Creating a Catalogue** ───────────────

- View the categories you have created as a collection. What different *sorts* of things are there? Are there logical clusters of categories?

  Perhaps one group is about sources of information, one about roles. Make a node for each 'parent' category (sources of information) and place the 'children' (for example, gossip) at nodes below the 'parent'.

- View the whole as a *system* of trees. Do they, together, add up to the project? Aim for a tree of nodes for each major dimension of the project. Start with the whole - projects are wholes, and they have shapes. Now what are the different dimensions of your project? Fill in that shape by plotting out the basic branches, establishing a small set of very general and independent categories that may be needed for the parts of the research project:

  o roles (formal and informal)
  o attitudes (to work environment, to authority, etc.)
  o sources of information (procedure manuals, team meetings, gossip, etc.).

- If a node doesn't have a logical place in your catalogue, don't force it in. 'Park' it in a 'free' area, with other categories whose place you don't yet know. Every now and then, check the nodes that are still 'free' of organization and move them into trees as appropriate.

As you form a category system, the project changes radically. Your uncoordinated collection of ideas is transformed into a filing system, which, like the library catalogue, will ensure that you know where a node is, and where a new node should go. In the process you will have pruned or merged a lot of the categories you made earlier, and the result is a smaller, tighter and organized system of ideas.

Idea Sorting Exercises

Try the following (all of which also make good teamwork or class exercises):

- Tell the project to a colleague. Ask them to sketch the ideas as you talk – as a tree-structured catalogue of the things you are studying.
- Prepare a presentation on your project, outlining topics to be covered: they are potential nodes.
- Do it physically, using mobile items, such as Post-it notes stuck on a wall, coloured cards or labelled blocks on a table.
- Code your research design (as suggested in the previous chapter) and/or your literature review. By coding them, you will make a new node for each new topic those documents cover. A well-structured literature review will often create a neat starter node system, since the outline of the review will be logical.

Now for the nodes from your data.

Naming and Describing Categories

Bother to give categories clear and unambiguous names. *Do you mean 'attitudes to managers' or 'attitudes to management'?* Don't use mnemonics, as they don't talk to you and can be very misleading.

Use descriptions to help you think through how you want this category to work for you. In filing cabinets, we stuck cards with descriptions on the folders for categories. Software provides description fields that don't fall off, and are easy to edit if you change how you are using the category. (*'Any text about attitudes to the management of this company: good or bad management processes. To be revisited later; may need to code on to differentiate.'*). Always date your description.

If you are working in teams, agreement on naming and use of a coding category is very critical. This does not mean that the team members should (or can) think identically. But you will need to discuss categories which you are interpreting differently, and achieve agreement. Use descriptions to alert you to the agreed definition. If you don't agree, record this.

Using Your System

In Chapter 4, a simple process of thinking 'up' from the data took you from the detail of the document (*that's interesting*) to the concept (*why?*) and then to the focused abstraction (why will *this* project benefit from *that* concept?). Another question has now been added: '*Where does it go?*'

If the new category doesn't fit somewhere, then wonder why. This may be because you have encountered a new aspect to your study. *You've coded text about the much appreciated and self-styled 'company clown' who lightens conflicts. But this new category doesn't really go under 'company positions' along with 'CEO'. And the company clown has a formal position – she's actually the accountant. Perhaps you need two parent nodes, 'informal company roles' and 'formal company positions'?* Considering this may open out new possibilities. What other informal roles are you seeing and how do they interplay with the formal ones?

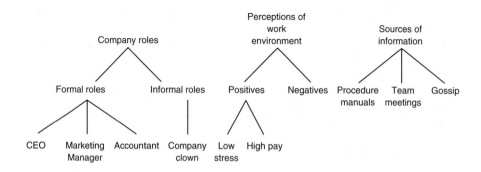

Note that you are shifting away from straightforward topic coding; *it's about the CEO. Now there is more analytical thinking: some roles aren't in the company structure plan, and they may be very important; they also may interact with the formal positions in interesting ways and I should look for those.*

Up from the Data and into the Category System

1. 'Why am *I* interested in *that*?' The answer is a category to be catalogued; in your project on computer, it will be placed at a node.
2. Now whenever you make a node, ask, '*Where does it go?*' If there is a logical place in your catalogue, place it there.
3. If the new category doesn't fit in the current catalogue, consider whether a new area should be opened up for it. Ask, '*What's this category a sort of?*' If the answer indicates a missing area in the catalogue, create that new tree and attach your new node to it.
4. If there is nowhere obvious for it to go, don't worry! Just leave the new category safely in an area for 'free' ones. Visit these often, repeating steps 1 and 2 for each.
5. Now return to the text to consider whether it should be coded again, at existing or new categories.

There is no need to 'fit' every category somewhere; and indeed you can't, since you will keep changing them. Think of the catalogue you are creating as work in progress.

The categories for thinking about the data will change throughout the project, since qualitative research is about theory discovery and theory exploration, not usually about testing a previously constructed theory. The system will be shaped, reshaped and examined in the months of test-driving it with more data. Quite normally, the nodes in a qualitative project will still be changing as the report is written, because writing, as previously remarked, is an analytical process. Above all, the dynamic system you are devising must work to represent properly the ideas you are gathering and stimulate the emergence of new ones. The validity of your study will depend on you adequately representing ideas and their relation to the data.

Working Your Category System

- Like any housework, this is never-ending: constantly tidy up. As each new category is given a place, check for redundant ones. Especially early in a project, you will store a lot of ideas that just might matter. Once you know they don't, delete them. (Or if you are nervous, move them into a 'retirement' area in your system!)
- Make each category earn its space. A good habit is to question the usefulness of a node if, over some time, it codes only one passage of text. This is possibly representing an oddity in the data, rather than a theme, but check that this oddity is not the tip of a bigger puzzle.
- If two categories mean much the same, check the data coded there, and if you are satisfied they have the same meaning, merge the nodes into one. You won't lose work; the coding information comes too. (If you are working in a team, check first that your colleagues agree these categories should be merged.)
- In the early stages, as those ideas 'emerge', allow them to stay 'free' for a short while. At the end of every coding session, review your free categories and ask each where it goes in the system. (No clear answer? Leave it 'free'.)
- Get in the habit of looking for things that go together and things that don't. Move them around if you are unsure of their place. (Back up the project before you make dramatic changes!)

The system should be simple, easy to use and documented – and you need to like it! Write a report on it to someone, to clarify how it works and to see it through their eyes.

Go to the **Harassment Complaints** project for a lively account of creative work to rejuvenate a project by reorganizing and sharpening a category system. Details include how recoding was done without losing any work, and the project was brought back into focus by 'lumping and coding down vs. splitting and coding up'.

Teamwork and Ideas

All the above advice applies to a team project, and team-mates are a great asset as you design and adapt the system of categories. Ensure that you are communicating well about these processes. Meetings, memos and other processes may be needed to ensure agreement.

The creativity/efficiency challenges hit teams sharply. It is important that nobody feels their creative initiatives are being forced inappropriately into someone else's efficient structure. A team has to learn of adventurous ideas, interesting themes and possible concepts, and the process of managing ideas must not destroy such initiatives.

But team coding must also be reliable, efficient and stable. Familiarity with the system of coding categories is a necessary condition for efficient and flexible coding. If the system changes unexpectedly, the researcher will be unable to find the category needed or understand the new ordering. If two categories are merged, and they were seen by some team members as very different, a serious inconsistency in previous coding may be overlooked. The result will be inadequate coding, and very bad team relations!

Teamworking a Category System

Creativity is always challenging in a team situation, since it has to be negotiated. One of the greatest risks is that if one member creates a category system and it is imposed on others, their ideas will be lost:

- Every team member who is using the system should be able to place their own new ideas into it without being monitored and constrained; be very careful that 'teamwork' does not become a compulsory process of agreement. Celebrate difference. The simplest way is to give each team member their 'own' tree of nodes. (This shows clearly who is having the really radical ideas!) New ideas can be 'parked' there until discussed and agreed for the project as a whole.
- Flexibility of the categories and their coding is essential for teams, and bad communications can be highly problematic. Many members may be coding and creating categories, and the right mix of consistency and freedom may take some time to establish. You need an agreement on ways that a 'need to discuss' meeting can be summonsed.
- Prior organization is necessary for teams, and this conflicts with the qualitative research goals of flexibility, so you need to do it well. In all but the smallest teams, in the smallest projects, the best basis for continuing cooperative organization will be early agreement about a core system of categories. This is because every member when coding needs to be able to find existing categories easily, and be reasonably sure they will stay in the same place.
- Teams need to discuss, collaboratively create and agree on a minimal category system and agree on not changing it; this will mean that members can 'see' as logical the arrangement of nodes, and count on its staying constant.

- When nodes are rearranged, all the affected team members should be consulted about or informed of the rearrangements. If the node system is changed, it must be either by the unchallenged authority of one principal researcher (this is not, technically, a team situation) or by discussion and agreement.
- Around this minimalist agreed system, maximize flexibility, so that the node system will change, despite the need for agreement. If this is done well, the development of ideas is very exciting, since it always involves communication. Periodic meetings are essential to ensure that all changes needed by any member are discussed.

The **Youth Offender Program Evaluation** project faced all these problems of organization and cooperation.

Problem Category Systems and How to Avoid Them

It's a good system if it works for you. As your system starts taking shape, there are four risks to avoid: excessive size, bad logic, coding fetishism, and mistaking a catalogue for a model. It usually turns out that they are related. If it's gross, that is because it's illogical. If this has happened, it's usually because the researcher became obsessed with getting it right or is forcing the catalogue to become a model.

Size As in any data management task, size is a challenge. You must be able to find your way round the system. So be stern with proliferating categories, and mean about creating new ones unless they promise something. What does it have to do with your research question? What might you use it for? There is no point in a category if you are not going to use it for discovery that's relevant to your project.

Especially early in a project, there is a tension here, since you still may not know if it will matter. You'll be helped by not worrying, so create the node if the category seems 'node-worthy'. But make it earn its space: as you revisit the system, check if the coding and ideas there are growing.

Logic Keep it light, but keep it logical. An illogical catalogue will always hinder analysis. The simplest rule is to keep *like* things together, and *unlike* things apart:

- Check regularly that any group of subcategories are all 'sorts of' the parent category. 'Company clown' just is not the same sort of role as 'CEO'.
- Avoid the temptation to put one *sort* of thing under a different sort.

  Perhaps your question requires comparing the work done by people in five different positions. It is tempting to make subcategories for each relevant position under each area of work. Under 'company PR' you might have three nodes ('CEO', 'marketing manager' and 'sales assistant'). It seems logical until you go to the next area of activity, 'sales monitoring', and find you have to make the same three subcategories there as well, and the accountant belongs there too.

  This catalogue is already a problem. Compare with the tree on p. 132, where the roles were simply catalogued together. How to access what is said about the CEO's PR work? With that separation of roles and activities, it is easy: just ask for everything coded at both CEO and PR work. But when the activity is a subcategory of the role, the question is hard to ask.

Efficiency not fetishism Managing ideas is essential for qualitative research, but it can overtake the goal of exploring and reflecting. Like coding, a good management system for ideas is a means to an end, not an end in itself. Every time you're managing ideas check that they are enriching your thinking and improving your use of your categories – not just putting off analysis.

With experience, you will find you can be more playful and experimental with the category system for your project. (Back up first!) Meanwhile, if you get stuck in anxiety about the 'right' place for this category, relax. It's wrong only if it prevents you finding it and getting it right later. Just ensure that you don't lose something interesting because you didn't know where to put it. Options include:

- Park it for later coding.

  Make a node called 'something to do with company structure', which perhaps goes under one called 'things I can't yet place'. That deals with it and you'll know to go back to it later.

- Go back up one level and do 'broad-brush' coding. Simply code the large segments that contain all the data about, say, conflict, in the general category until you are confident you can usefully distinguish the different sorts of conflict - or that you don't need to. Then, code on to new categories as they become clearer.

A catalogue is not a model The relationship between items in a catalogue is simply logical: *what is gossip a sort of? It's a source of information.* The relationship between items in a model are different. *My model of all the effects gossip has on company process, and who participates in it with whom, has at least two types of relationships – causal ones and interactive ones.*

When you start organizing ideas, it is easy to confuse these very different ways of representing their relationships. The sign of trouble is when your catalogue is being stretched to express what you are seeing in the data, rather than the logical relationship of categories. *The gossip is that the marketing manager's (MM) responsibility for company PR is to be taken over by the CEO. This item should be coded at four nodes in three different trees – it's about source of information (gossip), two formal roles (MM and CEO) and a business activity (PR). By coding it at all four nodes you ensure that this item will be found whenever you look at everything about any of them, or ask for the data coded at more than one of them, for example, if you are looking for material where both the CEO and MM are discussed. But the coding does not store your understanding of the relationship.*

You can write about your suspicion that the relationship of these managers is hostile in a memo. But you need a model to picture it.

WRITING YOUR IDEAS

As the structure of the node system is established, it will increasingly 'tell' your project. You now need to write it. A colleague looking over your shoulder at the node system should be able to read from it what the project is about. Ask them to do so, and you learn a lot about where it is skewed and what's missing. Then write about what you learned from how they 'read' it.

The aim now is to see the big picture and the small. It is easy to be over-whelmed with the system as a whole, and find that you can't see the analytical wood for those well-crafted trees. The best antidote is to write memos about the individual concepts, the node system as a whole, the data coded there, the themes emerging, and the sense you have of what's going on. And, perhaps, to model what you are seeing.

By now, your category system will provide:

- A current statement of the elements in your account or theory. Like your plan for a paper, it shows where your preparation has led and where to go next.
- A means of exploring theory in abstract: you can now locate those patterns and extract new links between topics and growing theories.
- A report of the state of your data and data processing: it tells not only what's there but what to look for. Be sure to let the classification system do this.

More Memos

As you move up from the data and manage the ideas carefully, abstract categories will come more easily. You will need not only to name and describe them but also to write. As well as holding coding of data, they are storage places for thinking. Their memos are often what matters most. Many a node memo has grown into a thesis chapter.

As soon as there is an adequate system of nodes, their management will become far less of a problem to you, and ideas about the categories will flow. Memos are where you tell what you are seeing; these do not need to be elegant constructs or polished arguments.

Memos on categories A category may need its own memo. Not all are inter-esting enough to deserve one, but most analytical categories do. Aim to record, quickly and informally but very thoroughly, your thinking about the idea, the recurrent 'noises' you're hearing in the data, puzzles, contradictions, and so on.

Use memos to identify matters to be discussed and to record debate and thinking about the different interpretations of shared categories. Always author your contributions – mark them with your initials or nickname. Later it will matter who wrote this challenging comment!

If you are working collaboratively, each creating your 'own' categories, find an easy way to identify them by ownership, and flag them for discussion. If each member has, as suggested above, their 'own' tree for their proposed nodes, they are less likely to feel constrained in the construction of new categories and writing of new memos.

Memos on the category system The category system also needs memos that will tell the *stories* of your analytical categories and the system you are constructing. Log the changes in categories, in their definitions or in their significance. Dated entries record and monitor the *history* of your system. Once you can see it as a whole, with parts, write about it. Critique your existing categories; try to extend and elaborate them as you play the material off against them. Don't lose records of when and why you introduced this new category or where it seems fuzzy. Give these memos a special name, for example, 'category system memo'.

In some projects, the ability to tell the story of the ideas and their management is central to the report. If you need such an account, ensure these memos are linked to the nodes in the project or documents they refer to.

Keep copies of reports listing current nodes in your software project at different times and you will have a picture of the development of categories. This may be the most efficient way to account later for the emergence of your explanation of their data. Spread the reports on the category system out on the wall and you can see how some areas are developing, others being combined. You are on the way to that explanation.

To Do

These exercises are best started on a whiteboard or very large sheet of paper:

1. Review the categories you have created so far, 'data up'. Revisit the ones emerging during the coding process (Chapter 5). Are they named accurately and described adequately? Do they belong together in any logical order?
2. Now look 'top down' from your project design. Revisit the categories you started the project with (Chapters 1–3). Working with a colleague, conduct the catalogue exercises above. Try for a fit with the 'data up' categories.

Move to the computer and in your project, conduct the following exercises:

3. With your starter category system, code another document, working with the categories so you can find existing ones and place new ones.
4. Critique a colleague's catalogue – check for and deal with redundant categories and duplicates.

5. Visit the categories you have left 'free' of the catalogue and review them, placing them in the trees when appropriate. Write a memo about this first stage of catalogue construction.
6. If you are working in a team, design a common catalogue of categories and discuss how you will use it to ensure consistency but allow innovation.

Suggestions for Further Reading

Few texts discuss the managing of ideas in this context. The following are notable exceptions: Miles and Huberman (1994), Mason (2002), and Saldaña (2013).

See also C. Wright Mills' essay on intellectual craftsmanship (1959). On catalogue systems, see Richards and Richards (1994, 1995), and *Readme First* (Richards and Morse, 2013).

And as noted in earlier chapters, very detailed advice on managing codes is available in the texts addressing coding in particular software packages: see Lewins and Silver (2014), Di Gregorio and Davidson (2008), Bazeley and Jackson (2013), and Kuckhartz (2014). For more detail, go to the website.

III
Making sense of your data

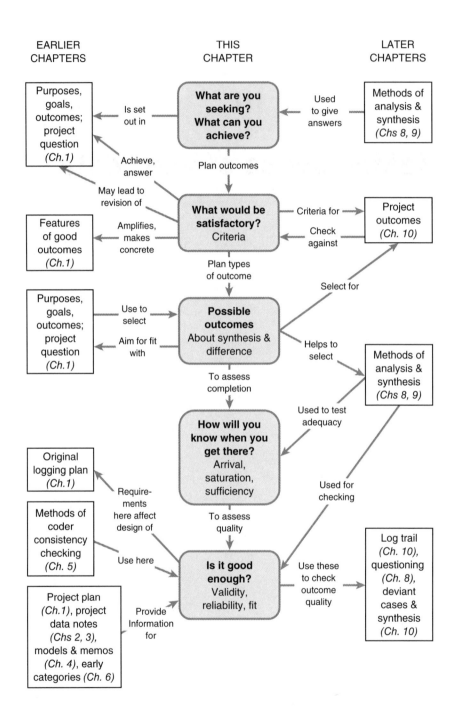

EARLIER
CHAPTERS

THIS
CHAPTER

LATER
CHAPTERS

Purposes, goals, outcomes; project question *(Ch.1)*

Is set out in →

What are you seeking? What can you achieve?

Used to give answers ←

Methods of analysis & synthesis *(Chs 8, 9)*

Achieve, answer

Plan outcomes

May lead to revision of

Features of good outcomes *(Ch. 1)*

Amplifies, makes concrete ←

What would be satisfactory? Criteria

Criteria for →

Project outcomes *(Ch. 10)*

Check against ←

Plan types of outcome

Select for

Purposes, goals, outcomes; project question *(Ch.1)*

Use to select

Possible outcomes About synthesis & difference

Helps to select

Aim for fit with

Methods of analysis & synthesis *(Chs 8, 9)*

To assess completion

Used to test adequacy

How will you know when you get there? Arrival, saturation, sufficiency

Original logging plan *(Ch.1)*

Require-ments here affect design of

Used for checking

Methods of coder consistency checking *(Ch. 5)*

Use here

To assess quality

Is it good enough? Validity, reliability, fit

Use these to check outcome quality

Log trail *(Ch. 10)*, questioning *(Ch. 8)*, deviant cases & synthesis *(Ch. 10)*

Project plan *(Ch.1)*, project data notes *(Chs 2, 3)*, models & memos *(Ch. 4)*, early categories *(Ch. 6)*

Provide Information for

SEVEN

What are you aiming for?

This chapter asks a question qualitative researchers are often unable to ask or answer until it's too late. Researchers need to be able to see how their projects may end. With a project set up and underway, you can now revisit the goals and design, and start seeing an achievable and good outcome. Possible outcomes are compared, with discussion of what you can expect on the way and how you will know when you get there.

The ultimate excitement and terror of a qualitative project is that you can't know at the start where it will end.

Researchers trained to test a clear hypothesis don't have this problem, since the project is set up to address and test a specific bit of theory. A qualitative project will not be set up that way, whatever its methodology. In each chapter of this book, the emphasis has been on learning from your data about what matters in this project, and adjusting your enquiry as you learn.

But not knowing what you will find is fine, so long as you *do* know what sort of an outcome you might be aiming for. At the start (Chapter 1) you framed a general statement of the purpose, goal and outcome aimed for. As the project progresses, it becomes both possible and necessary to firm up the picture of the outcome desired. Look for the right time to do this (rather as a hiker aims for a high patch of level ground, with a good view). With the first data records considered, coding underway and ideas being handled, take time out to assess where you have come from, how you arrived here, where you are going and the possible tracks to get there.

To direct your analysis, you now need to know what is sought, what is achievable, what will be satisfactory and how you will be able to tell that it is. Here are six questions to keep in front of you throughout the rest of your project:

1. What are you seeking?
2. What can you realistically achieve?
3. What would be satisfactory? (Or good enough, or incredibly good, depending on your goals.)

4. What might it look like?

And then, as you work towards this goal:

5. How will you know when you get there?
6. How will you know if it is good enough?

This chapter is about those questions. Once you can answer them, you can much more confidently name and frame what you are aiming for. This is the start of the last stage of the project. Chapters 8 and 9 are about how to handle the data in order to achieve that desired outcome. Then Chapter 10 is on reporting it.

WHAT ARE YOU SEEKING?

A novice qualitative researcher can easily get stuck at this question. Even after the project is underway, the question specified, design approved, data records abounding, you may still have no clear picture of what sort of an answer you are trying to produce.

In Chapter 1, a distinction was made between purpose, goal and outcome. It helps to clarify these different aspects of what you are trying for:

- Purpose: Why were you doing this?
- Goal: What are you trying to answer?
- Outcome: What sort of a product is required to achieve that purpose, and that goal?

Can you picture an appropriate report that answers your research question, and thereby meets your purpose? It must answer the research question, or do a good job of explaining why it couldn't, or why the question shifted in response to what you learned. And in almost all projects, it must do more than just describe the data.

Well, What Were You Asking?

This you know if you followed the advice in Chapter 1. Or at least you know what you were trying to ask. The project started with not just a topic, but a researchable question. This may have changed, as you learned more about your research field.

At that stage, you probably were not able to specify what sort of an answer you were trying for. Now that the project is underway, the question you asked is being addressed by appropriate data, handled in such a way that you are heading for a good answer to that question. Of course, expectations about what will be a good answer will depend on the methodological framework within which you are working. As in previous chapters, the advice offered must be put in that context. Revisit the issue of 'fit' of question, data, method and outcome in Chapter 1, and in *Readme First* (Richards and Morse, 2013). Remember that if you are working in a setting where issues of methodological congruence are not asserted, you still need to achieve that fit. The question asked should be addressed by the data it requires, handled appropriately so the question can be answered. Now is the time to check that this is so – do you have the data that question needed?

> Perhaps you are studying health behaviours, and your question was, 'How are mainstream and 'alternative' practices perceived by parents in this suburb?' You've sought perceptions through interviews and participant observation, read and coded the data records, and while it is too early to predict what the data are saying, you at least know that a report which merely indicates that there is a falling demand for mainstream medical clinics in this suburb would not satisfy the question. You're committed to saying something new about the range and patterns of those perceptions, and an account of their sources and their effects on behaviour.

Description and Analysis

Whatever the goal of a qualitative project, it is usually not *only* to describe the data. If you are doing highly focused funded research, the task may firmly be defined as description. But even in that context, the outcome should not be limited to just churning out summaries. *What are the responses of patients to a change in health provider?* Your answer can offer much more than a printout of the patients' answers because you have read and reflected on them. *There were three sorts of responses, patterned by socio-economic status …*

You have to be able to distinguish between description and analysis in order to analyse. Along the way to a theory or account of your data, you will require very rich descriptions, and they may be deeply interesting. Perhaps in that study of mainstream and 'alternative' practices, you've coded at 'trust' everything people say about trusting doctors, alternative practitioners and treatments. 'What do people say about this topic?' is a likely first step to thinking about the elusive concept of trust. To retrieve all these varied statements and describe them may be a substantial task. The description might inform, surprising with the passion and partisanship expressed in the statements you can quote. Your description may also indicate some patterns: perhaps women were much more likely to express unquestioning trust in alternative medicines than men. This has taken you beyond the original data. But you are still describing. Women say these sorts of things, men those.

To stop at describing the data is rather like describing the scene of a crime without trying to solve the crime. 'Somebody's dead, they were shot and there's a gun on the ground' is the beginning of a detective's questions. We hardly expect the enquiry to end with the facts of a dead body and discarded gun.

Consider the data on trust. The quotes from women and men are dead data, decontextualized. Your task is to ask live questions. What's going on? How did this situation come about and what might happen next? Is there something about these women's experiences that makes them more trusting of 'alternative' medicine? Or about that sort of health practice that makes it less comfortable for men?

Recall the discussion in Chapter 5 of the uses of coding. Simply to report all the text coded at a category will provide impressive descriptions. But it is only the first step to analysis. If you find you are printing out reams of reports on all the text coded at each category, worry. You are describing the data, topic by topic. Stop, and ask: how are these topics related? Coding, remember, is for a purpose. It gives you access to the data, so you can work with all the data on a topic – and go beyond it.

To move up from description of those topics, you need to start asking 'why' questions. Why is 'trust' applied to such disparate situations? Is it that there are several meanings given to the same term? (Browse and reflect on the different passages coded there.) Is it that trust requires preconditions that, perhaps bizarrely, are differently met in these different situations? (Modelling may find this answer.)

WHAT CAN YOU ACHIEVE?

Just as you set a researchable question at the start of the study, so too you should set an achievable goal for the end.

The first step is to read reports from similar studies. Go back to your literature review. Ask why some (but not all) reports are convincing, or intriguing. Focus on studies in your area, where you now feel you have some authority. Be cruelly critical of qualitative reports that you find boring, trivial or skewed by the position of the researcher. How can you do better?

Then, you need to assess what you now think you can achieve, given what you now know about your data, the richness of the records, the comparative grit in them, and your own interpretative processes and construction of categories. Given that knowledge, you can reflect on the possible outcomes for your study. To do so, you need to consider the ways *good* qualitative research can come out.

Can You Make a Theory?

In Chapter 4, I commented on the phrase 'emerging from the data'. Themes and ideas don't ever just emerge. Nor do theories. To sit looking at descriptions of data, like a cat at a mouse hole, will never produce a theory. Theories (and, indeed, the hunches, ideas, themes from which they are made) are constructed by researchers.

Novice researchers too often have been taught to see theory as a formidable intellectual construction, created by philosophers and embedded in scholarship. But theories come in all shapes and sizes. Our everyday life is informed by theories. You know how to dodge if you run across a street in traffic, or how to avoid an unwanted encounter. In there is a theory about the relation between distance, speed and impact, or the likelihood of your colleague's being in the office on Tuesday. These little theories are more or less useful, depending on how well crafted they are, and on your attention to evidence and consideration of possible factors in the predicted outcomes. Such little, local theories are usually the goal of qualitative research.

The tantalizing goal of 'grounded theory' has become part of the accepted vocabulary of qualitative method – though often used out of the context of the increasingly diverse techniques taught under that label. (For more on the goals and varieties of grounded theory, see *Readme First*.) But whether or not they are working in those methods, almost all qualitative researchers share a goal of accessible, understandable theory that is derived from, and justified by, their data. If you are puzzled by the goal of making theory, this account may assist:

> Theory in sociology is a strategy for handling data in research, providing modes of conceptualization for describing and explaining. The theory should provide clear enough categories and hypotheses so that crucial ones can be verified in present and future research; they must be clear enough to be readily operationalized in quantitative studies when these are appropriate. The theory must also be readily understandable to sociologists of any viewpoint, to students and to significant laymen. Theory that can meet these requirements must fit the situation being researched, and work when put into use. By 'fit' we mean that the categories must be readily (not forcibly) applicable to and indicated by the data under study: by 'work' we mean that they must be meaningfully relevant to and be able to explain the behavior under study. (Glaser and Strauss, 1967: 3)

Three of the 'Methods in Practice' reports are described by the researchers as grounded theory projects: **Handling Sexual Attraction**, **Leading Improvement in Primary Care Practices** and the **Sexuality-Spirituality** project. What do they have in common? Compare their methods and outcomes. For each, ask whether they follow the 'rules' of texts on grounded theory method. For each, ask: what new theory was created and how was it justified?

What Level of Theory Are You Creating?

If you feel it inappropriate to use the term 'theory', find other words and descriptions that fit the intended outcome of your study. Some really satisfying and useful outcomes are best described as *explanations* or *understandings*. But 'theory' is a perfectly good word, and there is no need to duck for cover when it is mentioned.

The social science literature has useful terms for the levels of theory. In writings since C. Wright Mills (1959) there is a distinction between 'grand theory', not related to any particular situation, and 'middle-range' theories, which reach beyond a particular situation to generalize. In grounded theory writing, the distinction is made lower down, between 'formal theories', which are more general, and *substantive theories*, ones that are particular to the substance of their data. The substantive sort of theory is the most usual in a qualitative study, and probably what you are aiming for. It's local to your data, but that does not mean it's no use to anyone else. If it is to be satisfactory, it will encompass the larger picture and allow you to see the whole, not just the detail of the data. It's like the detective's theory about *this* crime, not the criminologist's theory about what causes this *sort* of crime. But the detective's theory may be useful in solving past crimes and anticipating future ones by the suspect.

It is useful to distinguish between the tasks of theory emergence and theory construction. Turner (1981), making this distinction, pointed out that to make concepts 'emerge' from data was only the first step. The researcher still has to *construct* theory. As data are explored and coded, the categories may indeed come 'up from' the data (you have been doing that since Chapter 4). Managed well, they will give you a strong feeling that you are certainly not going to end up with nothing to say. But these threads still have to be woven into a fabric of argument, an account that will allow you to make sense of the data. That will be a local theory.

The next chapter is about the construction work. Here we first ask what sort of a construct you can hope to build.

WHAT WOULD BE SATISFACTORY?

In my experience, this is the least well-tackled challenge in qualitative research. The mythology of theory emerging from data, fully and beautifully formed, like Botticelli's Venus from the sea, makes it churlish to ask when your theory will be good enough. But you must ask that. Any old theory won't do.

──────────── **What Would Be Satisfactory?** ────────────

The discussion so far suggests three requirements for a satisfactory outcome:

1. It should meet the goals of your project, answering your research question.
2. It should offer analysis, not just description.
3. It should offer at least a new local theory or explanation.

Add to these requirements the three characteristics of a good outcome suggested in Chapter 1:

1. It should offer something more than the participants in your research could have reported.
2. It should *account* for your data. This has to be an adequate account, so you will be able to claim that it 'makes sense' of what's going on in the data.
3. It should be *usable*; you should be able to do something with the outcome. This may be to project it to other theories (which you have considered in your literature review) and expand or develop them, or to compare with other findings and examine why they are differently explained. Or you may put the outcome to a practical use, in a policy programme or a social action.

Now, spend some time describing, or picturing in a model, an outcome for your project that would qualify on all of these criteria as satisfactory.

WHAT MIGHT IT LOOK LIKE? POSSIBLE OUTCOMES

Qualitative researchers aim to construct projects that bring together the ideas generated from the data with questions and insights from elsewhere (previous knowledge, literature, imaginative comparisons and metaphors). They are local, in the sense that the discoveries and accounts are not usually generalizable beyond the small study, but the construct created can usually be tried out in other settings. To do so is important. Other researchers may respond to your work by adapting theirs or challenging yours. Participants may discover in your analysis ways they can move forward to deal with problems. And you will get more sure-footed in your claims that the work is trustworthy as you see it used.

There are many highly respected ways of constructing useful outcomes (and room beside them for innovative experiments). Most of the literature of qualitative research suggests the researcher is usually seeking a *synthesis*, a core theme or single story. Here, the researcher is distilling the complexity of their data to a story or an account of what's central or crucial. But *difference* may in fact be the big story, an account of how the research discovered patterns or contrasts. Both bringing it together and teasing it apart are highly productive of ideas.

Eight such possible outcomes are in the boxes below, divided into synthesis outcomes and difference outcomes. This is of course an artificial divide. Typically, a project will move between these types: seeking and exploring a pattern, as the researcher discovers the underlying big picture. Nor are the types of construct here exclusive or definitive. To nail a project to one outcome would be foolish; you will find that yours changes course as you work with the data. Treat these outcome pictures as line drawings of the possible construction (to assist this, I have given them nicknames).

Try these very different constructs on your project as you currently know it. 'Would this outcome best help those I am studying?' 'Might this be what I am moving towards?' You are now working at the last part of the 'fit' of question, methods and data – towards an outcome, a construct, that fits with your project's purpose and progress.

―――――――――― Project Constructs about Synthesis ――――――――――

- **The big picture:** Create from a mass of data a *unified account* of 'what's going on', distilling the central issue or character of the situation. Here the theory construction task is synthesis and clarification. Such studies re-present the situation vividly because they reduce it to the essential features, clarifying and explaining why these are central. (The analysis works on the data rather as a glass-bottomed boat works on choppy water – suddenly, you can see clearly.)

(Continued)

(Continued)

By identifying core aspects of trust and authority of health advice, you aim to bring all the complexity of your data together.

 From years of data in multiple sites, the **Youth Offender Program Evaluation** project set out to picture the impact of such programmes.

- **The pathway:** Analyse the steps taken in a social *career* or *journey*, with focus on identifying and specifying the stages, contributing factors and results of people taking this path, for example, the 'career' to illness, drug use, parenthood, crime or fame.

Case studies will track how women lost trust in traditional medicine when they had young children.

 By studying the **Elderly Survivors of the Hanshin Earthquake**, the researcher sought a picture of the processes of adaption and recovery in disaster management.

- **The x-ray view:** Construct and test through your data an *explanation* of a puzzling behaviour or social phenomenon, reducing the complex picture to what matters, to just the bones and sinews. Where are the fractures and the strains? Sometimes the explanation will draw on higher level theory. Sometimes it will be causal, but usually the model of cause and effect will be very complex.

Many aspects of women's daily lives make traditional medicine unattractive.

 The **Handling Sexual Attraction** project studied psychotherapists' handling of sexual attraction to their clients – but the project sought a grounded theory explaining other situations.

- **The music not the dance:** Show why the phenomena studied (perhaps an organization, institution or ideology) *work*, establishing the processes behind that explain why they operate together. This approach is very effective in analysis of situations we normally take for granted. It aims at discovery of mechanisms and processes.

Might you be able to identify an affinity between the ideologies of family life and of alternative health?

 From sparse records of recorded complaints, the **Harassment Complaints** project derived an explanation of processes.

The promise of a single storyline, a big picture, 'career' or a 'core theme' that brings everything together is seductive. It is also highly dangerous, since a single storyline can of course very easily be achieved by ignoring everything else. Often it is not possible to give a 'big picture' unitary account without making it so general it is trivial. Showing *why* the data don't come together under one theme, and what explains divergences, may be far more powerful than describing the theme.

In a study where contrast or pattern is embedded in the research question, or dominant in the data, you of course have to start there. The contrast or pattern may prove to be dominant, leading to an outcome that is about difference. Qualitative studies do not always seek a single – or even any – storyline. But the analysis will usually achieve something other than mere description.

A good example is the **REMS** project. On the surface, this is merely a data storage exercise, which then provided an evidence service via a coding system - which of course, like any coding, incorporated analytical thinking.

So consider for your study whether you should aim at making sense of diversity. Never see this as a less attractive outcome. Difference constructs can be far more useful than apparently seamless single-story constructs, and just as satisfying and elegant. Showing the points of divergence of pathways, or the possibilities for different policies, will highlight contrasts, and most studies thrive on them.

Project Constructs about Difference

In the examples above, comparison might be used as a way to distilling commonality. But comparison can be the climax of a study. If your original question, or your data, direct you to exploring and explaining, you may seek an analytical outcome that is about difference. Some possible outcomes include:

- **The dominant pattern:** Use a *systematic comparison* of cases or sites to create a theory of why they are different, or what common processes or characteristics override the differences.

  When women's stories of health emergencies are compared with men's, the strong differences lead you to asking about the ways women with young children in your setting learn health messages through informal social networks. You relate this to their acceptance of 'alternative' messages, using the literature on acceptance of medical authority.

  From case studies compared, the researcher in the **Sexuality-Spirituality Project** concludes that across very different stories, becoming straight is paradoxically a rite of passage to becoming gay.

- **The animated model:** Develop a *model* of the interplay of factors, by teasing out the relationship between elements of your study and explaining complex processes behind it. Such analysis often offers a dramatic elaboration of a situation that in the literature appeared simple. Alternatively, the model might be a first step towards a 'single-story' outcome, or the construction of a wider and more generalizable theory.

(Continued)

(Continued)

Teasing out the model, and interrogating the assumptions behind it, you may come to a more wide-ranging account.

The pattern is not simply of gender, but of the complex interplay of gender, life stage and social support.

 It was appropriate that the **Mapping Caregiving** project should work from participants' maps to a model of the factors in care networks.

- **Clarification by typology:** Identify (and specify from the data) *types* of responses or behaviours representing the varieties exposed by your study. These may be real (represented by some of your cases) or 'ideal' types (which, like caricatures, distil what's central to a type). Rich descriptions of representative cases can make a vivid report, often the most important for policy work, since it alerts the practitioner to the range of needs they will meet.

 In the **Inside Companionship** project, one outcome was to break up the single notion of companionship into three main dimensions: *companionship I*, institutional and instituted action; *companionship II*, action as 'pharmakon'; and *companionship III*, social and profane action.

 In the **Wedding Work** study, you see an example of detailed coding and analysis further developing and breaking open typologies from an earlier study.

- **Zooming in:** Explore and challenge or extend *an existing theory* (in the literature or real life) using your complex data to show the need for more subtle explanations or understandings. This is often the reason for doing a qualitative study, to show the richer picture. The existing theory, say, *of the patriarchal authority given to doctors*, provides a general picture, since all behaviours look the same from a distance. But zoom in to the detail of your study and you see much finer differentiators and more interesting processes, with which you can elaborate the theory.

It's not that all women accept the authority of all doctors, but that there are several sorts of authority here, and trust accompanies a different sort, more developed in women's networks.

 From the qualitative study of **Leading Improvement in Primary Care Practices**, the researchers revised the initial model to provide a more complete explanation of the process of change actually used within practices.

HOW WILL YOU KNOW WHEN YOU GET THERE?

This is a question which researchers are often ashamed to ask. If you had a good enough explanation or theory, would you recognize it as such? Are you at risk of discarding a useful theory because you didn't see it as a theory, or of walking right past the core theme, because you were too busy coding? The next two chapters discuss some of the ways that qualitative theory is constructed, as you search through and see through the complexity of the data. But many researchers need to know at the start what it is they should expect as an end of those processes.

I have argued above that theories come in all sizes, and the tasks of constructing small theories are not very formidable. This is comforting to the small-theory builder, but it may make them worry more about the issue of theory recognition. Would you know a good but local theory if you met it?

The usual answers are either that the researcher will know clearly when they get there, or that the 'saturation' of the data will indicate arrival. Both these signs of completeness are welcome, but in practice pretty untrustworthy. Fortunately, you don't have to wait for an 'aha' or rely on 'saturation'. You can evaluate what you have constructed by checking on focus and sufficiency.

Aha? Or Ho-hum?

Most experienced qualitative researchers will recall (always fondly) a moment of 'arrival', sometimes described by the discovery noise, 'Aha!' These are good moments, and not to be dismissed! They are also not guaranteed, and not trustworthy.

Don't wait for the 'aha', as it probably will not happen, don't feel cheated if it doesn't come, and don't trust it if it does! The majority of projects arrive at a good conclusion by steady steps through analysis processes rather than a grand moment of discovery. Arrival will be confirmed by growing confidence that you really know what's going on. It happens, in other words, over time, through thinking and working with the data.

And don't trust every 'aha' – it may represent wishful thinking or a skewed focus on just one aspect of the data. (Please revisit the discussion of you and your data in Chapter 2.) Like every other contribution to your theory construction, it has to be validated through the data. Just because it's exciting doesn't mean it's even useful, let alone right. Suspect it, especially if the 'discovery' is in your interests, because it fits what you wanted to find or the trendy or politically correct interpretation of the situation, or because you have a deadline!

Suspect, but don't dismiss it. Such moments may be the reward for excellent handling of the data. If so, they signify that the researcher has succeeded in getting above the 'noise' of the data to see an overriding theme or pattern, something that could be seen by participants in the situation. In my experience, these marvellous moments happen to those who have been working very deeply and sensitively with their data, paying due attention to every theme, worrying at the inconsistencies and puzzles. The recognition of a cohering theory or a crucial divider is the last stage in this work. Because you have in your head (and of course well managed in your project) the full story of all the categories and threads, your concentration on making sense of them overwhelms everything else on your mind. The clarification tends to happen when you are thinking about something else entirely – a colleague's research, a wider theoretical issue or the basketball game – and something in that context triggers recognition of a clue that was in your data.

 There are cheerful accounts of 'aha' moments and their subsequent uses in the **Wedding Work** project report on 'Analysis'.

So don't *seek* the 'aha' – if this happens to you, it will be by surprise, a minor or major eruption of discovery from your well-handled data and ideas. It may come when you are in the shower, on top of a high hill or writing a totally unrelated report. Of course, if it's exciting, celebrate, but also write it down, revisit it in the cold light of morning, and then subject it to the testing and grounding processes that any other theme is subjected to (see next chapter). It will have to survive rigorous testing to ensure it is not just an artefact of your own political convictions or a boring over-simplification.

Saturation

This term is variously used in qualitative research to describe arrival at a stage when nothing new is coming up. Earlier chapters have advised that your research processes will be to some extent driven by the data. You will expand the reach of your project, seek new sources of data or material on newly discovered topics, as these are required by what you learn. This has to stop if you are ever to conclude the project!

It will stop, and you will conclude, because the data will saturate. If the data records and the categories coming out of the data are well handled, both will stop expanding. As you take off from the data, expansion seems uncontrollable, but with carefully monitored investigations of the new areas the data demand, you will find the project levels off, fewer new questions arise with each document, fewer new categories are created and require investigation. Your catalogue of ideas is likely to shrink, as it becomes clearer to you what matters and what is extraneous. You'll be merging categories that are similar and deleting irrelevancies.

Be careful not to seek saturation in the interests of meeting deadlines. If each new document requires more memos about new ideas, more new categories for coding data raising new issues, you are definitely not there! Either the data are too disparate to support focus, or the processes of creating and exploring ideas are not working for you. Resist the temptation to force focus by ignoring variety or deleting the categories that are not fitting in. If you don't have saturation, you have more data handling to do. The next chapter is about ways of doing it.

Saturation occurs, in other words, not by magic, but by good data handling. But be clear about what it shows. Saturation can be easily arrived at by triviality. It may indicate that your data are too shallow to raise the issues that matter or that the analysis process is shallow – you are not getting anything new because you're not asking the questions that would scratch the surface of the data. Saturation says nothing about whether you are going to arrive at a synthesis that is significant.

Put simply, saturation indicates that you have covered the *breadth* of your data. From this spread of data, nothing new is coming up. Now there is the question of *depth*. To judge the adequacy of the depth of your data, you will need to evaluate the focus you can get.

Examine the account of achieving saturation in the **Handling Sexual Attraction** report.

Focus

Exploring the types of project construct above, I used the analogy of the zoom lens. As you read, reflect, code, compare, write and order concepts, you have been zooming in on the detail of your data and then out, taking off, up to a more general level. Moving in and out of detail is by now a familiar experience, and good researchers do it all the time. From Chapter 2, the processes described involved such movement ('that's interesting' is zooming in, then 'why am I interested in that?' is zooming out).

Being able to show clearly what is going on at each level, zooming in or out, is always a very strong sign that you are getting there. To show this needs focus, and focus needs depth.

By focus I mean simply the ability to adjust the way you are looking so you have a clear picture. Focus is harder to measure than saturation. It may require subtle judgement to decide whether a picture is clear, or clear enough. Many of the pictures you draw will be unclear; you lack the data or the depth to show them in focus. Trying unsuccessfully to focus may lead you to more theoretical sampling – to improve the depth of data and the sharpness of your picture.

When you have an account that is satisfactory, one indicator will be that in each of the areas you are analysing, there is a sharp focus. You are not reduced to generality ('some of the women felt ...') or to diffidence ('it would seem a problem for the younger men ...').

Sufficiency

It is exasperating for a researcher convinced that they will never make sense of 'all this stuff' to hear descriptions of excellent studies in terms of their simplicity, elegance and sufficiency. But the time will come, as you arrive at a good account of your data, when you will be confident that you have literally arrived somewhere *else*, that you climbed above the muddle and confusion of complex data and could clearly account for what they were about.

For a clear claim of sufficiency visit the account of second analysis of the **Harassment Complaints** project.

What would your account be like if it was sufficient? Five qualities add up to sufficiency for me.

Signs of Sufficiency

- *Simplicity!* The theory or explanation will get progressively simpler, often alarmingly so. You may find you doubt if it is very significant. Isn't this just glaringly obvious? Isn't it trivial? It won't be, if you have worked the data against this simplified statement until you are sure it is a small polished gem of a theory, not a mere pebble of truism.
- *Elegance and balance* are signs of a well-crafted theory that has been well grounded in the data. It should be a coherent story, one that 'hangs together'. If you need to cobble an extra 'ad hoc' theory onto the main story to explain part of the data, try reworking it, aiming to mould it again into a whole.
- *Completeness* is an essential feature. To satisfy, your story has to reach across all the confusing and complex data of your study, and all the categories created from that data if they are relevant to this theory. Nothing is left sticking out, unconsidered or unexplained. (The techniques in the next chapter will help you to identify exceptions.)
- *Robustness* will be established as you progressively challenge and adapt the theory. When it's sufficient, it doesn't fall over if different data appear. Cases that don't fit are explained. (How to find them and deal with them is another topic for the next chapter.)
- *It makes sense* when you tell it to the relevant audiences. These include colleagues and participants. If it is ethically acceptable to discuss with them (see below) your explanation of their behaviour, you have an excellent indicator of its making sense, at least to them. You may find they disagree, and that what you offer is not something they knew. But it should make sense to them. You are seeking 'Oh yes!', 'Now I see why ...' or 'I disagree but I can see that it could be explained that way'.

This is where teams have a huge advantage; there is always a group to tell it to, and the option of a workshop on the possible meanings. If it makes sense to the team, it probably makes sense.

The sufficient account of your data will *work*. When you lay this well-crafted interpretation over the data, it will make sense. When your confidence in the account is strong enough, you will find you can *tell* the project. That dreaded question, 'What's your study about?' can be answered in five minutes, not 50.

Note that sufficiency does not require a unitary construct. An account of differences can be simple, elegant, complete, robust and make sense of the whole project. (Most elegant artwork is complex not unitary. If you doubt the sufficiency of a story about diversity, consider the complex elegance of mosaics.)

Researchers who have experienced this extraordinary arrival know to expect it. The analysis steadily reduced noise, removed hunches and guesses that didn't hold up, brought together clues that increasingly pointed to a denouement, tested and dealt with alternative explanations, strengthened the fabric of theory. Metaphors for this process are common. One colleague describes a good project as like a good detective story, where at the end you see that all the clues led there. To another, it is like the arrival at a particular house, following sparse directions: clock the distance from the station, locate the supermarket on the corner, check the colour of the door and yes! – the right people open it.

HOW WILL YOU KNOW IF IT IS GOOD ENOUGH?

How can we be sure that an 'earthy', 'undeniable', 'serendipitous' finding is not, in fact, wrong? (Miles, 1979: 591)

This last topic is a major area of debate in qualitative research, since it raises philosophical issues of the nature of realities and their perception. Start there. You are almost certainly not setting out to claim you have the only 'right' answer to your research question. (And the answer is almost certainly not going to be plainly, simply, wrong.) It's not likely to be a question answerable in that way. If you discover conflicting understandings of the situation studied, as researcher you are not choosing between them, to conclude one was 'wrong'. You may report on how it was that the views so diverged, or show that one was based on a far more partial experience. But you do want to convince your reader that your explanation is not itself partial, that you have explored all possibilities, that it is sufficient. It is very useful to ask how you would know if it was a poor, misleading or inadequate explanation.

Follow the suggested readings to find out more about these issues. It is important to address them, and not allow them to freeze your interpretation. You must be able to move on with your project, confident that you know how you would discover if the analysis did not do justice to your data. If you know this, you can show it to the reader, and your account will be believed. You need to establish why you have confidence in that account, and why your reader should share that confidence.

When Could You Say It Was 'Valid'?

If you quail at the discussions of validity, move from the noun to the verb. To validate an argument or explanation, you check it step by step. In this way, you can establish that it is properly rooted in the data and soundly constructed. This is exactly how qualitative theory is built – step by step.

> Valid: ... Of arguments, assertions etc.: well founded and applicable; sound and to the point; against which no objection can fairly be brought. Validate: ... To make valid or of good authority; to confirm, corroborate, substantiate, support.
>
> Validity: ... The quality of being well-founded and applicable to the case or circumstances; soundness and strength (of argument, proof, authority etc.)
>
> *The Shorter Oxford English Dictionary*

We know what we mean when we judge an argument or an objection to be valid. If it's valid, it's well founded and sound (the Latin it comes from means 'strong'). So too with research. If we agree that your argument or research process is valid, it will be because the steps you have taken were firm and sound, and the logical progression from one stage to the next is well grounded, and we can see what those steps were.

'Validity' is one of the most discussed issues in qualitative research, because it involves the existence of objective reality and the truth of assertions about it. With 'reliability' (see below) it has been the bloodiest battleground in the hundred-year war against inflexible criteria for quantitative research. If you are working in a setting where these debates are relevant, there is a considerable literature to cover. You will find a recent literature offering new and interesting ways of gauging validity in qualitative research, and new words for them (credibility, transferability, dependability, confirmability).

For now, the important question is: how would you, and your reader, know if the argument or explanation you propose is valid? This is a good question, and you need to be able to see the answer if you are not prepared to risk having significant audiences dismiss your work as merely your opinion.

Validity Checks – and What They Tell You

Building validity checks into the research design is a highly attractive option, especially for researchers working in a setting where the norms of quantitative research dominate.

Two ways of 'checking' validity are commonly advocated. These are 'triangulation' and 'member checking' aka 'respondent validation' (designing for these was discussed in Chapter 1). Both are very interesting design approaches for many projects, and may support a more multifaceted analysis. But as 'checks' on validity, both are highly problematic, and for the same reasons. Either a research design bringing different sorts of data together or a design for feedback from respondents will raise the same questions: how will we now interpret either agreement or disagreement?

Triangulation 'Triangulation' is the term widely used for research designs where different sorts of data or methods of handling data are brought to bear on the research question.

Several of the projects report use of triangulation. Contrast the **Youth Offender Program Evaluation**, the **Wedding Work** and the **Elderly Survivors of the Hanshin Earthquake** projects.

Often, using multiple approaches promises very interesting results; it's always interesting to see the same question different ways. The advantages of doing so will depend on your topic and they must always be balanced against the splitting of resources into several sub-projects. In particular, when careful mixed methods approaches are designed, bringing quantitative data into play with qualitative, very rigorous analysis of the qualitative data can result.

But those advantages will not automatically convey validity. Indeed, the splitting of resources may, ironically, lessen the claims to valid results from any of the sub-projects, since there will be less time to do very thorough testing of ideas or pursuit of cases that don't fit, and less time to log these processes.

It is useful to reflect on the metaphor for 'triangulation'. The term comes from surveying. By taking two readings with a calibrated instrument from known positions, the surveyor, with mathematical precision, can locate the exact position of a third object. This is not the sort of checking you are doing in a qualitative project. If you designed several ways of making data about your research question, what were you hoping to locate? The research question is unlikely to be about a simple matter of fact, let alone a physical object. Probably, two different sorts of data will give two (or more) different interpretations of the situation. Unlike the surveyor, you are likely to have strong reasons for supposing that one of your 'readings' will be more useful than the others. This will be very interesting indeed, but you may have no reason to treat any of these ways of looking as more 'valid'. If the different sub-studies give a similar picture, this may strengthen your argument for that picture, but you will need to consider very carefully the factors that might have distorted them all similarly.

Member checking Techniques for providing feedback on your interpretations offer a 'check' on validity in a different way from triangulation and, importantly, at a different stage of the project. Design for 'triangulation' requires the researcher to view the situation through different methods or data types as part of the analysis process. 'Member checking', by contrast, typically happens at the end. The design usually proposes that the researcher produces the report, and subsequently has it reviewed by those studied, revisiting it in the light of their judgement. Do 'they' see the situation as you, at the conclusion of your project, now see it?

The questions of how you (or they) 'see' a situation, making sense of it, and how you can trust such accounts, are discussed in detail in Chapter 9. In that context, it is important to think through the very many possible interpretations of members having either agreed or disagreed with how you see it. Here, the important point to make is that while respondent feedback is always very useful, it never provides a simple process of 'validation'.

When Would It Be 'Reliable'?

'Reliability' is another of those abstract nouns with long reading lists. Like 'validity', it is more approachable via its verb.

We refer to our ability to 'rely' on people, services or the weather forecast. The verb means to depend on or put our confidence in the relevant husbands, buses or sunshine to do what we were expecting them to do (pick up the kids, arrive on time or dry the laundry). It's worth noting that regularity is implied to different degrees (those assigned to picking up should *always* do it, or else; buses are expected to arrive on time, within reasonable traffic-related range; and frankly, the weather bureau does its best with available resources). None of these statements mean that regular behaviour is invariably predicted.

Regularity and standardized procedures fit poorly with life and qualitative research. Qualitative researchers protest (very reliably and validly!) against having the standards of randomized control trials applied to naturalistic field research. There are very few situations in a qualitative project, as in life, that can be replicated in a controlled way. The goal of standardized 'measures' which return consistent measurement in a controlled setting is obviously incompatible with qualitative work. (Nor is it in any of the definitions of reliability in ordinary dictionaries; it is a particular use of the term for a narrow range of research methods.)

So aim for a result your audience can rely on. Do not assume this is easy – it's just different from consistency in a controlled setting. It absolutely is a goal of good qualitative research that the audience should be able to depend on it, to put confidence in the research result, that it should be seen to be trustworthy. If you always set this standard, you will be able to assure your readers that you have reliably examined the data records, that they can count on your locating and consistently using the categories created, that you are responsibly storing and using all information available and that the processes of your questioning and cohering the data in explanations are transparent and well documented. In other words, the best way to assure that your work is reliable is to have well-validated procedures in all that you do, so people can see that you always 'deliver the goods'.

Coder Reliability 'Checking'

> Consistency requires you to be as ignorant today as you were a year ago. (Bernard Berenson)

When coding is used in qualitative research in some disciplines, researchers strongly rely [*sic*] on tests for coder consistency. In Chapter 5, ways of establishing degree of consistency over time or across coders were described. These are highly useful exercises, especially for team projects. But be sure to interpret the results appropriately. Like the validity 'checks' just discussed, they establish that there are different interpretations, and leave you the task of establishing what this means and whether it matters.

Colleague checking was used for codes in the **Leading Improvement in Primary Care Practices** project. Both the large governmental projects on the site, **REMS** and the **Youth Offender Program Evaluation** project report detailed efforts to establish and maintain coding consistency across large teams.

Given the significance of coding in many of the processes discussed so far, consistency, or the exploration of reasons for inconsistency, are important issues. If your coding is inconsistent, or if you are working with a colleague and coding differently from them, the processes that rely on coding will obviously be affected.

Funding bodies or quantitative colleagues may demand coder consistency tests for your project, with the goal of minimizing disagreement. It can be done, and can be useful – but reflect on that goal. Some sorts of qualitative projects do require consistency. For example, in a long-term study of service failures, final reports on each failure must be able to be accepted as constructed and tested in the same way, yielding comparable results each time. In cases like these, the design may include a way of checking each coder's work with feedback on deviations until the coder conforms to the test case requirements. 'Consistency testing' is a better term for this process than 'reliability testing', since having two coders reliably inconsistent won't do.

Fit of the Outcome to the Data

The rest of this book is about the ways of working with data to establish what can confidently be concluded, and what can credibly be claimed. Each of the processes for searching data and seeing the project as a whole provide a basis for the final outcome. In each, an audience must be able to validate what you have done by checking how detailed your data records were, and how you conducted enquiries, how you tested them against exceptions and explained these, reflected on them and on your part in their construction.

Logging for validity claims Of course, a record of all these processes and reviews should be in the log trail, and from this stage, the evidence from logs becomes essential. We may need to check that you have done the testing openly and honestly and documented the pursuit of any assumptions that might mask alternative explanations and any exceptions that might hide a weakness in your case. More memos needed. The reader should be able to find documentation of each step (or be convinced that you could find it). It must be clear how you reached your conclusion. This all, of course, means work. It is far easier to produce a result that is labelled as 'just my view' than to construct a strong, well-founded outcome.

There are many sources of our judgement that an explanation is valid. Watch for them as you read other studies. Keep them in mind as you carefully explore your own data, build enquiries to make sense of them, and record what happened. To have your research recognized as valid – sound and strong – requires constant vigilance against unquestioned assumptions, narrowing of viewpoints, avoiding of alternative possibilities.

Beware emotional claims that a study 'rings true' or that by gaining access to a vivid account of a terrible experience you have validated the conclusions. This is Hollywood validity. Be very sceptical of claiming that you 'know' because you are there, or that the 'voice' of your participants (or their agreement to your account) validates your claims. You and they are the least likely observers to notice cracks in the evidence or counter-instances, and most likely to accept an outcome that represents a partial view.

Good qualitative research gets much of its claim to validity from its emphasis on reflexivity. The researcher who can show convincingly how they got there, and how they built confidence that this was the best account possible, is best able to make such claims. This is why qualitative research has a special need for project history, in the form of a diary or log of your reflections on your relation to the data and your research experience. Since Chapter 1, the trail of your project 'logs' has recorded the journey you take through processes of working the data; now it must log exploration and testing of interpretations. In the final chapter, there is advice for bringing all these records together to assess the basis for your argument.

Trailing Validity

Often, diaries and log trails record only what was done to achieve entry into the field, or the detail of interview questions. What needs most to be audited is the handling of your data.

By now you will have a wealth of writing about the creation of your data and the ways you have worked with data records. Each of the following will be highly relevant to your claim that your conclusions are valid:

- The log you have built up since the beginning of the project (Chapter 1), recording at each step why it was taken, what were the alternatives and why rejected, and what you then saw as the likely results for the final project.
- Project notes, setting notes and interpretative notes, which accompany each data record (Chapters 2 and 3).
- Archived models from the early stages showing what you think is going on. Layers in those models might show different views of the project.
- Records of theoretical sampling explaining decisions to widen a sample, or move into another area, and what encouraged this decision.
- Memos that are dated with each entry (see Chapter 4), offering a history of the changes in method, a document and its interpretation, an idea and your ideas about it.
- Archived copies of the catalogues of ideas created at different stages (Chapter 5), telling how they grew and changed during the project. Such archives, if kept at regular intervals, give a vivid picture of the development of ideas.

In the next chapters, this impressive record will be expanded by a log of:

- o the questions asked of the data, and the ways you sought and obtained answers, and built on them to ask new questions (see Chapter 8)
- o what didn't fit – themes that don't weave into the whole, 'deviant cases' not explained by your theory, and your attempts to account for these
- o the accounts of the project as a 'whole' or a 'pattern' through which you draw concepts and ideas together into theories.

The final outcome will be 'right' only in the sense that you can show it fits your data. This last criterion is of course by far the most important.

Theories are not right or wrong. They do a better or worse job of accounting for the situation, or answering the questions, and of fitting the data. Explanations are more or less adequate. You want your theories to be useful and your explanations adequate. So establishing the grounds for your claims requires adequately knowing, exploring, searching and making sense of your data.

To Do

1. Revisit your statement from Chapter 1 of your project's purpose, goal and intended outcome. Write a paper reviewing the original statement of outcome, reflecting and revising it. Tell what you are aiming for!
2. In a memo, present eight possible *and useful* outcomes for your project – one in each of the ways sketched as synthesis and difference in this chapter. What might each offer as an answer to your research question? How would each fit your purpose? On the basis of this review, choose a preferred outcome.
3. Write a paper discussing for your project how you might use any two of the three 'validity checks' discussed in this chapter – triangulation of method, member checking and coder reliability checking. In your project, what assurance would you expect to gain from the two methods discussed?
4. On paper or on computer, create layered models indicating the possible outcomes and how they would work for your project.

Suggestions for Further Reading

Aim to be comfortable with the idea of theory from data, and with the many modes of theory and uses of theory in your research. See Flick (2014) and Ely et al. (1997). On working towards theory, see Harding (2013) Chapter 6 and Bazeley (2013) Part 4. And be sure that if you are working within a specific qualitative method, you have a clear picture of the sort of theory it aims for. See *Readme First* (Richards and Morse, 2013).

(Continued)

(Continued)

On issues of the validity of your account, a web search is a good place to start, as the topic of validity in qualitative research is of growing interest. Historically, Lincoln and Guba's (1985) alternative 'naturalistic axioms' (credibility, transferability, dependability, confirmability) threw the debate open. But more recently, Eisner (1998) offered an uplifting account of 'credibility', a term which is also used in the thorough exploration of issues by Silverman (2001). Flick (2014) provides an impressive and practical summary, and gives references to the major contributions to the debate over validity and reliability. For forthright contributions to that debate, see Kirk and Miller (1986), Seale (1999) and Wolcott (1994). There is a specific literature on case studies, see especially Ragin and Becker (1992) and Yin (1989).

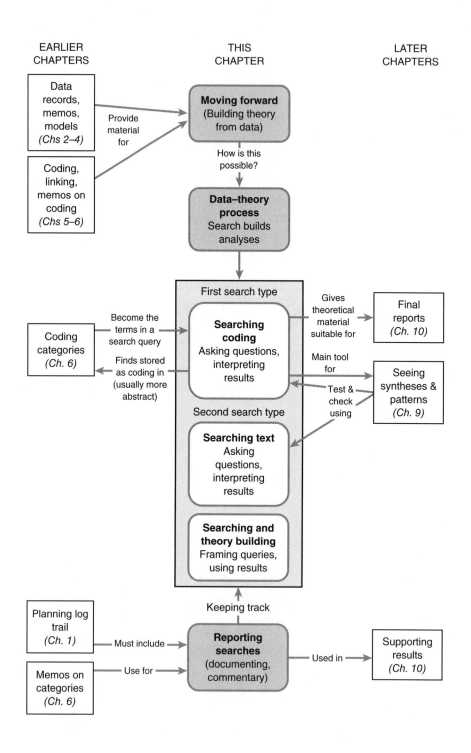

EARLIER CHAPTERS

Data records, memos, models (Chs 2–4)

Coding, linking, memos on coding (Chs 5–6)

Provide material for

THIS CHAPTER

Moving forward (Building theory from data)

How is this possible?

Data–theory process Search builds analyses

First search type

Searching coding Asking questions, interpreting results

Second search type

Searching text Asking questions, interpreting results

Searching and theory building Framing queries, using results

LATER CHAPTERS

Coding categories (Ch. 6)

Become the terms in a search query

Finds stored as coding in (usually more abstract)

Gives theoretical material suitable for

Final reports (Ch. 10)

Main tool for

Seeing syntheses & patterns (Ch. 9)

Test & check using

Keeping track

Planning log trail (Ch. 1)

Memos on categories (Ch. 6)

Must include

Use for

Reporting searches (documenting, commentary)

Used in

Supporting results (Ch. 10)

EIGHT
Searching the data

How do you work up from the data and ideas discovered to small theories, from which grow bigger ones and strong conclusions? One way (of many) is to search the data, to explore how coding categories are related and how ideas occur in the text. This chapter turns to tasks that are available with software, which provides the ability to search for and test relationships between coding categories and the data they code. It also allows you to search for the words in the text that indicate patterns or themes. This chapter explores searching techniques, how to interpret what they find and how to use those finds to reach for theories.

You have set up a project, you are handling the data and ideas, you can see more clearly the possible outcomes. Now, how will you get there?

One of the pieces of advice throughout this book has been that analysis is ongoing from the start of a qualitative project. But the processes of analysis used will of course change as you move through the early stages of exploration, firming the research question, gaining the confidence to specify what outcome you are trying for, and then drawing the project to that conclusion. You may get there by continuing work with the data records, reading, reflecting, writing, coding and creating and handling ideas about them, making increasingly sure-footed decisions about what matters, what doesn't, how issues are related and how the research question can best be addressed.

Some projects proceed in that manner until, from all this steady work, a clear picture emerges. It is a process that contains its own reality testing, and as you grow more confident, you can test your ideas back through the data. But in most projects, the ways of handling data that have been described so far will not suffice to take the project through to a convincing outcome. A common experience is to get through a tumultuous early stage of climbing up from the data, innovative memo writing, category exploration and reading, thinking, coding evidence, only to arrive at a bad sense that you are becalmed, unable to get past merely knowing your data thoroughly. 'So what?' is not a good outcome.

MOVING FORWARD

Becoming becalmed, you need ways to get moving away from the early work, to see your project as a whole, or find significant patterns:

- This chapter is about ways of *searching* to discover and test relationships between the categories you have been coding at; or to discover words in the text that usefully indicate patterns or themes. Searching coding usually requires specialist software. Searching text can be done with many digital tools, though specialist software gives you ways of coding results. Both sorts of searching are 'fetch' processes that require you to specify what you are searching *for*.
- The next chapter is on ways of *seeing*, rather than searching. It explores different techniques to assist you in the discovery of themes, linkages or patterns. These offer both ways of *seeing* the data differently, alerting yourself to core issues or shapes in the project, and ways of testing how well they represent the data. These are techniques that show and surprise, rather than fetch on demand.

These two groups of techniques are very different. *Searches* are directed by you, ways of *seeing* surprise you. While you can search through your data on paper, fine-detailed search techniques are a new phenomenon, available because of computers. Most of the ways of seeing your data anew are as old as the hills.

By now, some of the techniques described in these chapters may be familiar – at many stages they have been suggested as ways of checking or exploring data. Experienced researchers use them from the start of a project. If you are moving sequentially through the steps of data handling, these steps often made sense only because of the promise that such techniques would be available. (Would you code, for example, if you couldn't search patterns of coding?)

 Two of the projects tell of search processes unsupported by software. The researcher in **Inside Companionship** reports that he used software but only 'as an interactive big folder or a filing cabinet. I ordered texts, subtexts, divisions and sub-divisions. I moved and recovered them according to my new and "floating" criteria. But I can not say that I managed my analytic thought by this software.' Searches were done in classic ethnographic method, reading and rereading the diaries and field notes. The **Handling Sexual Attraction** project sought grounded theory, using traditional methods of searching without computer software.

Computers and Searching

For the first time in this book, we meet a group of techniques that appeared, in this form, only with software. They cannot be done, or can be done only very simply, using manual methods. This is a place where you need to check the techniques supported by your software; different software packages offer very different functions and processes of searching.

You also need now to check possibly familiar digital tools outside specialized qualitative software. Many of these support searching. For a wide-ranging review of these options, see Paulus et al. (2014).

In the past, we of course searched for patterns and words manually, through our transcripts, field notes or other records. But the limitations of human memory and access restricted us to reading through records and putting them in heaps, so searches were slow, simple and small-scale. With software, both the text and your coding can be searched, either in simple searches or using sophisticated tools for asking very detailed questions. The computer can tell you immediately if there are finds, and show them or code them. So the method is far easier, and far more powerful, and most importantly, you can do far more with it.

But the fact that the computer *can* do such searching does not mean you *should*. Always, as with all data-handling methods, ask why you would want to do this. Both coding searches and text searches are of course mechanical processes. Like all mechanical techniques, they do not directly support interpretative processes, and they will never substitute for those. And these processes when conducted by qualitative software have the now familiar effect that they restrict you to searching the contents of the project 'box'. So you need constantly to ask whether the search you can send the software to do is addressing the question your analysis raised, what is being searched, what the results will mean and how you can use those results so that your question is addressed. Here we meet again the apparent dilemmas of efficiency and creativity. How do you use such mechanical processes to support an interpretative method?

THE DATA-THEORY PROCESS

The outcomes pictured in Chapter 7 all require the building and testing of a theoretical account of your data. The process of construction is substantial, however small the theory, because it is attached to a big goal – to make it as good an account of your data as possible. Searching processes are required throughout this task, to build and to test what is built at each stage.

Making this sort of theory is like making most complex structures – you start small and build up:

- Rather as a child builds with a wood and plastic construction set, you take apparently unconnected items and connect them, test the strength and fit of this first stage construct, and then build on it.
- Think about your project in this way, and you realize that at each stage you will need to search for co-occurrences, things that don't fit, themes that interrelate.
- If the fit is good, a next construct will be supported, tested for strength and fit, and in turn built upon.

- The resultant construct may have been unpredictable at the start, ungainly during the early stages, but if you can search all the materials and test relations between themes, step by increasingly stable step, it will do.
- Like the child's tower, your tentative theory will become unbalanced, doomed to collapse if too much stands on it. The fact that those first pieces did fit together does not guarantee a stable structure. Each may fit better with different pieces – you won't know till you try, and again you will need ways of searching for different relations.
- As you build, the testing process will tell if you have lost a strong base structure, and are pursuing a theory that explains only partially. If so, pull it down and start again. If the task of building the final construct is daunting, it is helpful to think as the child does, of the small unit that's the task for now.

Qualitative theories are built in this way up, out of very little, in a process T.J. Richards has termed 'data–theory bootstrapping'. (To 'bootstrap' a program or a computer means to get its software running using that software itself without reliance on outside help.)

Data-Theory Bootstrapping

We often get going by finding little things that relate in some meaningful way – perhaps, if our interest is in stress, that certain topics get discussed in anxious ways (and that is something that good coding and retrieval can find for us). So then we start looking for components in those topics that might cause anxiety, often by studying the text, finding or guessing the components and coding for them, recalling situational facts not in the text and looking for suggestive co-occurrences of codes. We might on a hunch start looking at text passages on people's personal security and how they arrange it (research on background theory here, and lots of coding again), to see if there is some possible connection between components occurring in the anxiety topics and security arrangements. If we find one, the theory is still thin, so we embark on a search for others, and thereby look for a pattern. The result of this is a little group of chunked-together coded text, ideas and hypotheses that, provided they can be kept and accessed as a chunk, can become an ingredient in further more abstracted or wide-ranging explorations. This chunk is said to be of larger 'grain size' than its component codings, and it may in turn become an ingredient of a later theorizing of larger grain size still that is built out of existing chunks. (Big fleas are made out of smaller fleas.)

And so the web – of code, explore, relate, study the text – grows, resulting in little explorations, little tests, little ideas hardly worth calling theories but that need to be hung onto as wholes, to be further data for further study. Together they link together with other theories and make the story, the understanding of the text. The strength of this growing interpretation lies to a considerable extent in the fine grain size and tight inter-knittedness of all these steps; and the job of qualitative data handling (and software) is to help in the development of such growing interpretations. (Richards and Richards, 1994: 448)

Approaching Search Tools

The two groups of searching tools – coding search and text search – work with very different aspects of your project. If used thoughtfully, they can be combined in ways that strongly assist the processes of building up and testing ideas. Both groups contain many varieties of searches, not explored here.

The coding search tools find relationships and patterns in your coding (descriptive coding that stores the attributes of cases, topic coding and/or analytical coding). *So far as your coding represents this*, they indicate relationships between the information expressed by the attribute values and the categories of topics or concepts where you are coding. And so far as the coding you have done and stored in your boxed project represents what you need to know, these are very powerful tools. If you stored information about the attributes of cases or coded what your records say, it's probably because you want to find what one category had to do with another (*stress* and *security*, for example), or how different sorts of people saw a problem (*women's and men's accounts of personal security*). There are many ways to do this. You might write about, or record in a model, the possible relationship or pattern. But usually you want to find the passages of text coded at those categories, to read and think about the relationship of categories or test that a hunch is represented by the coding of the data; *women's images of personal security are quite different from men's.*

The second set of tools is for searching the text in your data records to locate where certain words or phrases occur. *So far as the text in data records represents this*, they indicate the content of the records. And these tools can be combined with coding to search for and explore patterns. *Who uses that word 'stress'? When women do, is it ever in the context of text coded at 'security'?*

At least some, and usually many, of these techniques are relevant in most projects, and there will always be many ways in which they can be combined, far more ways than you will ever use. While the two sets of tools access your data in very different ways, they have in common that the researcher directs these searches, choosing the tool to ask the question that makes sense for growing theory, pointing it at a specific search and testing it back through the data. As you build up your knowledge of the data, you can move forward, testing the ground beneath you, learning from where you have been and at each stage checking how surefooted you are.

Many of the steps described above come from now familiar aspects of your normal data-handling processes – gathering material by coding, reviewing it and seeking the dimensions of a category, writing about them. But to construct a higher structure, you will need to evaluate your coding critically, to explore it and go beyond it.

SEARCHING CODING

Coding brings data together and distributes data. Search processes build on both these results.

Coding *gathers material* by category. It is one important way of creating the small grain size of analysis. 'This is something I am interested in, and this is the material I have about it.' Chapter 5 showed how you can then distribute as you browse that material, thinking in terms of the possibly multiple meanings it contains. *With all the material on stress in one place, you might read, reflect and discover the different dimensions of stress and code on to create those new precious categories to hold the discovered dimensions.* For some research questions, this might be sufficient. You are on your way to creating a typology.

The account of working with data for the **Harassment Complaints** project tells the story of using several different styles of coding, to explore the data, to gather data in broad categories for later coding on into finer ones as themes emerged.

Coding also *spreads* material out. As your coding develops, you see the project via many (sometimes far too many) such categories, and gain an overall picture of what's going on. As discussed in Chapter 6, this handling of topics is essential for managing the ideas about your project efficiently. *Perhaps as you handle the data on stress you realize the accounts are always in a social context, and you code for each of the different contexts discussed (family, work, etc.).* For some projects, this may be an adequate outcome. Your task might only have been to identify all of the contexts within which stress occurs.

Were you to do only coding, and to stop at coding, you would see the project as a logically linked array of categories. Their range, and all the data on any of them, could be described. This is a major advance on seeing the project only as a series of interviews or field trips. But it still offers description, rather than analysis. Few research questions are answered well by *only* describing the data at each code. For most researchers, it is essential also to explore the relationships of those categories, and to build on them. Searches of coding are one way (and often the most direct way) of building up from small hunches to the bigger grain size of little theories. But you need a way of talking through what you are asking to ensure the search is doing what you need.

Asking Questions with Coding Searches

Start by phrasing in ordinary language the questions you want to ask and then explore the search tools in your software to find if you can ask them. *How serious are the experiences of stress for employees in this company, and are they addressed adequately in the procedures?* First ask: do you have categories for the things you want to ask about? (If not, should you? This may loop you back to creating new categories, as in Chapter 6.)

Now, can your ordinary language question be asked by exploring the relationships between categories? *What passages are coded at 'stress' and at 'seeking medical advice'? Where does coding at 'feelings of panic' occur with coding at 'work context'?* If your goal is to explore the relationship between stress and health risk, or serious stress and work context (bigger grains of theory), such searching gets you one step further.

Now think about where it gets you. That search identified – reliably – all passages of coded text and, importantly, the software knows the sources of those passages. *I can read and think about all the data from my interviews that I have coded at both 'feelings of panic' and 'context: work' and about which cases they come from.* No other data passages are coded at both, so we can also ask, who didn't have such feelings in that context? Back to the ordinary language question: is that what you were asking? If not, can you frame a different ordinary language question? *I'm really trying to find out about different work contexts; did anyone talk of such feelings in the context of work if they had a senior position?* Check the ways your software provides for asking about coding. *Ask that question again, but take out anything from those cases where job level is junior.*

At first (and maybe later) you will be helped by writing out the questions and searches and noting when one fits the other and when it doesn't. Never lose the habit of first framing the ordinary language question, then asking how adequately (given your categories, your coding and the search tools) you can ask it by coding search. That habit allows you to picture clearly what the search is doing and what it can contribute.

From the start, use the full range of search tools available in your software. Asking *'What's coded at "feelings of panic" and "context: work"?'* will have obviously different results from asking *'What's coded at "feelings of panic" but not at "context: work"?'* You will want the first search when you need to read everything on workplace stress, the second when you want everything on stress in any other context. These are both different from the far more generous, *'What's coded at "feelings of panic" or at "context: work"?'* Different again would be questions about the proximity of coding at two topics, or the sequence in which they occur. None of the computer searches will exactly ask your ordinary language question, but you will quickly identify the most useful.

From the start, maximize the focus of your searches. Any of these different questions can be asked of any chosen part of your data. You might restrict the scope to a particularly meaningful group. *'What's coded at "feelings of panic" and "context: work" from interviewees with management positions?' You can compare this with the same search conducted across all staff. Or you might create a qualitative matrix (cross-tabulation) of all of the contexts (home, work, personal relations, social life, etc.) by the different experience of stress (or panic). Now you can read what is said about each experience of stress (so long as you coded it) in each context.* The matrix has split the data, so you see it a different way. Now, ask for the text from each cell, read and compare. If it makes sense, export the table to a spreadsheet or statistics package to test for associations.

For examples of the use of qualitative matrix displays, see the **Wedding Work** and **Harassment Complaints** projects.

When you do any of these searches, the result is data. The software will give you back, coded, the data that are the answer to your question, so you can ask another question. *What did those stressed managers say about leave entitlements?* Often, as you are building an account of the data, you will be much helped by searches that gather material together. Consider what you get from an 'or' search like *'What's coded at "feelings of panic" or at "claimed disability"?'* All the data coded at either will be returned, *so now you can read together what was said by those who had experienced panic feelings or a self-diagnosis of stress. You see for the first time that the medical certification is associated with only some sources or sorts of stress.*

Whether or not you use such questioning ability to inform your interpretations, you will certainly need it to test them. *Which staff claiming stress sought medical certification and which didn't? Which cases don't fit?* Those are easy questions to ask – *so long as your coding supports them.*

Uses of Coding Searches

Searches of coding can be used for five quite different purposes:

1. For querying the data records and the categories you are constructing out of the data. You can ask any of a logical set of questions about the relations between two or more categories by asking about the data coded at each.
2. For *coding* at a new category the material found by a search, so you can ask another question. (The finds from any search are the passages answering the search question. They can be stored as coded data, ready to be queried further.)
3. For gathering material coded in combinations of categories, to re-see and rethink it.
4. To show or pursue a pattern, increasing the grain size of your theory. You might ask to show the bigger picture of how one group of categories relates to another.
5. For theory testing: to test hunches or interpretations by locating material that fits or fails to fit the theory, and pursuing the case or behaviour that still needs explaining.

Interpreting Coding Searches

As remarked above, searching of coding patterns was difficult and unreliable before computers. With software it is perilously easy! Since the computer stores all the coding information you provide, it can immediately tell you how attributes of cases or coding at topics are related. *You can run the matrix search above for managers in each age group, or by gender, and be reading what the younger women said on this stress topic in seconds.* Already, the questioning is far beyond what could have been done with paper records. But always go back to the ordinary language question. Why did you want to do this?

Like coding, these processes should be purposive. As with any analytical process, you need to reflect on what you are doing, and to make sure it is what you need to do. As you use search tools, the following alerts will assist you to evaluate their results.

In using and interpreting any search of coding, carefully describe your results to take into account the ingredients in the search – your categories, your coding, what it represents and what is being asked.

Always be very careful to 'say' a search accurately, to see clearly what you are searching for and then to read the passages found and (as in Chapter 5) delete coding that is irrelevant. And of course, log it well.

Interpreting Coding Searches

Consider, first, four issues about your own handling of data:

1. How good is the catalogue of categories? Coding searches rely on there being the appropriate categories to search. You can't ask a question if you don't have the categories to ask it, or the coding at those categories.

   You created categories for issues like leave entitlements later in the project. Unless you return to find data on those topics in previously coded documents, a search for what women say about leave entitlement will find nothing from early documents. How much reliance can be placed on the categories?

2. How good is your coding? For these powerful searches, the weak link is you, since the computer is searching for patterns of your coding. If you are relying on coding search, you must be clear about the adequacy, reliability and consistency of your coding. If you were tired, changed your interpretation of a category or only sometimes coded at it, the results of the search should be clearly evaluated with these conditions taken into account. (Recall the advice in Chapter 6 to review the categories and their coding periodically, so you can see ones that are being underused or have been forgotten.)

3. How adequate is the context coded? Remember the mechanical nature of the search. If you coded only very short phrases at each of two categories, the coded passages may not overlap at all, and a search for overlap will fail to indicate that both topics were discussed in this passage.

4. Never forget, coding searches are limited, if you are using qualitative software, to the project 'boxed' within that software. If as previous chapters have urged, you wish to include data not stored in that project, you'll need a way of storing pointers to that data, or descriptions, and coding those so searches will find them. Check how to do this in your software.

(Continued)

(Continued)

Now consider three issues about the meanings of coding:

1. What does your coding represent? You interpreted a data record which indirectly records the meanings someone else put on their experience. The coding is certainly not a direct representation of the experiences or perceptions of the participants in your project. Interpret it accordingly.
2. What did this search actually find? Coding searches report on where you have found passages coded (or not) at each topic. Literally, they are asking questions about the structure of the data record.
3. Since those coding searches were directed by you, they 'fetch' only what you think to ask for. If you rely on such user-directed searches, they must be combined with exploratory work, whereby you can be surprised, discover by serendipity, 'see' rather than search. (See next chapter.)

Searching for the passages coded at 'seeking medical advice' and 'workplace bullying' will find you any passages which were coded at both. It won't find passages elsewhere in the document that were coded by one or other and it won't find passages you didn't code. If all the finds are from women, resist the temptation to report, 'Only women sought medical advice in the context of workplace bullying': some men may have been unwilling to speak about these subjects in that context. Use a different search (for any documents which have coding anywhere in them at these two categories) to find the men who confessed later in the interview that they had been bullied. But note, this search will gather anyone (if you coded them accordingly) who talks about bullying in one place and in another place discusses seeking medical advice for anything.

SEARCHING THE TEXT

So searching your patterns of coding relies on coding having been done and done well. With those tools, the weak link is you the coder, and the boundary is the boxed project. Tools that will search the *text* of your data records offer quite different ways into the data. Here the critical question is whether the records will contain the strings of characters you specify to direct your search.

The ability to search documents for strings of characters in their text is familiar to any user of a word processor or search engine. All such tools may be of use to you. But think differently about text search in qualitative software: it doesn't just take you to each place where a word occurs, it (optionally) shows you the context and *codes* those finds and their context. Usually researchers save not just the words found, but those words in some helpful chunk of context, such as the paragraph. And the software can later take you back to the context.

A historical note: the first qualitative software did not have text search capability. This was because qualitative researchers didn't think to ask for it. When our craft is interpretation, why would a mechanical process help? You are looking, surely, for meaningful statements, people's complex perceptions, not every time they say the words 'leave entitlement'. But with the advent of sophisticated searches of text, entirely new ways of exploring and checking appeared.

What Can You Ask with Text Searches?

If you want to get in one place all the comments about leave entitlement, and if those words, or a small number of alternative phrases, will always be used when the subject is discussed, mechanical coding is a great time saver. And this can be a serious saving of time, since text search can also be used to do simple coding of sections that occur with recognizable labels. (If you later find a passage on leave entitlement where those words were not used, you add coding to this passage at the category.) Of course it is not a substitute for reading all your data records and noticing whenever people talk about leave, in these or other words. But it can be used early in a project, or late, to find and display all occurrences of those strings of characters.

Text searches may appropriately be used as a first step prior to reading and coding the data, if your records don't easily give you access to material on a topic. Text searches for questions in a structured interview, for example, often commence a project by bringing together all the answers to each question. Now the researcher can read them together, assessing and coding their content. (Early on, this is a great way to check if your questions are providing useful answers!) Programs that include word count functions can also give you early access to the data by reporting which are the most commonly occurring words. (See, for example, the technique Dempster et al. (2013) developed to tackle very large data sets with word count and text search tools in advance of reading and coding.)

Text search also can thus be used alongside coding, or for checking or expanding coding. When you realize, belatedly, that you have not been coding for something that now appears significant, you may be greatly helped by using a mechanical text search 'scoop' to get all the material that might be about that topic, then cleaning it up. (I call this 'dragnet' coding, since the researcher is working, rather as fishing fleets do, to scoop up everything in an area for later sorting. Like dragnet fishing, it scoops a lot of stuff you don't want, and must then clean out. But it is less environmentally hazardous.) With such scoop tools, when you are making claims for what the data say, you can test them by asking if those words occur across the data or in any particular part.

Most importantly, text search can assist in creating and testing theory because it can bring together material to test hunches and expand results. Don't underestimate text search as a tough test of the 'dominant theme' that you are 'seeing' throughout your data. Every researcher has a war story of a 'dominant theme' that grabbed their attention, a word that seemed to occur everywhere, but which in the hard light of day was being contributed seldom and then mainly by the members of the research team!

Uses of Text Search

Text searches can be used for many quite different purposes:

1. To discover *and code* all the material on a topic that can be reliably identified via a string or pattern of characters occurring wherever the topic occurs in the data records (either because those words always occur in the required context, or because the researcher has inserted them).

Note that one way of identifying material that a team member needs to discuss is for them to insert keywords (for example, their name) into the text, so the problem passages can be rapidly found.

2. To 'autocode' sections of data records that can be identified by text: for example, names of speakers, numbered questions, named stages of an interview.
3. For gathering material that might be on a topic so it can be reviewed, cleaned up, the irrelevant material deleted.
4. For analysis of discourse or patterns of expression, study of metaphors or other word studies.
5. To test any hunch or suspicion about the data that involves the words people use.

You're sure stress for women is about career curtailment. The theme dominates your interviews with women and contrasts with men's accounts. Well we can check that. Search for 'stress', or a range of synonyms, through all the text coded at career curtailment where the speaker was female. Now run the search again scoping it to males. Now rethink!

Text search is your friend when there is mechanical work to do, or tough testing of hunches so long as the words in your data record are an adequate indicator of the presence of the theme you are seeking. (Relevant here are the reflections on the making of good data records in Chapter 3.)

Always report the ways you used searches, the relevance to your method and to its credibility.

 Go to **Elderly Survivors of the Hanshin Earthquake** for an account of the use of text search as documents are introduced, to gain an overview of themes and also to gather contributions of each speaker.

Interpreting Text Searches

Text search, like any other mechanical process, has to be honed to the qualitative task underway. Never rely on a mechanical process to do interpretative coding.

Interpreting Text Searches

Consider, first, three issues about the mechanical nature of these searches:

1. The computer neither reads nor interprets; use text search only for processes that are appropriately handled by mechanical recognition of strings of characters or patterns of strings. Interpret them accordingly.

   If you search for 'doctor' and they used the term 'GP', expect to find only 'doctor'.

2. As in any mechanical 'find' procedure, the computer will find unintended results: 'stress' will find 'distress' and 'mistress', for example. You could specify that the find should be a whole word, but to do so would disallow 'stressed', 'stressful', etc. Learn your software's tools for using wildcards and specifying search criteria. (Computers have no sense of humour and no imagination.)

3. Like coding searches, these are limited, if you are using qualitative software, to the project 'boxed' within that software. If as previous chapters have urged, you wish to include data not stored in the software project, you'll need a way of storing pointers to that data in words that can be usefully searched, or of separately handling digital searches outside the 'box'.

And add three concerns about the researcher's handling and uses of search results:

1. Text search results must be reviewed and cleaned of finds that are not as intended. Once they are coded, you can treat them as any other coded data, reviewing, uncoding inappropriate finds, adding context as needed. Or you can review each find as it is made. Either technique takes time; the near-instant retrieval of finds is only the first step in a process of reading, interpretation and analysis.

2. Never interpret text search finds without their context. It's not illuminating to get back dozens of occurrences of the single word 'stress'. When you do a text search, you can specify the relevant 'chunk' to be shown or coded automatically along with each find, such as the paragraph it's in. Then the results of the text search will contain all paragraphs with 'stress' in them. (If you had to return to each find of just the word 'stress' to locate its context, the time saved by text search will disappear. But often you will wish to return to the document where the text was found and work some more with the data.)

3. Forgive the repetition, but it's essential to remember that, like coding searches, these are 'fetch' tasks directed by you. If you rely on such user-directed searches, they must be combined with exploratory work, whereby you can be surprised, discover by serendipity, 'see' rather than search. (See next chapter.)

Now, thus forewarned, you can explore the very powerful tools of searching.

BUILDING ON SEARCHES

As you work towards a good account of your data, it is useful to be clear what you can (and can't) ask a tool to do – and that you do the asking. Both coding search and text search are ways of sending the software to 'fetch' the answer to a question *you* pose, and test your ideas in ways *you* ask it to, by 'fetching' the material that fits or doesn't fit. Directed well by the researcher, software searches allow us to focus on a growing interpretation, seeking and verifying the bits of an emerging picture and driving a project forward.

Revisit the account of data–theory 'boot-strapping' above. In building up from the small hunch to the larger grain size of a little theory, it is important that the results of a search are coded, so they go back in as more data. (The term for this is system closure: you are incorporating the answer to each question in the whole system of your data and your thinking about the data.) Since your searches can be of any combinations of attributes or topic or analytical coding or text, and the results are again coding, you can build with them and on them:

- Ask a question by text search of a restricted scope: *What do women say about leave entitlement?* You don't just get a heap of quotations. The answer is coded data; we have a new category for women's statements about leave entitlement. *Make a partner category for what men say about leave entitlement and browse it alongside what women say. How do they differ?*
- Now you can build on this to ask another question. When women are coded as talking about stress, what do they say about leave entitlement? This is simply asking for data coded at both of those two categories. For the women who talk about stress, what do they say about leave entitlement? How about the women who don't talk about stress? Here are two searches, for 'leave entitlement' in different scopes.
- The answers to searches are new categories, and you can read the text coded there, think, write memos, code on from there or ask another question. *Which women who talk about stress are not talking at all about leave entitlements? Is it those who have indicated they give high priority to work commitment?* If your hunch is confirmed, check it out and climb on it to ask another question. Falsification sends you up to the next grain size. *Okay, there are few women who even mention leave entitlements in this context, whatever their commitment, whereas men always do. So there's no simple answer to stress in the work context, and gender is now strongly inserted in our thinking. We need another way of looking.*

Note that it is still up to you to ask the next question, but often the result of the search is the prompt needed to pursue the iterative nature of theory building and testing.

The search process can also, of course, be applied to the researcher's own comments and observations. Search memos to track the development of an idea. Search documents for what the interviewer said in order to find if a 'core' category is actually mentioned only by the interviewer, not the participants.

REPORTING SEARCHES

As you become familiar with search tools, you will find that you use them in many ways in one session. Your question is rephrased, the scope of the search changed, and another hunch pursued.

> It's not only gender, surely, that divides these cases? Some women seem to be seeing the situation very much as the men do. What is the intervening factor? If we take out the women with young children, do we see a different pattern?

Your software will record for each search what the requirements were and what was found. But you need to document the chase – what you were asking, what hunch you were following, what clues came from a case study, and so on. Most search sessions are of this nature, and the story should be recorded with the usual attention to 'why' questions required of any logging operation. Why did you chase that hunch? Why was the search result unconvincing? What cases didn't fit and can you explain why?

A simple method is to keep an area of your memos for search memos, and write up each of these chases. Each will be a series of searches and reports, so a memo on each chase may report a dozen search procedures. Date each 'chase' memo, and carefully record detail, as they may matter later (see Chapter 10). Code memos, and link them to other documents and nodes, knitting together related search results into valuable theoretical knots, relating parallel results, and pointing to exceptions.

Log also the ways these mechanical searches re-present your data to you, and even reshape data. It is easy, when you are moving fast, to create what Gilbert (2002) calls 'unmindful transformations', and sometimes these are so subtle as to escape notice. (A useful habit is to check the characteristics of the scope of a search before you jump to conclusions about what it found.)

Searches directed by you may come up with important surprises, hunches and shifts in thinking. They may send you out on a quite different path. It is important to document how you started on this new enquiry.

> Actually, none of the extremely stressed male interviewees was concerned about leave entitlements. They see stress quite differently from the way it is managed in the proper procedures of the company.

But you also need different techniques, for seeing things you had not seen in the data before. These techniques are the subject of the next chapter.

--- **To Do** ---

1. Revisit the preferred outcome you proposed in Chapter 7, and now set out in a flowchart what would be necessary for getting there, from where you currently are in your project. How will you go about building and testing a theoretical account of your data?
2. Back to your software: study tutorials and examples to learn the range of search techniques and try them in your own data.
3. Identify an area of your project where you could pursue a hunch or question. State what you are asking in ordinary language and then plan the searches that would ask it. Conduct and report on the searches in a search log memo about this.

--------------- **Suggestions for Further Reading** ---------------

There are many texts now addressing the building and testing of theory in qualitative research: see, for example, Flick (2013), Lofland and Lofland (1995), Seale (1999) and Silverman (2001). On the 'boot-strapping' of theory, see Richards and Richards (1994). On the role of computers in changing analysis processes, see Davidson and Di Gregorio (2011) and Lewins and Silver (2014).

On issues of searching, you need to go to the literature concerning computers. For an overview of digital tools for qualitative research, see Paulus et al. (2014) and for the most authoritative account of qualitative software tools for searching, Lewins and Silver (2014) and its website. Coding searches and text searches are covered in all texts focused on particular software packages, for example, Friese (2012), Bazeley and Jackson (2013), Di Gregorio and Davidson (2008), Kuckartz (2014). See the website for further advice. Gibbs (2002) offers further reflections on computer searching. For the classic, and still inspiring, account of the uses of matrix displays, pre-computer, see Miles and Huberman (1994), updated in Miles et al. (2013).

Detailed reports of analysis processes using searches, and comparisons of different software packages across one data set, resulted from the KWALON conference in 2010 and were published in the online *Forum: Qualitative Social Research*; see Evers et al. (2011).

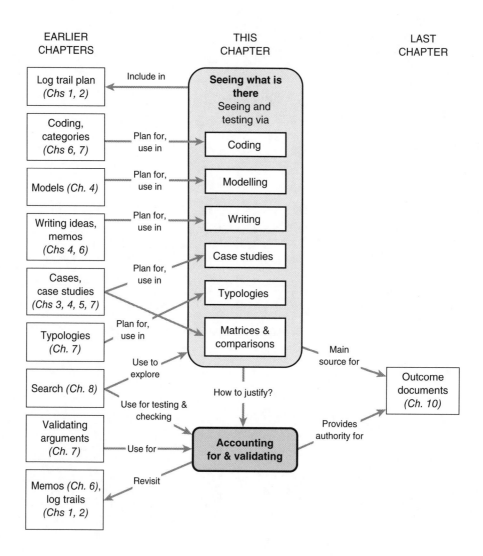

EARLIER
CHAPTERS

THIS
CHAPTER

LAST
CHAPTER

Log trail plan
(Chs 1, 2)

Include in

**Seeing what is
there**
Seeing and
testing via

Coding,
categories
(Chs 6, 7)

Plan for,
use in

Coding

Models *(Ch. 4)*

Plan for,
use in

Modelling

Writing ideas,
memos
(Chs 4, 6)

Plan for,
use in

Writing

Case studies

Cases,
case studies
(Chs 3, 4, 5, 7)

Plan for,
use in

Typologies

Typologies
(Ch. 7)

Plan for,
use in

Matrices &
comparisons

Main
source for

Use to
explore

Search *(Ch. 8)*

How to justify?

Outcome
documents
(Ch. 10)

Use for testing &
checking

Validating
arguments
(Ch. 7)

Use for

**Accounting
for & validating**

Provides
authority for

Memos *(Ch. 6)*,
log trails
(Chs 1, 2)

Revisit

NINE

Seeing a whole

Arriving at a satisfying theory or explanation requires seeing the 'big picture', making sense of your data, discovering the core themes or the overriding pattern. Some of the many ways of seeing, and techniques for achieving these, are brought together in this chapter, with advice on ways of chasing and checking themes, seeking synthesis or patterns, and on justifying what you claim to see.

Searching your data is different from *seeing* things in data. And searching is also, importantly, a less qualitative exercise. The tools for searching 'fetch' the answer to a question *you* posed. But qualitative research is about discovering meanings 'up' from the data. So while searches are essential tools for exploring data, you also need techniques for generating new ways of looking at your data, asking questions that emerge from the data, questions that you didn't know to ask before. As for many of the processes in earlier chapters, these techniques are about complexity *and* simplicity. They aim to make things more complicated, to help you be surprised, seeing your data records in a new way. But the goal is synthesis of these discoveries, seeing the project as a whole, making sense of it.

SEEING WHAT'S THERE - AND WHAT'S NOT THERE

Qualitative research has many such techniques. Some are very simple, common-sense tactics, tricks you can play on your tired mind. Some are sophisticated uses of search techniques for discovery.

Like the tricks of most skilled trades, these techniques are not well documented. They can be hard to find and learn unless you sit at the knee of an experienced player. Some texts record some such techniques (see the suggested readings at the end of this chapter). But the crucial stage of a project, the step where you most need ways of seeing, may have no recognized procedure to follow.

Specific methods may nominate their own techniques, sometimes almost in rulebook form. If you are working in such a context, there will be clear instructions to tell you what to do next, how to discover and justify a theory. If this is your context, you are well advised to follow the instructions, as this will give you the best chance of finding the appropriate tools, fitting together your question, method and outcome (and the expectations of your funder, client or examiner). But no method is exclusive. Any of the techniques discussed below may assist you – consider them all!

If you are able to work with experienced researchers, encourage them to talk about the times that data 'fell into place' or 'made sense', and to reminisce about why this might have happened. Then try creating such a situation in your project. At this stage, it often helps to be playful. Rather than follow a rulebook, try playing with different ways of looking. Often the best advice is, 'Why don't you try this?' rather than 'This is how it is done.'

Many experienced qualitative researchers are unaware of using received techniques for handling or analysing data, or of having combined techniques in an unusual way. Rather, they discover or adopt things that seem to work, or did work for colleagues, for generating ideas and checking them out. Methods chapters rarely describe these processes. (Make a note that you should describe yours.)

 The 'Methods in Practice' site was designed partly to rectify this lack of discussion, with stories from what happened in real projects, and partly to encourage others to give such detail. Comparing the sections on 'Working with Data and Analysis', you will find great variety in the researchers' accounts of what worked for them in making sense of their data.

As you move on with your project, checking and steadying each step, seek combinations of techniques for each stage and record what works and what doesn't. Don't expect software to do it for you, though it will help you keep good records of what you did and where you arrived. Insight combines with mechanical searching; the ghost of a memory of a recurrent theme informs a search for cases that are different. It is important to be aware of how many different ways you can work with the data, and how you can mix them – you are rarely stuck without some technique that will get you out of the brambles and onto a firm path again. Log how you came to see the data this way. Record the trail of these logs and link what you say to the categories, especially search result categories, where you used software techniques.

WAYS OF SEEING

This section offers a sort of 'shelf display' of things you might try to assist you in seeing what's going on in your data. As with the searching tools in the previous chapter, these are all ways both of finding and of testing ideas about what's going on.

In Chapter 7, the sketches of possible outcomes were (very loosely) divided into those showing and accounting for synthesis, and those discovering and exploring a pattern. Moving towards synthesis and/or pattern(s), the researcher needs ways of seeking the theme or the pattern and also, importantly, needs ways of testing it. Table 9.1 simply displays some tactics that work. Make a habit of looking up from a task to skim the table to identify the tools most likely to generate a new way of seeing, or tests most likely to expose a simplistic story.

Six major groups of techniques are summarized in the table. The rest of this chapter expands on these.

Note in particular:

Table 9.1 Seeing and testing synthesis and patterns

Seeing	Testing
1. Via coding and category handling	
Cataloguing categories, drawing together the different sorts of categories	Grouping data; seeking meaningful groups, patterns to challenge syntheses; searching for counter-instances, finding what doesn't fit the theme; determining what categories have been left out
Integration of categories: moving, merging, memo writing, seeking generalities, classes	
Searching coding, asking what's related, what's alike	Testing for intervening factors; using to challenge generalizations
2. Via modelling	
Displaying relationships and how they recur	Using layers to show different ways it makes sense
What hangs together? Seeking clusters of factors and their contexts	Identify and model what doesn't link up
Finding where a category fits in a model	Present to a sceptical audience, if possible to your research participants
Presenting the synthesis to an audience	
3. Via writing	
Telling it as an integrated story - plausible accounting; using metaphors or analogies to portray the whole and help you see it differently	Questioning 'dominant' themes and integration that's too easy; how well do the themes relate to the details of the data - are they just vague generalizations?
Overlaying explanations from elsewhere - the literature, other studies	Actively seeking rival themes; shocking it: forcing extensions, reinterpretations
Fleshing out themes, stories; explaining and reflecting on recurrences	Dumping metaphors that strain the data
	Trialling and disposing of alternative explanations (including ones from other studies)
4. Via case studies	
In-depth case studies showing within-case integration: making sense of the variety in the data through how it works in a case	Working with the data in case studies: seeking within-case puzzles and between-case differences
Spreading-it-out techniques - cross-case review, to find how much variety and what centrally explains it	Testing a theme with negative cases
	Reshaping the data with an 'imported' order, e.g. narratives in timelines

(Continued)

Table 9.1 (Continued)

Seeing	Testing
5. Via typologies	
Discovering meaningful subgroups, subclasses of things	Questioning whether the groups are meaningful
Using detailed illustrative case studies to describe 'ideal types'	Testing the typology by seeking underlying commonalities
Making sense of the data with this typology – completeness assessment	Filtering and assaying the data, to test if the pattern holds through significant issues
6. Via matrices	
Seeing and displaying an explanatory pattern in behaviour or interpretations	Validating the pattern by reading, reflecting and searching the data coded in each cell
Reshaping the data deliberately to allow you to see the bigger picture	Trialling the matrices through different cuts of the data to ensure that the pattern is not particular to one group
Patterning theme occurrence as a way to a 'bigger' theme; showing the patterning factors	Checking frequencies of occurrences and the specific cases that occur

- There is no clear distinction between tools for seeing the story and tools for testing it. These are techniques for handling data in such a way that important themes are discovered *and* challenged by the data, or patterns located *and* clarified by the data.
- You can use these tools at every stage of a project – analysis is ongoing.
- The table starts with ways of using the tools from Chapters 5 and 6 for this next stage. New suggestions can be incorporated in those processes.
- Most tools have many uses: never pre-emptively reduce the uses of a good tool. (That screwdriver was not designed to take the lid off a paint can, but when you need to take off the lid, it's better than a blunt stick!)
- Some of these techniques assist you in seeing a whole; some direct you to patterns. Don't see these as different paths. Looking for a pattern is a way of testing the apparent synthesis. Testing a pattern to destruction may show you an integrating theme.

Seeing and Testing via Coding and Category Handling

Start by reviewing and rethinking the tools you have been using all along. Many of the techniques suggested in Chapters 4–6 for integration are ways of seeing the whole. Once the process is working for you, you can actively use it in the data–theory bootstrapping processes discussed in the previous chapter, not only for searching but for seeing possibilities. Often search tools, as in the example of the previous chapter, have clarified what isn't the central explanation and this takes the project further.

> It's not just about leave entitlements and it's not just women. Women and men see stress quite differently from the way it is managed in the proper procedures of the company. Where to go from here? Focus on the multiple meanings of stress and ways people talk about the contexts, rather than just where they are.

Now we need to revisit the data and look for a different story.

─────── **Making Coding Work Towards Synthesis** ───────

- Welcome abstract categories, ones that interpret the data, and be increasingly suspicious of proliferating categories that seem merely to describe topics. Keep memos on both sorts.

  The phrase 'personal security' occurs frequently; an *in vivo* code.

- Focus especially on things that recur. If a thing comes up again, don't just code it, wonder why. Develop a habit of watching the recurrences and thinking (and writing) about those categories that seem to gather things together.

  You notice recurring words that indicate surveillance. Collect the phrases people use for being watched or monitored and the ways they find to cope.

- Organizing the categories for thinking about your data is a major integrating process. Every time you ask 'What's this a sort of?' you are integrating. The 'sorts' of categories are the dimensions of your project. These 'higher level' categories bring things together.

  When someone comments they have 'no space', is that a sort of surveillance? Or could they mean either physical space or freedom of opinion? And are these also new important categories?

- From the start, treat the category system as the growing conceptual structure of your project, not a mere filing cabinet. While processing each record, do it in consultation with that catalogue. Alert yourself to what you need to look for, skim the categories you've prepared, check you haven't missed something. Ask why it's not there. Keep methodological memos on the state of the category system and the ways it changes.

  Perhaps a working category of 'space' is needed, and a note to keep looking for these themes. This young, overloaded staff member didn't say anything about stress in the context of the workplace – why not? What did she say about space?

These processes can all run alongside continued coding. Don't rely on coding to give you ideas, but desert your coding once ideas are forming! Never allow the seductive soaring of memos towards an attractive theme bring about a premature end to your coding, even when it appears that the data 'make sense'. That's the time to read and interrogate the data even more thoroughly; that's the time to doubt the hunch and to revisit coding categories and rethink them, explore their dimensions, to ensure that you are not missing anything new.

These processes require documentation. In the not too distant future, you will be reporting the synthesis you discovered, and how you discovered and tested it. In Chapter 6, I noted that a valuable habit is keeping reports on the state of your node system. These reports record your thinking in action, and tell the story of how you brought the project to a conclusion. Write about the ways that the categories seem to assist synthesis – or impede it.

The uses of searching are critical here, as the search tools will allow you to identify exceptions to the account you are proposing. *Take time to look for counter-instances and intervening factors, using search processes to identify those who are not stressed in situations that seem stress generating.*

 For examples of the uses of coding in seeing and testing patterns, see the **Wedding Work** and the **Harassment Complaints** projects.

Making Coding Work to Show and Test Patterns

- Seek and constantly check out patterns.

  Read, reflect on everything about 'stress' (and code on to new categories for different sorts of stress). Look for a patterning of stress experience and solutions.

- Maximize the patterns found, but combine this with a plan for warding off, guarding against, the power of each pattern. Check them out, distinguishing fleeting themes from ones that appear throughout the data. Always suspect a strong pattern, if only because life (and hence qualitative data) is not that easy. Actively seek counter-instances and inner patterns especially when all you have seen so far seems uniform.

  Trial that first guess that there will be different stress types in different contexts. Not surprisingly, there will, but are these the groups that matter for your question?

- Check your pattern not merely for descriptive relevance but also for theoretical focus.

  Was it just about work contexts or was it about experience of stress? If the latter, don't settle for a breakdown by work context; what factors may lie behind this? Go back to the text: as you read the text coded at each stress type, tease out all its variety.

- Specify the location of the pattern.

  Don't settle for a generalization – do your different stress types align exactly with different contexts? Probably not.

Seeing and Testing via Modelling

Modelling of qualitative research was introduced in Chapter 4, with an open invitation to use models for practically any sort of display or presentation of what you are seeing and doing. If you have found modelling useful, it is worth reading about it as a technique for analysis: there is a considerable literature on qualitative modelling, and the purposes and types of models. Whether or not you pursue that literature, do retain modelling as a free-form, sometimes escapist, mode of expression.

But modelling has more specific purposes at the stage when you are trying to see the project as a whole. Pictorial representation can be more effective than words for expressing what, in your interpretation, is going on.

----------- **Some Uses of Models for Seeing the Whole** -----------

- Decide whether you wish your models to be merely drawings of things that have something to do with other things, or whether they represent specified sorts of relationships between objects in your project. Stay consistent with that decision. There is nothing wrong with models that are just sketches of what you think is going on. But make a clear separation of these from models specifying relationships that can be explored in the data.
- Use a model much as a detective does, to draw the many clues and what they seem to lead to.
- Use a model for simplifying, discarding 'noise' - and then reflect on the data confusing the pattern. Gather the things that matter. Layer your models to show different simplified 'strata' of the big picture.

  Show in different layers the ways different sorts of stress are experienced, then bring the layers together to show how they interrelate - or don't.

- If you are modelling particular sorts of relationships, always name and specify them, so you can see causal chains or affective networks, etc. Use all the abilities of your software to identify and define the nature of the relationship, so you are not later trapped into misrepresenting it. (Be especially careful of 'causes': most qualitative data are not about causal relationships but about things that go together.)

  A young woman talks of 'surveillance' - does surveillance mean lack of space to her? Is this another meaning for the model? A tentative link.

- Models are most helpful when the researcher is most unsure of what is going on. Drawing it assists telling it, and drawing it in many versions will often clarify which way of looking is most productive. Beware of qualitative computer packages that offer modelling tools if they constrain you to working always within the software project. For flying ideas, you may do better with large pieces of paper or freeform modelling online.

Go to the **Handling of Sexual Attraction** project for a vivid account of the desertion of software tools for paper and pins!

Models are a valuable teamwork tool. If your qualitative software can layer a model, give each member a layer, to draw what they are seeing as the essential aspects of the project, or simply as what is going on. (Not using software? Then draw layers on transparencies to show on an old-fashioned overhead projector.) Now, in a team meeting, show one layer after another, with the team members explaining their view and, as needed, returning to the relevant data.

Never delete a working model. These are valuable records of your thinking or exploring at that stage.

Seeing and Testing via Writing

At all stages in the project, telling what you are seeing will be important. Writing is a way of clarifying ideas and seeing through complex data. It is necessary often to write about data in order to get to the other side of complexity, and be able to start writing a report. To delay writing until you can 'write it up' is to miss this advantage.

Most of the processes discussed so far involve writing. You create good data records by writing in them and about them, create categories for thinking about your data and write descriptions of them or memos about them and their relationships. You write in your diary or log about the methods you've used and what worked, and the trail of tests and questions you've followed. Or record them on tape, and later (but not much later) transcribe them.

Some of this writing is stored in memos. If you have followed this way of writing, you will have a lot of memos, and they too should be handled well. In Chapter 4, a loose typology of memos was proposed – memos about method, about documents and about ideas. As you start asking the bigger questions, with larger grain size, you will be writing less about the individual items in your project and more about the answer to your research question.

More Roles for Memos

- Memos should occur more often now, about anything really interesting, including recurrent 'noises' in the data, puzzles or contradictions. Be generous with memos. A little hunch may not seem memo-worthy, but if now you note your vague ideas, later they are there to build on. And link them always to the other memos on which they build.

  Your memo on 'surveillance' now links with the memo on the multiple meanings of getting 'space'. Though the category remains particular, the memos are beginning to draw lines between categories.

- Memos will now be written on the emerging story. So a memo will no longer belong to one document or idea. A model leads to a memo. A run of searches leads to a memo. Develop *early* a routine for actively seeking new link-ups - this is much more useful than waiting to accept them grudgingly when they force themselves through your way of thinking. And find a way of storing these 'meta-memos', thinking of them always as possibly growing analyses.
- Develop *early* a routine of writing challenges: as you write about any theme or synthesis you are seeing, challenge it. Counterbalance by looking for rival themes or writing how it would be if the opposite were the case. You need to fight the tendency of known themes to dominate perception and skew coding away from as-yet unborn ones.

  If 'surveillance' had been a theme only for those who reported no stress at all, how would you see it then? Could it be interpreted as giving comfort or security?

Teasing it out and weaving it together Another sort of writing will serve you well at this stage – sketch pieces, or reflective notes. Writing is a way of running with an idea and trying it out. (Remember Turner's phrase: we have to *goad* data into saying things (Turner, 1981).) Qualitative researchers have many ways of stretching data records, challenging them, fracturing them so the meanings will be seen differently. And this is done best by writing them out.

Ways of Goading Data

- Run with a theme: if a thread seems to loop through the data, take it as far as possible, actively searching for more occurrences and seeking plausible explanations in terms of it. Be generous in its extension and application – allow it full rein. Only then set about challenging it.

  Getting 'space' seems always portrayed as a good thing. Isn't there such a thing as too much space?

- Shock tactics! Try imaginative reconstructions, forcing extensions or reinterpretations. Group work assists in the search for robustness – your goal is not just to get new ideas, but to establish ideas that withstand challenge. (This means you are greatly helped by challengers. Ask a friend to play critic or examiner.) As you write, pay attention to loose threads, bringing constant interaction between theory and data until the theory is robust, satisfying.

- Use metaphors and analogies and pursue them. Sometimes chase them to the point of absurdity. When the metaphor no longer fits, you will find ideas flowing. Pay particular attention to metaphors used by participants in your research; run with them and explore their implications. Carefully withdraw from the metaphor, reflecting on its messages, when it no longer is in contact with the situation.

  The young staff member says she is feeling caged in this job; this leads you from the everyday contexts of family and work-related stress, to thinking about the different sort of stress a caged animal feels. Is family actually more like a cage? You can't change it easily, even get away from it for the weekend. But whoa, neither of these social 'cages' is locked. So what do we learn from thinking about locks and the agents who use them?

- Exploit comparisons – within the project and with other unrelated studies or everyday phenomena.

  How different is the caged experience of this bored, restricted worker from the cage of earlier social control over women's independence? Drawn in two layers of a model, these situations appear strikingly similar, but the outstanding differences say a lot.

- 'Try on' a theory that works in another area, just as you might try on a different garment.

  You were reading about prisons, and the theory of total institutions. What aspects of that theory might fit the workplace you are studying? And how are they different? Are the interviewees stripped of previous identity? Can they dress and express themselves freely? Is their use of time externally prescribed?

- Write reflexively. Particularly about your confidence and doubts. Start with what doesn't fit. (Always, keep a record of which cases were different; don't just slip into phrases like 'most people said'.) Exceptions probe the rule, forcing you to find a better and more encompassing rule. So exceptions are precious route indicators. Write about them, worry if there are no exceptions (most data are not like that). Keep footnotes on the people who didn't say this, and reflect on them. These are basic, commonsense questions – you just need to ask them.

  Why should this (otherwise unexceptional) woman be an exception? How can I explain her different responses? And how can I test that account, or is it really just a guess?

To arrive at an adequate account may not require a single integrating statement. That adequate account may be a statement of a pattern that explains and encompasses the variety of your data. But it does require confidence that you don't have to keep searching for more themes – and can start shedding the irrelevant ones and checking out the theory. And the best way to arrive at that confidence is to write about your steps, tests, degree of confidence and the puzzles remaining. Writing now is far better than waiting until you know what you wish to write.

Seeing and Testing via Case Studies

Focus on a case is entirely different from focus on a theme. In one person's story, or the experience at one site, you can try to see how all the themes, issues and processes interplay, or don't. This single-case focus (*within-case analysis*) can be highly productive. Or alternatively, comparison between cases (or *cross-case analysis*) can highlight common issues and central themes. Either is supported by search processes if you have coded all the material about a case, as suggested in Chapter 5.

   Case studies are often written up at the end of a project to illustrate what has been concluded (and they make vivid illustrations – see next chapter). But early in the analysis, they can be a valuable stimulus to integration. Especially if your project is growing rapidly and you feel you are losing the vivid recall of people and their experiences, it can be very rewarding to focus on just one case, or a sharp comparison of cases. Treat yourself to a case study not as an end in itself, but as a way-station on the road to bringing it all together.

 Case studies were central in the final round of the **Youth Offender Program Evaluation**.

──────────────── **Doing Useful Case Studies** ────────────────

- Use case studies as a special event, a relief from the rigours of coding and memo writing.
- Always write a case up (or talk it up, loosely, on tape). Get an audience – talk it out, explain about that person and how their experience brings together the threads of your argument. Developing and writing case studies provides one of the most attractive ways of going into 'depth' of description and critical reflection.
- Don't let the case lead you into only one corner of the theoretical yard. Before you come out of the case, ask what it has to say about other aspects of the project.
- Aim for classy case studies. Like coffee and chocolate, case studies should always be high quality. Go back to all the sources of data available – listen to the tape, look at photos, drive back past the house where you conducted an interview. If possible, drop

back to talk to the person. Read your field notes from that episode and try adding to them yet again from new memories.

- Try to use cases you particularly remember - the ones you keep talking about, or that puzzle or bug you, sites that troubled you or people you really felt close to.
- Model the case and write it! Even if (especially if!) your case still puzzles you, get it down and ensure that later you return to make sense of it.

Never forget the ethics of it all. A good case study is far more intrusive and far more recognizable than your account of one participant among many.

Seeing and Testing via Typologies

A typology is simply a systematic classification of types. But to do this with qualitative data is not simple. Beware of a too-easy typology. A nifty typology with neat names for the types makes a quick and memorable presentation for marketing, or sound-bite for the TV interview. If you are really successful, your types will be informing, surprising, remembered and cited by those concerned with your topic.

> The study showed four types in the workforce, 'the shrinking violet', 'the caged songbird', 'the bully boy', 'the stress-worker'. Which are you, and which is your boss?

But a small complication – do they represent your data? The trouble with typologies is that they present a misleading sense of understanding. Most typologies are in fact merely descriptive of (some of) the data, and, worse, smudge the detail of diversity.

If you are working towards a typology, it should be because the data demand it and the data support it. Your detailed analysis consistently indicates that there are several very different approaches represented. Or participants indicate that they see several types. If you have appropriate data, one very powerful indication of a typology is through a quantitative analysis of the cases for which you have qualitative data.

If your data analysis seems to lead to types, think carefully about the ways they are constructed. Systematic classification of types in qualitative research requires skill and very careful attention to what is highlighted, and to what was shed or cast off in the classifying process.

Pay attention, too, to the explication of the types. In the sketches of possible outcomes in Chapter 7 (itself a loose typology), one possible outcome was nicknamed 'the talking typology'. The memorable typologies of qualitative research offer vivid portrayals of different clusters of factors and the ways they are represented in the data.

Constructing and Using Typologies

Constructing any typology takes time and requires thorough knowledge of the data.

- On the basis of your growing understanding of the data, identify the related features or properties of people, sites, processes or behaviours that are to be distinguished. Don't settle for just one property.
- Now the task is to explore the ways these properties or dimensions co-occur or are connected. We want to know what web of factors is being explicated. Explore relationships and patterns to identify why and where the pattern originates. Meaningful groupings may result (meaningful to participants and to your theory). Do these occur elsewhere? Thus to the data again: how do your cases or situations distribute over this complex mosaic of factors? Types with only one case are to be suspected, as is forcing the data into types that misrepresent them. As in all pattern-finding processes, the best advice is to look for contradictions and deviant cases for analysis, because they're theoretically exciting.
- Now back to the typology – how adequate is its spread and coverage? Are you sure it is not merely a collection of catchy images? Check that you are asking *all* the data, not discarding what doesn't fit. Can you construct types that are *not* represented in your data and should be? How does that inform the next stage of your project?
- If your story provides too 'good' a coverage of the data, keep worrying at whether it is self-evident. What, if anything, is new about this typology? What, if anything, does it say or send you off asking? If it merely gives you a framework into which everything can be fitted, it's not very interesting. (The world, reputedly, is divided into two sorts of people, those who think the world is divided into two sorts of people and those who don't. The latter will be the better qualitative researchers.)

Seeing and Testing via Matrices

Much of the advice above applies to the use of qualitative cross-tabulations, or matrices. Matrix work is, like typology construction, a task of systematic comparison in order to arrive at a pattern. It also provides a new way of seeing sharply whether and where a pattern dominates.

> Run a matrix of the different sorts of stress by different gender. The table tells you how many cases are represented in each cell and gives you the text of what women and men said about each stress type (so long as your coding is good enough).

Matrix work and computers In manual methods, matrices are often used as a means to display a suspected or discovered pattern, or outcome of a project. But when a matrix is constructed by computer, three very different processes are supported:

1. The matrix can show all the data extracts that belong in any cell, not merely a summary. If you draw a matrix on a whiteboard or paper, its cells of course can contain only a summary. On computer, you can click on a cell and see all the data coded at this cell. *Read everything from women on what you coded as 'space stress'. Now read what was coded as 'space stress' from men.*

2. You can use the ability that the software provides to change the scope of a search. So you could run that matrix for each of a number of workplaces in turn and see whether the patterns are different.
3. If it is appropriate for your project, you can display counts of cases, passages or even words in each cell and (if it makes sense to do so) export them to a statistics or spreadsheet package for further analysis.

For use of matrix analysis with software to establish differences in data sets, see **Harassment Complaints**.

A special sort of reflection is required by matrix work (qualitative or quantitative). What sort of association are we asserting here? The mere layout of a cross-tabulation tells us nothing about the supposed relationship between factors or variables. The interpretation is still to be done. Working qualitatively, you can now read the text that belongs in the cells and explore what that relationship involves.

As you write, suspect the too clear picture – qualitative data aren't like that. Most qualitative questions don't fit into a two-dimensional table. What have you overlooked? In your writing up of a matrix, always assess sharply the dominance of the pattern you are pursuing.

A note on constructive comparison Some projects start out with a comparative design: the decisions about where you go and the sorts of data you seek will be driven by the importance of picturing the two sites or cases in ways that support thorough comparison. Designed that way, they are more likely to provide consistently comparative data.

Some Uses of a Matrix for Seeing a Pattern

Matrix displays can be a crucial way of spreading out and arriving at a pattern:

- Matrix layouts present evidence in a way that helps pattern discovery or pattern testing. Often, you know there is a pattern there but you can't locate it; a matrix will help you narrow it down.
- A matrix is a highly useful tool for spurring further enquiry, whether or not it shows a pattern. If the pattern isn't clear, ask: why not? *There seems no firm relation between different stress types and gender. Perhaps your stress types are just too crude? Or the type of stress isn't related to gender but the severity is? Is there an intervening variable - the low status of women's jobs means surveillance hits them harder? Type of stress may be more about social support sources than about role context?*
- Setting out a cross-tabulation is, of course, a way of relating two different variables or factors. But it will help you ask if there are indeed two, and only two, significant factors here. The possibilities of others need exploring. *No it's not just about gender (actually, most things aren't). But there do seem to be gendered patterns in ways of dealing with stress. Perhaps the missing dimension is social networking skills?*

Building systematic comparison into your study, especially a bigger study, is contentious in some research traditions, regarded as more appropriate for a quantitative study. Qualitative designs tend to happen upon comparison rather than set up for it. As noted in Chapter 1, designing qualitative research for comparison requires more organization and preconceived record-keeping than is usual, and runs the risk that the project will lose flexibility. In particular, comparative projects will usually require more information storage, and control of sampling to ensure balance and similarities of characteristics. Such a project can very easily begin to resemble a design for quantitative analysis – not of course a bad thing, but different.

All projects, however, use comparison, and it could be said of all qualitative research, indeed all research in all disciplines, that it thrives on comparison done well.

When in doubt, quantify! Adding up is not the last resort for qualitative research. If you are uncertain about what the data are saying, a very useful way of asking is to count – how many men say this, as opposed to women? Merely counting, of course, gives mere description. But armed with a clear picture of a pattern, you can inform and design your pursuit of it. Make sure you're counting the same things, and then set out to understand the occurrences as well as the absences.

Exploit ways you can compare views of different team members. If they come from different social or professional settings, comparison may give a multilayered picture of the whole.

—————— Uses of Comparison in Qualitative Research ——————

There are many very different ways of using comparison within qualitative projects (and very many variants on each). To use it well, you need to be clear what sort of comparative processes you are intending. Compare these three ways of generating ideas:

- Specific comparison of two like cases or situations, where there is some explicit controlling of other factors; where used, this tends to be the goal of the project.

  How do these businesses, all in the same industry and the same size, deal with stress in these different cultural settings?

'Same' is hard to achieve in qualitative research, since controlling of contextual complexity of course limits the richness of the data. To the researcher interested in everything, identical situations just don't exist. But a thoughtful analysis of difference can certainly be done.

- Comparison within the themes emerging from the data: this can happen only as themes emerge, so can't be designed into the project.

  In this one situation, we have identified contrasting behaviours – why would that be, and what does it tell us about the meanings people put on the situation?

- Imaginative comparison – *how would she have responded if the situation had been different?* Where else might this happen and what would it be like there? Or how does this discovered behaviour compare with something known and understood? Or cultural comparison – how might members of one culture perceive this situation, compared to members of another?

With all the discussion above, a general principle emerges: doubt integration (the sense that you have seen the whole) until you have proved it. One piece of very good advice is to seek integration only after you have sought variety. Suspect early integration. Interrogate apparently emerging themes.

ACCOUNTING FOR AND VALIDATING YOUR 'SEEING'

Whatever the outcome, your goal is that the project should 'make sense'. Integration may be achieved by a core theme or an overlying pattern. Either integrates in the sense that the outcome sufficiently accounts for all the significant detail.

Note that some, but not all, of the ways of 'seeing' look like reportable techniques. Here, you enter an interesting area of methods that are normally not recorded, simply because they are not seen as methods. It matters for the credibility of your account that you should find ways of telling the discovery, and to do so, of course, will help researchers who follow. If you find yourself saying 'I suddenly realized', or 'I just knew', try to play back the mental tape that will show you why you felt you recognized an explanation then, or why you felt that at this stage you could confidently say 'I know'.

Respondent 'Validation'

In the present context, as you attempt to bring the data together and see the overall picture or pattern, other ways of seeing are of course highly relevant. Revisit the discussions in Chapter 1 on designing for respondent feedback ('member checking' or 'respondent validation'), and in Chapter 7 on 'checking' that an argument is valid. If you have placed a feedback loop in your design, reflect on different interpretations and what they mean. Such questions usefully raise all of the issues of reflexivity, and if tackled well will heighten awareness of your part in making your data and the layered processes of interpretation of people's worlds.

The complexity of these issues very often prevents researchers from achieving ethically appropriate communication with respondents and using available feedback loops. You need to think and talk through the issues for your project (your research question, your design, your context, your relationships with your topic and the respondents and your method of analysis). If you are working within a methodological literature, it should assist you in dealing with the questions of interpretation that this situation involves. Whatever your context, the following issues must be raised.

It is almost always useful, sometimes essential, to know if your explanation makes sense to participants in the research field. But this does not mean the respondents have to approve it. Recall from Chapter 7 the original account of what a grounded theory would be like:

> The theory must also be readily understandable to sociologists of any viewpoint, to students and to significant laymen. Theory that can meet these requirements must fit the situation being researched, and work when put into use. (Glaser and Strauss, 1967: 3)

Being understandable to significant laymen is different from being agreed by the members of your sample. Both they and you will have strong views about whether your account fits the situation. Theirs must now be treated as new data as you work to establish that there is such a fit or to explain why there is no fit. Like all the processes of qualitative research, these require closure; the feedback data must be integrated with your current understanding, so it all fits.

Interpreting 'Member Checking'

Before you begin 'member checking' consider and answer each of the following questions:

- **What is being checked?** If it is simply a check that the participants have the demographic characteristics you recorded for them, or recall a discussion as you do, the task may be simple, but this is hardly validating your interpretation. Most commonly what is being 'checked' is how you have 'seen' the situation. What account of this interpretation are you to give out for checking? You are unlikely to ask the participants to read your whole book, report or thesis. But to read a chapter out of context will not give them the broader picture.
- **With whom are you checking?** Who are the relevant 'members' and what is their relation to you and to your research topic? By now, you know the diversity of the research area, of power, influence and interest, of perceptions and meanings people put on the topic. (That's what you are studying.) It is very unlikely that 'members' are a homogeneous group.
- **And who is checking whom?** It is never appropriate to think in terms of an 'us and them' dichotomy, in which you are 'doing research on' them. Would you expect some respondents to be closer to the research and researcher(s) than others, who are more likely to stand back and analyse? (In most ongoing field research projects, some participants become close advisers or informants.)
- **How would you interpret agreement?** This is a crucial question. If the participants agree with your analysis, given that they are probably not researchers, this would be surprising. (It may be a matter for concern. One of the goals set for a good project back in Chapter 1 was that it showed something the participants could not see.)

- **What follows if 'they' agree?** This is a major ethical issue. If a participant agrees to your account and even to its publication, this does not clear you of the responsibility of considering the implications of publishing. Perhaps they are unable to see future fallout from your report. Perhaps those consulted have an interest in your publishing a critique of others.
- **How to interpret disagreement?** There are of course two different situations to consider: everyone disagrees with you, or (a different issue) there is disagreement between members on your interpretation. By now it should be very clear that respondent checking does not establish the truth of your report. Think through, before you start feedback processes, all the different reasons why disagreement might appear. It is very likely that if you have made a good job of your research, the report exposes or even hurts some participants. You may have probed motives and interests, revealed the ways high intentions disguise messy politics or fear. Perhaps your task includes confronting the participants with this analysis, but do you expect them to agree and, if they did, what would that tell you?
- Whatever the response to the interpretation you present to your participants, **what was it they responded to?** How partial was that interpretation? A group meeting with a flip chart cannot possibly present a well-integrated theory. Examine with brutal honesty your own motives in presenting and what you presented.

The **Handling Sexual Attraction** project took interpretations back to the participants.

Writing about the Fit of Theory

Fit of theory to the situation requires that you integrate all the ideas and bring the integrated account consistently into play with your data. Such integration is often very hard to achieve. You've put effort into representing what you are studying with a rich variety of data, many voices and different ways of seeing things. Most researchers know the increasing desperation of efforts to turn this multi-coloured data into a unified account – preferably before the deadline. And they know, too, the subsequent doubt: did the explanation find you or did you, in desperation, impose it on the data?

To deal with these doubts, record honestly what you have done, what you tried, how you decided to discard or pursue a theory, where and how a significant theme emerged. Always note the failures as well as the successes, since all 'failures' are themselves explorations of the data. At the end of the project, you will be able to offer, in full detail, the story of how you arrived at your conclusion. Now you only have to write it.

Here, as in so many other areas, there are contradictory priorities. You need to worry about themes that hang out loose, unconnected. But you also should worry about integration that's too easy. Skilled researchers work rather as weavers do, drawing in as many threads as possible while watching the picture of the whole. Experiment with and critique the integrative mechanisms used by different 'experts' and try them all. Always use more than one and invent your own. Write the combination up as yours.

In this writing, constantly examine what it is you did. When did you realize these issues were linked, and what helped you to get closure around them? Try very hard not to think of, or write of, any of these stages as mysteries!

The Software Didn't Do It

In all this exciting process, never forget, or forget to report, your agency.

Qualitative researchers were more likely to take credit and responsibility for their products when their tools were very low tech. The advent of computer tools has hugely improved the range and rigour of methods for searching, and added new ways of seeing and testing. But it has also brought a risk of hiding behind the tools, or relying on them to do the thinking. 'Will your software analyse my data?' is a question often asked of developers. No, it won't. (I usually add that it won't write your thesis either.) Software doesn't see and doesn't analyse – you do. Each of the techniques for searching and seeing will assist you in the trek towards a satisfying account of your data. If arrival at the fit of theory and data took a series of carefully crafted iterative searches, describe them. Acknowledge their limitations (they depended on the coding you had done or the occurrence of phrases in the text) and document how you pursued and accounted for the exceptions.

Revisit, in the previous chapter, the goals for your research outcome. They are all qualities assessed by human evaluation: simplicity, elegance and balance, completeness, robustness and the ultimate accolade: it makes sense. Now, making sense of it to an audience is the task of the final chapter.

--- **To Do** ---

1. Work through the table of techniques for seeing and testing synthesis and patterns. Write a proposal for using one technique in each of the six groups (coding, modelling, writing, case studies, typologies, matrices and comparisons).
2. Treat yourself to a very thorough case study; choose a case (a person or a site) in your project and use all the data available to you to write a within-case account of how the factors and processes being studied are experienced by and affect that case.
3. In software or on paper, make a matrix of an important pattern in your data and explore it critically. If you are working in a software package, make that matrix and then take a big piece of paper and draw up the pattern you are chasing. Critique what you could do in software.

 Read the accounts in the **Inside Companionship** project of the relation of researcher to data in an ethnography. Reflect on your agency within your own project and write a comparison of the two.

--- **Suggestions for Further Reading** ---

The ways of seeing synthesis and patterns in this chapter reach into many specific methods. Miles and Huberman (1994) provided detailed advice on techniques for seeing patterns in data in their classic collection of things to do to data, with particular emphasis on modelling and matrices, both pre-computer. That classic has been updated with increasing emphasis on display with models and matrices: Miles et al. (2013). Recently, other texts have again turned to practical techniques: for examples see Bazeley (2013), Harding (2013), and Kuckartz (2014).

For techniques specific to grounded theory, see Strauss (1987). On case studies, see Ragin and Becker (1992), and Yin (1989). Within ethnography, there is a new emphasis on the agency of the researcher and the ethical issues of their relation to data: Hammersley and Traianou (2012). *Readme First* (Richards and Morse, 2013) has a chapter on abstracting.

There is an increasingly active debate on theory in qualitative research; start with Seale (1999), Silverman (2001), and Strauss (1995), and follow their references. For diverse techniques, there is much to be learned by browsing the big collections, for example, Denzin and Lincoln (1994, 2000), and Seale et al. (2004).

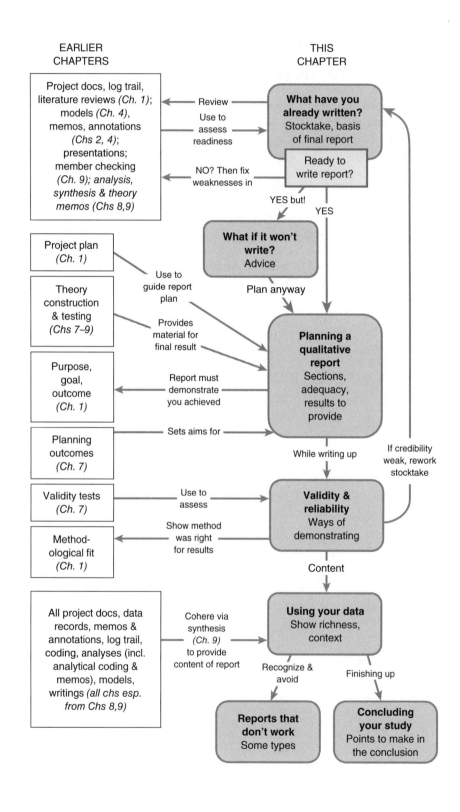

EARLIER
CHAPTERS

THIS
CHAPTER

Project docs, log trail,
literature reviews *(Ch. 1)*;
models *(Ch. 4)*,
memos, annotations
(Chs 2, 4);
presentations;
member checking
*(Ch. 9); analysis,
synthesis & theory
memos (Chs 8,9)*

**What have you
already written?**
Stocktake, basis
of final report

Review
Use to
assess
readiness

Ready to
write report?

NO? Then fix
weaknesses in

YES but!

YES

Project plan
(Ch. 1)

**What if it won't
write?**
Advice

Use to
guide report
plan

Plan anyway

Theory
construction
& testing
(Chs 7–9)

Provides
material for
final result

**Planning a
qualitative
report**
Sections,
adequacy,
results to
provide

Purpose,
goal,
outcome
(Ch. 1)

Report must
demonstrate
you achieved

Planning
outcomes
(Ch. 7)

Sets aims for

While writing up

If credibility
weak, rework
stocktake

Validity tests
(Ch. 7)

Use to
assess

**Validity &
reliability**
Ways of
demonstrating

Method-
ological fit
(Ch. 1)

Show method
was right
for results

Content

All project docs, data
records, memos &
annotations, log trail,
coding, analyses (incl.
analytical coding &
memos), models,
writings *(all chs esp.
from Chs 8,9)*

Cohere via
synthesis
(Ch. 9)
to provide
content of report

Using your data
Show richness,
context

Recognize &
avoid

Finishing up

**Reports that
don't work**
Some types

**Concluding
your study**
Points to make in
the conclusion

TEN
Telling it

That writing is a way of analysis, and necessary for justifying analysis, has been argued from the start of this book. This chapter is about the tasks of writing what you have discovered, showing how you discovered it and why it should be taken seriously. The chapter starts with the task of assessing the adequacy of your log trail and your readiness to conclude. It finishes with advice on planning and creating a report that properly represents the research you have conducted and convincingly presents the analysis you have achieved.

This chapter is not titled 'writing it up'. That common phrase carries a misleading message, that writing is a once-off conclusion to a project. Writing it up, like wrapping it up, also suggests a neatening, hiding the difficult bits, smoothing the rough. Your reflections and reports need the rough with the smooth. And importantly, since the start of the project, you have been writing it, steadily and regularly, as you recorded and clarified your understanding of the data. The final report is only a last stage of the writing.

In Chapter 2, when writing for logging the research process was advised, a distinction was made between 'telling' what's going on and 'writing it up'. Telling is easier, because it's informal, takes less time and is interactive. And it is flexible: it is much more natural to tell why the story has changed than to rewrite a written-up report. As your project matures, you will be helped by mixing writing with talking and modelling.

By the late stages of the project, if you have been writing about it in progress, the account will at last have crystallized. You will know what you are aiming for, and be able to use all the relevant techniques for getting there. As you work towards an outcome that brings the loose threads together, you will have a firm answer to that question 'What is your project about?' *This is what I tried to answer, this is what I learned, this is why it matters, and here is a useful account.*

Thus we return to the purpose, goal and outcome of a project. All three now have to be addressed. Why were you doing this: for what purpose are you now writing a report? What were you trying to answer and what answer do you now have to offer? What sort of a product is required to achieve that purpose, and that goal?

START WITH WHAT YOU HAVE WRITTEN

In each chapter, there have been things to tell about the project, in the spoken or written word, to yourself, your team, your diary, your software, your supervisor, your client or, if appropriate, to your research participants or your friends. If your logging processes have been thoughtful, much of the work is already done. This is how you find if you are ready to write it up, and how you bring together what you will need in order to give credibility to your report. And if you find you are not ready, this is how you identify what still needs to be done.

From the start of this project, you have written about data, ideas, puzzles, descriptions, links – in annotations, memos, reflective documents, field notes and changing descriptions of your categories. As you designed the project, set it up, managed the emerging ideas, you logged change and reflected, regularly, on what you might be aiming for. Now view this writing as a whole. It is time to take stock.

Like the 'live' browsing of coded passages, a full writing stocktake was not feasible without the computer. Then, your little thoughts were written in the document margins, or filed with the ideas, or, worse, distributed around your environment, on yellow stickers that fell off in the bus. Bringing the writings together took too much time and meant removing them from their proper context. The result was so incomplete that it was not worth the effort, so they never could be reviewed in this way. But if you are using any software, use it now to muster these disparate writings.

Mustering memos and other ways you have been telling your project can be both encouraging (you've written a lot!) and exciting (you've discovered a lot!). It will also give you a chance to assess the strengths and weaknesses in your material. Just as you see the data records differently when you browse together all the passages coded at one category, so too will you re-see your reflections when you read them together.

Set aside time to identify and actually *read* all of the writing *you* have done in this project. Don't get sucked back from this task to rereading the other data records. And commit to reading it all: don't discard in disgust naïve ideas from early on – treat them as data.

Telling It in Teams

For teams, this stage of assessment can be a formidable task, since there will be so many log items. To share it is productive, especially if you can create divisions of labour that bring new ways of seeing the data. One option is for the team members each to take 'ownership' of a category appearing in the analysis, rather than, or as well as, revisiting only their own writing. Now you all see what everyone contributed. You may discover unknown resources diffidently hidden in memos by less confident members of the team. It is quite likely that you will find that some members wrote far less than others; at this stage they can be encouraged to contribute overviews.

Go to the **Handling of Sexual Attraction** project for a detailed account of the use of computer and paper in displaying and discussion leading to the writing up. The two authors report the process of working towards a 'storyline': 'Using our diagrams (pinned to a noticeboard) as orientation, we created a series of headings and subheadings reflecting the concepts and sub-concepts we had discovered. Under these headings we pasted the corresponding parts of our 'storyline', which we then formalised and elaborated upon by reviewing our memos and methodological file to ensure that all concepts were accounted for and represented appropriately.'

A Writing Stocktake

Bring together and read together and distil, in turn, each different group of your writings and other ways of telling the project. You probably have writing devoted to each of the following categories:

- Project proposals, design documents and discussions.
- Literature reviews and discussion notes on books and/or papers.
- Models and diagrams, ranging from the earliest, messiest ones to layered, impressive (and possibly over-optimistic) presentations of what you at that stage thought was the overall story.
- Annotations on data records (don't read the record again).
- Descriptions of the categories you have created (don't revisit the categories or browse the data coded at them: just reflect on their representation of your ideas).
- Memos of all sorts. Read separately and summarize your memos about method, your memos about documents, and your memos about emerging ideas. Reading them together will show you the ways you discovered clumps of ideas and how you began constructing possible theories, where and why you gave up on a theory.
- The new data from 'member checking' (see previous chapter) and your reflections on what you learned from the participants.
- All the other stuff! This may include any tapes or notes of discussions you have had or thoughts after you drove round the corner from an interview; diary records of progress or problems and counselling sessions with colleagues.

But What Can You Tell? Confronting the Ethics of Research Reporting

From now to the submission of your report, the issues of ethics we raised in the early chapters are paramount. As you write, every memo, and every extract from your data, will threaten the requirements of anonymity and confidentiality that were almost certainly faced in your research design. If you haven't already 'anonymized' your data records, using pseudonyms and avoiding definite descriptions of individuals, you will need to do so now. As you assess your log trail, keep notes on all such issues.

Now that you can front up to the data you have acquired, it may be time to revisit those issues of ethics in the context of your project. What personal material has been entrusted to you? How can it be properly, ethically, reported?

 In the report of the **Sexuality-Spirituality** project, the researcher concludes: 'A lasting impression that I take away with me is the implicit faith of interviewees in entrusting me with their stories. I am also humbled by their lack of judgement of my privileged social positioning as researcher and heterosexual within a hetero-sexist ordering of society. Most in turn, were intrigued that someone was willing to listen to their stories even transcribe and study them.'

Most qualitative researchers confront at least once the dilemma that their rich data and vivid accounts they produced during the project will be less rich, less vivid, if the reports avoid exposing identities. Confronting this always hurts, and there are no perfect answers to the problem. It is worse when participants are easily identifiable, as public figures, or by others in the study. All writers of qualitative reports have resorted to modes of obscuring identity, and almost always they feel the report is less because of the ethical requirements. But those requirements of course are commitments you can't avoid.

 Go to the **Harassment Complaints** project for thoughts on how the researchers managed the 'balancing act' of anonymizing rich and personal data.

Assessing Your Log Trail

Despite your best efforts, it is unlikely that these mustered materials offer a perfect account of the project. (In fact, it's impossible.) You are assessing the trail, not attempting to prove it's perfect. Can you show how the materials now link up? Can you show what each step or stage contributed, and its relevance now?

Many memos will have been dropped or neglected (some deserved to be, but others languished undeveloped). Reflections on method got lost in your excitement with a theme that occurred (but the memo about method may have warned you to test the theme). Your energy went into coding your data records at the expense of annotating them, or into writing about the searches you completed, rather than your changing understanding of a theme. An evaluation of these materials will tell you where the holes in your argument remain, and what needs to be done either to repair them or to explain them.

Your ideas are more easily overtaken by the scale of data in larger projects. A stocktake of writing may well show gaps, places where there was no consideration of an alternative interpretation, or where the data simply were not read. Most of the processes recommended here will help, but be particularly on the lookout for gaps in the writing, and attempt at this stage to fill them.

Assessing the adequacy of the logs will give you the basis for moving towards writing a final report. Importantly, it will also tell you if you are not yet ready to do so.

How Good Is the Log Trail?

- You will probably be startled to find how much writing there is. Keep a summary of the significant items as you go. Be alert to gaps and inconsistencies, to inadequate explanations or thinking that tailed off.
- A table display gives a useful log summary. Make a row for each theme, concept or 'chase' of searches, for example. Make columns for comments about your confidence, the completeness of the analysis, what still needed testing at this point, etc. That last column is where a red alert goes if you find a hole in your argument, or an area requiring new thinking.
- As you read, write. Of course, you will not report on every bubble on this muddy river of material. From skim-reading every little annotation and every minor change to a category definition, you will rapidly select what matters. Write about the flow of the project. Make sense of how you built up your understanding of the data and your answer to the research question.
- As you write the history, *add* to the record. Importantly, you should never alter the record of what you did or thought in the past, but rather write *on* from that, adding how you now see this memo or why you now know your assessment of this problem was inadequate.

Whether or not each team member does a stocktake of their own log items, it is very important that the team meeting assesses the whole body of items together. As a team, you need to confront missing pieces and weaknesses sometime; it's better to do so now, while they can be discussed, than later when the team is set on final reporting and any hitch holds everyone up.

Using the Log Trail

The outcome of this stocktake could be that you start writing the final report, and come up for breath only when you've finished the first draft. (It's been known to happen.) As you reread and rethink earlier thoughts, you discover that the synthesis you were seeking was there already, and you feel it will 'write itself'. It won't, but this is a good start. But even if there is no immediate flow of writing, you will have achieved two major steps.

The first is that you have written the project in your own voice, 'telling it straight'. In your final report, this straight statement will of course be lost, as at each step you will document and illustrate your conclusions. Once you have written in your voice, you will find it much easier to hold a strong statement of your account through the final, fuller report.

The second achievement is that you now know whether you are ready to write that final report. The stocktake has saved you from attempting a conclusion that would have been inadequate, requiring retreat or, worse, failure to convince. If you are not ready, the stocktake will have identified the topics to revisit, questions still to be asked, perhaps even new data to be sought to fill a gap.

If you assess that you are ready, you have a firm basis for starting. The stocktake of writing shows how much reflecting has already been done, how ideas have linked up. As you work on the stocktake, you have probably gathered very many clusters of little ideas into bigger ones. Revisit Chapter 7 on data–theory bootstrapping. Think about your little writings as very small grain size theory and the stocktake as maximizing the chance that they will clump into greater grains.

And Actually Writing in Teams!

Once you start writing, a quite different challenge is to be met if you are working with a team. The stocktake includes their materials and yours. The data are open to their interpretations as well as your preferred ones. Of course you can agree to differ, and write a set of differing accounts, but to do so would waste the benefits of team research.

 Go to the **Youth Offender Program Evaluation** project for detailed accounts of the procedures set up for teamwork work during analysis and reporting.

Explore the options in software – not just qualitative software! – for sharing the data and the drafts: see especially Chapter 9 in Paulus et al. (2014).

WHAT IF IT WON'T WRITE?

Qualitative researchers have a quite different challenge in writing a report from that faced by quantitative colleagues. Compare their journal papers: the qualitative papers are far longer, they have no pre-set structure, they rarely have summary illustrations like tables or diagrams and they are full of quotations. The qualitative report has to persuade, convince and illustrate with words. There is no neat template to fill in. This is often a major obstacle to writing.

There's No One Right Write-Up

It's an indicator of the lack of confidence plaguing qualitative research that Howard Becker is still cited for arguing in 1986 that there is no one right way to write up research. Of course there isn't; for each project, there will be a choice of ways to write up, and for your project, the choice is yours. If the search for a right way is your problem, read the reflections on the idiosyncrasy of qualitative reports in the readings at the end of this chapter.

As qualitative research becomes more acceptable and thoughtfully debated across disciplines, researchers working with qualitative data are much more likely to be advised that their way will necessarily be different from someone else's. Revisit the discussion of 'reflexivity' in Chapters 3 and 4. Once you have become aware of your own part in making and interpreting the data, you are freed of any suggestion that there is a right way to report your project. It will be somebody's report.

Yes, You Can Do It Justice!

Expelling the myth of the right way is a lot easier than dealing with the fear of not doing the analysis well enough. One of the major contributors to writer's block is the feeling that your data are too rich, your project too amazingly complex, the participants' needs too unanswerable, the variety of meanings too dazzling, for you (or indeed anyone) to do them justice.

Being overwhelmed by the richness of data is a common and necessary (and often enjoyable) experience for qualitative researchers, but by this stage in a project, you should be able to deal with it. You have developed reliable techniques for handling that richness and complexity. If at the reporting stage you start to feel overwhelmed again, don't retreat to 'poor little old me' apologetics. Just review those processes until you discover the source of your discomfort. Your stocktake of writings should identify sharply where you are unconfident. Are there significant categories you still feel unsure about? Return to browse all that data, recode, rethink and rewrite the issues. Are there types of data that you feel you have not handled well, perhaps the photographic records, or newspaper cuttings? Review and report on these.

A different version of this block, and one deserving respect, is the fear that you may impact what you studied, and change things for the worse. This can be a serious problem if you intended to, and will, contribute to policy or practice for real people in real, sometimes serious situations. As the time to report comes nearer, so too does the fear that you might misinform, mislead or even mistake the messages in your data. Worse is the fear that your report may be misinterpreted or misused. If these concerns confront you, they must be answered, since failure to report would also have very undesirable consequences. The report must be made, and it must be unambiguous and useful. Revisit all the ways of being sure you're justified in claims you make, and ensure that each step in your argument is clearly documented. Now do the analysis, presenting in your report a careful assessment of the implications for action, avoiding over-simplistic headlining of conclusions.

Tell It in Instalments

Start somewhere, anywhere other than the beginning. (The first chapter is almost always best finished last.) Write small glowing pieces that are good in themselves, treating them as pictures to hang on the wall, rather than pieces of a jigsaw. Write small papers for conferences and leave them isolated; later you will find if and where they fit. Store the pieces with any clues about what you think they will link to, and leave them to mature while you write other pieces.

At this stage, a seminar series can assist to produce the final report. Invite an informed audience and present a series of papers on different stages of the project. If other team members become part of a general audience, the authors will find it easier to tell what they see, rather than assume everyone also sees it. Prepare the working papers for publication, with the seminar discussion record after each paper.

PLANNING A QUALITATIVE REPORT

As with any paper or essay, a qualitative research final report will require outlining and planning. This may be a challenge if your reporting hitherto has been in 'scientific' mode. It takes great ingenuity to fit a qualitative project into the framework of Introduction, Hypothesis, Methods, Results, Conclusion. If such constraints are imposed on your task, or if the requirements of your institution specify segmentation, plan within those sections to shape the report more qualitatively.

To identify the relevant parts for your report, use the skills you have developed for categorizing and drawing together categories. You have built a theory or an explanation up from the data. Now build a report that presents it. If they are arranged so that they step the reader through the analysis, the sections and chapters of your report will *deliver* your conclusions and their validation.

─────────────── Plans That Work ───────────────

If you need a framework to start, adapt this four-part plan:

1. Introduction/overview: your purpose and goals and arrival at a 'researchable question'. Report styles differ over whether here you announce what you answered and the outcome you achieved.

2. A first section on the *location* of the study, with chapters reporting the four different contexts of the project:

- Where it is in the **literature**. Why is this study needed and new? The scale and detail of a literature review will be determined by your context.
- Where it is **methodologically** – the way it was done. The choice of methods, how these will affect the outcome. What other options were available and what would have come of those choices?
- The **setting** of the research, showing the reader the places and people, assessing the ways you entered and explored the research field.
- Yourself as **researcher**, your situation and your cultural and social location and ability to understand the different locations studied, the difficulties and how you dealt with them. Your involvement with the situation and participants studied, and reflection on the influence of this involvement, on them and your study.

3. The central analysis chapters: give these a strong thematic design. Possible arrangements for these all-important chapters or sections include:

- Chapters that step **sequentially** through stages in the story that is being told (either chronologically or logically).
- A chapter for each of the **dimensions** you have identified in the problem or situation studied.
- Units (chapters or sections) that are each a **case study**, through which each of the themes or patterns of your analysis are systematically explored.

4. The conclusion, which should be reported with full regard for the requirements of reflexivity and relevance. Here, consider sections on other ways of looking, unfinished business in the topic area and effects of the research.

Design each of these parts carefully to ensure it will combine description and analysis. No significant section should be only descriptive. By outlining with these goals, you will ensure that you never lose the momentum of analysis.

What Is an Adequate Report Like?

In Chapter 7, a good outcome was sketched as follows:

- It should address your purpose and goal, giving an answer to your 'researchable question'.
- It should offer analysis, not just description.
- It should offer at least a new local theory or explanation.
- It should offer something more than the participants in your research could have reported.
- And it should *account* for your data. This has to be an adequate account, so you will be able to claim that it 'makes sense' of what's going on in the data.

Your report just needs to show that it did!

──────────────── **So the Report Should Provide ...** ────────────────

On the basis of those requirements, an adequate qualitative report will offer (not necessarily in this order):

- A clear statement of your purpose and goal – why you proposed the project, what you asked and have found or concluded, with assessment of how (and to what extent) it answered the research question. This statement should include the ways the research question shifted, and why.
- A convincing account of how you proceeded with analysis of the data, and how you arrived at the conclusion – the processes of analysis. What sort of a 'construct' are you offering? How well does it explain, interpret or display the situation studied?
- An exploration of the conclusion and its importance, including an explanation of why it is new, and the implications for the previous literature or policy assumptions. The extent to which it challenges, extends or affirms an existing theory or practice.
- An explanation of the researcher view, and how it provides a clarification, development or interpretation of the view of the participants; an account of why and how you gained this viewpoint; and of the data and the processes you've used.
- A coherent account of the steps to your conclusion, the ways those steps were validated, the processes used to explore and question the data and how you know it is satisfactory.

However you segment the report, check at each stage that these five goals have been answered for that segment.

WHAT ABOUT VALIDITY AND RELIABILITY?

As you write, carefully make claims for validity in terms that are appropriate to your audience, but do make them.

Qualitative researchers are arguably at risk of throwing out the idea of validity with the rather murky and now decidedly tepid bathwater of the debate with quantitative research. The rejection of 'positivism' was an attempt to defend qualitative research against those who evaluated it in terms of irrelevant goals. In the context of academic debate, it seemed necessary to challenge research paradigms in which validity required large-scale research, statistical measures of reliability and assertions of truth. To free qualitative research from this defensiveness, some authors have argued that reliability and validity are terms that belong to the positivist paradigm, and qualitative researchers should avoid them. But beware!

Too much negativism about positivism can put at risk the acceptance of your qualitative research if you work in areas where validity is a standard clearly held.

Set your standard, and as you report, stick to the goal already set – to establish that your account of the data is valid (well founded and sound) and that your methods as a researcher were reliable (that the audience can trust that you have used thorough and consistent methods to produce a trustworthy outcome).

Revisit Chapter 7 and review the ways this can be done. You should be able to show a consistent trail of logs justifying (or noting the limitations of) each step in your project, examining alternatives and dealing with puzzles. As you start writing a final report, you can steadily draw on these materials to account for the arrival at your conclusion, establishing that it is grounded in your data, and is not a product of your biases or partial analysis.

You now need to state the concluding explanation, synthesis or pattern in a way that is clear to your audience, and to back that statement with convincing evidence and a robust account of the research process.

Stepping Up to Make Claims

This is another task that may be best done in instalments. Each of these instalments will contribute to your final report.

- Address the issues of evidence and soundness directly in everything you say and write about the project. To dodge them, merely relying on the attraction of your rich data, is a betrayal of the work you have done.
- Write a reflective piece on what the project did *not* cover or represent. With a broader scope to your data, what might you have been able to achieve? Such reflection helps you assess where you stopped, and why, as well as what you did explain.
- Write a paper on the process of your project and the ways you have sought to ensure robustness and trustworthiness, drawing carefully on your log trail. Examine where the gaps are, what challenges your account is still open to and what checks you could make to cover those risks.
- If the burden of evidence is too heavy to cite fully, take one small module in your theory and track its growth to establish how in this little bit of your account you show it is a valid one, well founded and sound.
- Take one method of enquiry you have used, and tell the story of using it, showing that your handling of the data and ideas has been transparent, consistent and thorough, so that a reader could rely on it.
- Write a methodological paper about what is still opaque and how you might have better documented the research process.
- Write about your log trail. Use your stocktake of memos and notes to write an overview of the methods used to contribute to the quality and trustworthiness of this research, critically assessing how adequately each served this purpose. You may wish to include a condensed version of the table summary of your log items as an appendix.

Writing the Methodological Fit

This book started with an assertion that, whatever your context, your study needs a *fit* between the question being asked, the design of the project and the methods being used to make the data with which that question is to be answered.

Now, you will need to show that you designed the project for methodological fit, adapting it to respond to discovered requirements, and how the methods chosen answered those requirements. Such a fit is never perfect, so don't try to present it as such. It is important to assess honestly the adequacy of your design and the sufficiency of the data you worked with. Use your log documents to report on the adjustments made as you discovered gaps and challenges.

Report also ways that you adapted or innovated techniques. No qualitative methodology is exclusive. If you have worked within a recognized methodology, your report should establish, to the extent that it is relevant to your audience, that you worked well with the techniques and methods set out in the literature. But to pretend that you worked exclusively therein is both unnecessary and almost certainly unwise. You will undoubtedly have invented or borrowed techniques from elsewhere, and your account should clearly indicate what they were and how they contributed (or didn't).

In the context of your method, report in detail that is appropriate for your target audience, on whether you used software, and if so, what program you used and how it contributed (or not) to your outcomes. Software is often not reported at all, or reported very inadequately, in qualitative reports. To omit what you did with software may seriously diminish the credibility of your claims to thorough analysis. Take care here that your agency and your use of software tools are accurately reported. High on the list of reporting blunders is the awful assertion that 'the analysis was done by [Software Package]'.

USING YOUR DATA

In qualitative work, the most serious and least acknowledged problem in writing is the requirement that you move from respecting, deeply studying and responding to your data to *using* data.

Whenever you tell or write your project, there is a tension between the richness of the data, the need to know everything 'in' the data, and the requirement that they be reduced to a clear outcome. You will experience this tension from the start of the project, but it really hits at the end.

Showing Richness

As you draft any section, ensure that you are representing the range and richness of the data. This does not require, indeed is often frustrated by, long quotations. Describing a situation vividly and referencing what was said may be more powerful than simply quoting.

Use the models drawn during the project, and develop them for the report, to confirm your knowledge of the data across each area of your argument. Talk out a model to an appropriate audience, showing at each stage that there is impressive data behind every box or line. If there isn't, revise the model! Include the relevant models in your report, either as an introduction to the issues to be discussed or as a way of summarizing an argument.

Use your case studies to steady your confidence that you really know these records and their variety. At moments of indecision, return to the data via a case study.

Using Quotations

A good project is laden with rich records, lengthy accounts of detailed narratives and long memos about complex relationships – how can this wealth of detail and mass of material possibly be represented in your book/thesis/paper/presentation? Most qualitative researchers have great trouble with any data reduction, partly because the criteria for reduction are never clear and partly because they are unwilling to let go of the detail. But reduction at the end of a project is excruciating. By now, you should have shed what didn't matter – so everything that remains clearly matters.

The goals of reporting require that you depart from the data but ground all the threads of your theory in data. Neither is easy. As you construct and test theories, you are constantly dragged back into the detail of particular cases. As you gather *just* the material that illustrates a critical concept, the whole paragraph of each quotation, indeed the whole record, seems relevant.

It is important to contextualize quoted material, and also to keep people and sites identifiable as wholes. Your wording needs to show for each passage used that it is appropriate and adequate for the purpose. Of course, where respondents could be recognized and should not be, you require a very careful and project-wide system of anonymity, if necessary using fictional details or splitting of described cases. Take time to develop this system fully, so anonymity if possible does not destroy the context of the data.

——————— Writing the Context of Your Data ———————

- In using material from your records, always locate its source if you can, indicate why you trust these data, and why they are pertinent in this context.
- If appropriate, tell what possible problems there might be with this data extract in this context, and how (not whether) it's coloured by your participation and other factors.
- If you have a small study, within the limitations of ethical practice, carefully devise a system of pseudonyms to identify each quote, so the reader can track how this person

(Continued)

(Continued)

is responding across a number of areas of the analysis, and get a sense of the 'whole' case. As you write, help the reader draw these links between even small illustrative quotations. *Maria, who had objected strongly to the amalgamation and still regretted it, now accepted the benefits of what she termed the 'sharpening of staff'.*

- If you are not able to identify 'whole' people or sites in this way, at least attach to the passages quoted the one or two attributes that matter for your argument. (Female, Manager, over 50 yrs.)

You may love every interview you conducted; you may see significant meaning in every phrase transcribed. That word for the effect on staff, 'sharpening', came in a flood of emotional rhetoric from Maria; you recall her body language expressing distress at losing friendships, anger at bad people management. It should surely all be in your report? The answer is: probably not. All that detail is needed in your written report only if the report is a case study of Maria's dilemmas. If, however, you created a new concept, 'staff sharpening', to take off from the data and construct a theory of the impact of amalgamations on human resources, you are using that term as a platform for theory building. To swamp it in the detail of Maria's account will lose the focus, and stop you moving up to the abstract concept you constructed. So what was your question, and what is the argument being made? If you are building a small cluster of theory around 'staff sharpening' we need only her phrase, 'sharpening of staff'.

Of course, in using your data you must never abuse them. The context and the intended meaning are carefully reported in the detail relevant to the argument and to the audience and setting. But in none of the probable outcomes will we need to include a long paragraph of Maria's interview.

REPORTS THAT DON'T WORK

There are, depressingly, many different unsatisfactory outcomes from any research. But qualitative research has four particularly common ones.

The Patchwork Quilt

The most common way of doing injustice to data is via a report that is a collection of long quotations, supposedly representing the data. These reports are easy to pick because, like bad journalism, they are studded with fuzzy generalities (*Most felt there had been difficulties*) stitched together by breathless partial summaries (*Many, on the other hand, disagreed*). Like badly made quilts, they have no common weave across the pieces stitched together.

There are many problems with this style of report. Note especially:

- Such an account is bad data reduction. You are purporting to describe your data fully, but of course the patches are cut from something bigger. You have lost context by cutting out the quotation but not giving details of origin. Your exasperated reader will immediately want to know: *Who felt this? How many?* and *Why those people, not the others?*
- You have also lost focus. You are seemingly exploring the variety, but in fact crudely reducing the data by clumping into 'most' and 'many', thereby losing the context and continuity of the cases. Within the long quotations the reader can see far more variety than you have identified: *that quote seems to be all about difficulties. Why is it in with the unidentified 'many' who disagreed?*
- The stitched extracts drag the reader back from the analysis to the individual person. This isn't a study of Maria, her experience or career. Your project's purpose was to inform the handling of restructuring.

In other words, this sort of report offers bad description and no analysis. You are gaining little ground from the quoted material and going nowhere from the data. You may be interested, moved or excited by these quotations (though, sadly, almost always others won't see the richness you do). But data don't speak for themselves.

Every time you insert a paragraph quotation, wonder if perhaps just one phrase of that paragraph would better make your point.

The Illuminated Description

Much more impressive than the patchwork quilt is a coloured, rich account that takes the reader deeply into the data in appropriately long passages of text. The reader is immersed in the situation, vividly pictures the people, hears the voices, and is moved by the experiences. Such a presentation of the data can be enthralling.

If moving and enthralling your reader is your goal, this writing style is effective. *Perhaps the purpose was to shock managers into seeing the HR results of restructuring; Maria will serve as an image for this purpose.* But it is convincing only in one sense: we are convinced that the author was there. Whether their account is adequate or their analysis insightful we just can't tell. So it is rare that a study can report only this way, and such a report always risks providing only description.

Aim to integrate data as part of the argument, not to flood the argument with data passages. Almost always, quotations will be more powerful if they are as brief as possible, pruned to express just what matters. As you illuminate your own report with the words of those you studied, select just the words that say what they meant, remove all words that don't make the point. This is hard, and you may require help. The best helper is a tough editor who will mercilessly cut extraneous words and show you how much clearer your chapter is now that it is half the length.

The Leap of Faith

How often have you followed, in the popular or professional literature, an account well provided with convincing evidence that suddenly launches into assertions of principle, prediction or politics? This is a very common outcome for a qualitative project whose original purpose was strongly driven by ideology or social commitment. If you are so driven, take care that the steps in your argument are firmly grounded in your data as far as possible, and that you clearly indicate the point at which the data no longer support the discussion.

Social research of course can inform speculation about processes beyond the scope of any particular project. In many contexts, a report will disappoint if it does not reach out to such discussion. The requirement is that the researcher clearly indicates what part of the argument is based on data and what part is not. To make such a clear distinction greatly assists the claim of qualitative research to be 'evidence based'. Not to make that distinction provides critics with examples of unjustified leaps and does a grave disfavour to the method.

Yourself as Hero

Throughout this book you have been urged to be reflexive, to write in the first person, to recognize your agency, to be aware of the ways you made these data records and handled them, the path you took to particular interpretations. As you move to reporting your research, you need to assess and thoughtfully evaluate and write about your effect on the outcome.

But you also need to be very careful in adjusting the focus on yourself so it informs the reader but does not merely feature your own performance.

Reflect for a moment on the term 'reflexive'. As explained in Chapters 2 and 3, it means more than 'reflective'. Variously defined, 'reflexivity' is widely used in the context of qualitative research to refer to the element of self-study in any such research, and to alert researchers to the need to question the taken-for-granted knowledge they take into a study and the many ways they influence what they record as data. Being reflexive has been a goal from the start of your project, and from the earliest chapters you have been encouraged to reflect on your making and your handling of data and ideas, your preconceptions and your interpretations. These memos kept you aware of the issues. But now, how much detail is required in a final report, to tell honestly this multilayered interpretation? How autobiographical should this report be?

As you move towards your account of the research, many new challenges appear.

- How do you interpret the input of your own knowledge and experience? How much does the reader need to know?
- Just how open, honest and excruciatingly revelatory should the account be?

Put simply, what's needed depends (like so much else) on your research question, your judgement of the audience and setting. You would be central if your research question were about researcher impact on the research situation. But otherwise, it is necessary to go back to the goal and purpose of the project, to ask: how much of your reflection on your impact is needed and useful? Wherever your writing starts to sound like self-promotion or self-pity, refer to your goal and purpose.

To do this well does not require a multi-volume diary of your research experience. In the contexting parts of your report, you should carefully assess – briefly – your part in what you are reporting. Set a tough standard for the selection and editing of material about your own agency. Be aware of your audience: in some academic settings, reports do not include thorough discussion of wrong pathways and early erroneous interpretations. And in some 'real-world' settings these may be simply irrelevant to the project's purpose. If convention or practical purposes prevent your reporting relevant issues, write a separate methodological paper for a qualitative journal on these aspects of your project.

CONCLUDING YOUR STUDY

Qualitative data can be handled, and can be managed, in such a way that you can make sense of them. This has been the message of this book. A convincing research report will conclude with that message. You wish to show that you have skilfully handled and carefully done justice to the data, and that your analysis makes sense.

From the earliest chapters of this book, there has been emphasis on the processes by which qualitative research builds testing and reflecting on the data into each stage of analysis. Each step in theory building is, in a sense, self-testing. Only when confident of a grain of theory will the researcher build onto it another grain. If you tell your project with conviction, your report will mirror that way of constructing conclusions.

So reporting qualitative research turns out to be yet another data-handling task.

A Concluding Box

The considered argument or evidence-based theory you are reporting certainly did not simply 'emerge' from the data. Your report has told what you did with the data and what happened when you did it. Even a brief report should give a clear story, in each of the sections of the report, of:

- where the ideas came from;
- what alternatives were discarded and why;
- what processes of pursuit were used;
- what ideas were brought together and how;
- what was tested and how it was tested;
- the degree of confidence being claimed.

In your concluding chapter, in good qualitative mode, you can firmly draw these themes about the analysis together. For the whole study, each should be assessed.

Without apology for the nature of qualitative research, the size of the study or the diversity of the data, establish that you designed and conducted a coherent study addressing the question you constructed after thoroughly reviewing the literature. Establish that you sought the appropriate sources of information, you made and responsibly recorded the relevant data, you handled those good data records skilfully and examined them reliably, you rigorously pursued ideas emerging from the data and you reliably documented your journey as they were developed and tested through the data. And that you have, as a result, something worth hearing.

To Do

1. Do a writing stocktake for your project. Prepare a table summarizing your writing so far, and report on any weaknesses or gaps revealed.
2. Plan the outline of your report, using and adapting the outline provided above.
3. Write a section of your report appropriately using quoted material to illustrate and strengthen your argument. With a colleague, or in a group, share samples of such writings, and discuss. Take another writer's section and edit its quotations, with the goals of making the quoted material as vivid and as brief as possible.
4. Write a report on the overall account you are offering, and why you are able to claim it is convincing.
5. Now you can aim for the final report!

Suggestions for Further Reading

Validity in qualitative research has its own substantial literature (see further readings to Chapter 7). For more specific discussion of validating your claims in reports, see Kirk and Miller (1986), Silverman (2010), Seale (1999), Yin (2010).

There is a startling amount of literature on writing qualitative research, compared with the paucity on handling data. See *Readme First* (Richards and Morse, 2013), Part 3. Most collections have chapters on writing, for example Seale et al. (2004). For very detailed advice, go to Wolcott (2009), Silverman (2010), Delamont and Atkinson (2008), and Flick (2014). Grounded theory texts advise in detail on writing, and are of use for many other methods as well; see particularly, Charmaz (2006) and Strauss and Corbin (1998).

For other books or chapters explicitly on writing, see especially the famous contribution by Becker (1986), Eisner (1998), Janesick (2000), Lofland and Lofland (1995), Mason (2002), Morse (1997), and Richardson (1994).

There are also very many works on writing theses, for example, Piantanida and Garman (1999). For others, as for so many of the tasks in this book, explore using digital tools! Read sample chapters to find a style and content that is useful to you.

References

Agar, M.H. (1996) *The Professional Stranger: An Informal Introduction to Ethnography*. San Diego, CA: Academic Press.

Atkinson, P., Coffey, A., Delamont, S., Lofland, J. and Lofland, L. (2001) *Handbook of Ethnography*. London: Sage.

Auerbach, C.F. and Silverstein, L.B. (2003) *Qualitative Data: An Introduction to Coding and Analysis*. New York: New York University Press.

Bazeley, P. (2013) *Qualitative Data Analysis: Practical Strategies*. London: Sage.

Bazeley, P. and Jackson, K. (2013) *Qualitative Data Analysis with NVivo* (2nd edn). London: Sage.

Becker, H.S. (1986) *Writing for Social Scientists: How to Finish your Thesis, Book or Article*. Chicago, IL: University of Chicago Press.

Bong, S.A. (2002) 'Debunking myths in qualitative data analysis', *Forum Qualitative Sozialforschung/Forum: Qualitative Social Research*, 3(2): Article 10.

Braun, V. and Clarke, V. (2013) *Successful Qualitative Research: A Practical Guide for Beginners*. London: Sage.

Bryant, A. and Charmaz, K. (eds) (2007) *The Sage Handbook of Grounded Theory*. London: Sage.

Busher, H. and James, N. (2009) *Online Interviewing*. London: Sage.

Charmaz, K. (2006) *Constructing Grounded Theory: A Practical Guide through Qualitative Analysis*. London: Sage.

Coffey, A. and Atkinson, P. (1996) *Making Sense of Qualitative Data*. London: Sage.

Creswell, J.W. (2013) *Qualitative Inquiry and Research Design: Choosing among Five Approaches* (3rd edn). Thousand Oaks, CA: Sage.

Davidson, J. and Di Gregorio, S. (2011) 'Qualitative research and technology: in the midst of a revolution', in Denzin, N.K. and Lincoln, Y.S. (eds), *Handbook of Qualitative Research* (4th edn). Thousand Oaks, CA: Sage, pp. 627–43.

Delamont, S. and Atkinson, P.A. (2008) *Representing Ethnography: Reading, Writing and Rhetoric in Qualitative Research*. London: Sage.

Dempster, P.G., Woods, D. and Wright, J.S.F. (2013) 'Using CAQDAS in the analysis of Foundation Trust hospitals in the National Health Service: mustard seed searches as an aid to analytic efficiency', *Forum Qualitative Sozialforschung/Forum: Qualitative Social Research*, 14(2), http://nbn-resolving.de/urn:nbn:de:0114-fqs130231.

Denzin, N.K. and Lincoln, Y.S. (eds) (1994) *Handbook of Qualitative Research.* Newbury Park, CA: Sage.

Denzin, N.K. and Lincoln, Y.S. (eds) (2000) *Handbook of Qualitative Research* (2nd edn). Thousand Oaks, CA: Sage.

Denzin, N.K. and Lincoln, Y.S. (eds) (2011) *Handbook of Qualitative Research* (4th edn). Thousand Oaks, CA: Sage.

Dey, I. (1995) *Qualitative Data Analysis: A User-friendly Guide for Social Scientists.* London: Routledge.

Dey, I. (1999) *Grounding Grounded Theory.* New York: Academic Press.

Di Gregorio, S. and Davidson, J. (2008) *Qualitative Research Design for Software Users.* Maidenhead: Open University Press.

Eisner, E.W. (1998) *The Enlightened Eye.* Englewood Cliffs, NJ: Merrill Prentice-Hall.

Ely, M., Vinz, R., Downing, M. and Anzul, M. (1997) *On Writing Qualitative Research: Living by Words.* London: Taylor and Francis.

Evers, J.C., Silver, C., Mruck, K. and Peeters, B. (2011) 'Introduction to the KWALON experiment: discussions on qualitative data analysis software by developers and users', *Forum Qualitative Sozialforschung/Forum: Qualitative Social Research, 12*(1), Article 40, http://nbn-resolving.de/urn:nbn:de:0114-fqs1101405.

Fern, E.F. (2001) *Advanced Focus Group Research.* London: Sage.

Fielding, N.G. and Lee, R.M. (eds) (1991) *Using Computers in Qualitative Research.* London: Sage.

Fielding, N.G., Lee, R.M. and Blank, G. (eds) (2008) *The Sage Handbook of Online Research Methods.* London: Sage.

Flick, U. (ed.) (2013) *The Sage Handbook of Qualitative Data Analysis.* London: Sage.

Flick, U. (2014) *An Introduction to Qualitative Research* (5th edn). London: Sage.

Forum Qualitative Sozialforschung/Forum: Qualitative Social Research (2005) *Secondary Analysis of Qualitative Data, 6*(1).

Friese, S. (2012) *Qualitative Data Analysis with ATLAS.ti.* London: Sage.

Geertz, C. (1973) *The Interpretation of Cultures.* New York: Basic Books.

Gibbs, G. (2002) *Qualitative Data Analysis: Explorations with NVivo.* London: Open University Press.

Gibbs, G.R., Friese, S. and Mangabeira, W.C. (2002) 'The use of new technology in qualitative research', *Forum Qualitative Sozialforschung/Forum: Qualitative Social Research, 3*(2), Article 8, http://nbn-resolving.de/urn:nbn:de:0114-fqs020287.

Gilbert, L. (2002) 'Going the distance: "closeness" in qualitative data analysis software', *International Journal of Social Research Methodology, 5*(3): 215–28.

Glaser, B.G. (1978) *Theoretical Sensitivity.* Mill Valley, CA: Sociology Press.

Glaser, B.G. and Strauss, A.L. (1967) *The Discovery of Grounded Theory: Strategies for Qualitative Research.* Chicago, IL: Aldine.

Goodall, H.L. (2000) *Writing the New Ethnography.* London: Rowman and Littlefield.

Hammersley, M. and Traianou, A. (2012) *Ethics in Qualitative Research: Controversies and Contexts.* London: Sage.

Harding, J. (2013) *Qualitative Data Analysis from Start to Finish.* London: Sage.

Hesse-Biber, S. (ed.) (2011) *The Handbook of Emergent Technologies in Social Research.* New York: Oxford University Press.

Holstein, J.A. and Gubrium, J.F. (1995) *The Active Interview.* Thousand Oaks, CA: Sage.

Humble, A.M. (2012) 'Qualitative data analysis software: a call for understanding, detail, intentionality, and thoughtfulness', *Journal of Family Theory and Review,* *4*(2): 122–37.

Janesick, V.J. (2000) 'The choreography of qualitative research design', in Denzin, N.K. and Lincoln, Y.S. (eds), *Handbook of Qualitative Research* (2nd edn). Newbury Park, CA: Sage.

Kelle, U. (ed.) (1995) *Computer-aided Qualitative Data Analysis.* London: Sage.

Kirk, J. and Miller, M. (1986) *Reliability and Validity in Qualitative Research.* London: Sage.

Krueger, R.A. (1988) *Focus Groups: A Practical Guide for Applied Research.* Newbury Park, CA: Sage.

Kuckartz, U. (2014) *Qualitative Text Analysis: A Guide to Methods, Practice and Using Software.* London: Sage.

Kvale, S. (1996) *Interviews: An Introduction to Qualitative Research Interviewing.* Thousand Oaks, CA: Sage.

Le Comte, M.D., Millroy, W.L. and Preissle, J. (1992) *The Handbook of Qualitative Research in Education.* London: Academic Press.

Lewins, A. and Silver, C. (2014) *Using Software in Qualitative Research: A Step-by-Step Guide* (2nd edn). London: Sage.

Lichtman, M. (2014) *Qualitative Research for the Social Sciences.* Thousand Oaks, CA: Sage.

Lincoln, Y.S. and Guba, E.G. (1985) *Naturalistic Inquiry.* Newbury Park, CA: Sage.

Lofland, J. and Lofland, L. (1995) *Analyzing Social Settings.* Belmont, CA: Wadsworth.

Machi, L.A. and McEvoy, B.T. (2012) *The Literature Review: Six Steps to Success* (2nd edn). Thousand Oaks, CA: Sage.

Mann, C. and Stewart, F. (2000) *Internet Communication and Qualitative Research: A Handbook for Researching Online.* London: Sage.

Marshall, C. and Rossman, G.B. (1999) *Designing Qualitative Research* (3rd edn). Thousand Oaks, CA: Sage.

Mason, J. (2002) *Qualitative Researching.* London: Sage.

Maxwell, J.A. (2013) *Qualitative Research Design* (3rd edn). Thousand Oaks, CA: Sage.

Miles, M.B. (1979) 'Qualitative data as an attractive nuisance: the problem of analysis', *Administrative Science Quarterly,* *24*: 590–601.

Miles, M.B. and Huberman, A.M. (1994) *Qualitative Data Analysis: An Expanded Sourcebook* (2nd edn). Thousand Oaks, CA: Sage.

Miles, M.B., Huberman, A.M. and Saldaña, J. (2013) *Qualitative Data Analysis: A Methods Sourcebook* (3rd edn). Thousand Oaks, CA: Sage.

Miller, T. and Birch, M. (eds) (2012) *Ethics in Qualitative Research.* London: Sage.

Mills, C.W. (1959) *The Sociological Imagination*. Oxford: Oxford University Press.

Morgan, D.L. (1997) *Focus Groups as Qualitative Research*. Newbury Park, CA: Sage.

Morse, J.M. (ed.) (1994) *Critical Issues in Qualitative Research Methods*. Thousand Oaks, CA: Sage.

Morse, J.M. (ed.) (1997) *Completing a Qualitative Project: Details and Dialogue*. Thousand Oaks, CA: Sage.

Patton, M.Q. (1997) *Utilization-Focused Evaluation: The New Century Text*. Thousand Oaks, CA: Sage.

Paulus, T., Lester, J.N. and Britt, V.G. (2013) 'Constructing hopes and fears around technology: a discourse analysis of introductory qualitative research texts', *Qualitative Inquiry*, *19*: 639–51.

Paulus, T., Lester, J.N. and Dempster, P. (2014) *Digital Tools for Qualitative Research*. London: Sage.

Piantanida, M. and Garman, N.B. (1999) *The Qualitative Dissertation*. Thousand Oaks, CA: Sage.

Punch, K.F. (2014) *Introduction to Social Research Quantitative and Qualitative Approaches* (3rd edn). London: Sage.

Ragin, C.C. and Becker, H.S. (eds) (1992) *What Is a Case? Exploring the Foundations of Social Inquiry*. New York: Cambridge University Press.

Richards, L. (1990) *Nobody's Home: Dreams and Realities in a New Suburb*. Melbourne: Oxford University Press.

Richards, L. and Morse, J.M. (2013) *Readme First for a User's Guide to Qualitative Methods* (3rd edn). Thousand Oaks, CA: Sage.

Richards, T.J. and Richards, L. (1994) 'Using computers in qualitative analysis', in Denzin, N.K. and Lincoln, Y.S. (eds), *Handbook of Qualitative Research*. Newbury Park, CA: Sage.

Richards, T.J. and Richards, L. (1995) 'Using hierarchical categories in qualitative data analysis', in Kelle, U. (ed.), *Computer-aided Qualitative Data Analysis*. London: Sage.

Richardson, L. (1994) 'Writing: a method of inquiry', in Denzin, N.K. and Lincoln, Y.S. (eds), *Handbook of Qualitative Research*. Thousand Oaks, CA: Sage.

Ridley, D. (2012) *The Literature Review: A Step-by-Step Guide for Students* (2nd edn). London: Sage.

Rubin, H. and Rubin, I. (2005) *Qualitative Interviewing: The Art of Hearing Data*. Thousand Oaks, CA: Sage.

Saldaña, J. (2013) *The Coding Manual for Qualitative Researchers* (2nd edn). London: Sage.

Schwandt, T.A. (1997) *Qualitative Inquiry: A Dictionary of Terms*. Thousand Oaks, CA: Sage.

Seale, C.F. (1999) *The Quality of Qualitative Research*. London: Sage.

Seale, C.F. (ed.) (2001) *Researching Society and Culture* (2nd edn). London: Sage.

Seale, C.F., Gobo, G., Gubrium, J.F. and Silverman, D. (eds) (2004) *Qualitative Research Practice*. London: Sage.

Silverman, D. (2001) 'Research and social theory', in Seale, C.F. (ed.), *Researching Society and Culture* (2nd edn). London: Sage, pp. 97–110.

Silverman, D. (2010) *Doing Qualitative Research* (3rd edn). London: Sage.

Silverman, D. (2011) *Interpreting Qualitative Data: Methods for Analyzing Talk, Text and Interaction* (4th edn). London: Sage.

Spradley, J.P. (1979) *The Ethnographic Interview*. New York: Holt, Rinehart and Winston.

Stewart, D.W., Shamdasani, P.N. and Rook, D.W. (2006) *Focus Groups: Theory and Practice*. Newbury Park, CA: Sage.

Strauss, A.L. (1987) *Qualitative Analysis for Social Scientists*. Cambridge: Cambridge University Press.

Strauss, A.L. (1995) 'Notes on the nature and development of general theories', *Qualitative Inquiry*, *1*(1): 7–18.

Strauss, A.L. and Corbin, J. (1998) *Basics of Qualitative Research: Grounded Theory Procedures and Techniques* (2nd edn). London: Sage.

Tesch, R. (1990) *Qualitative Research: Analysis Types and Software Tools*. Basingstoke: Falmer.

Turner, B.A. (1981) 'Some practical aspects of qualitative data analysis', *Quality and Quantity*, *15*: 225–47.

Weitzman, E. and Miles, M.B. (1995) *Computer Programs for Qualitative Data Analysis*. Newbury Park, CA: Sage.

Wolcott, H.F. (1994) *Transforming Qualitative Data*. Thousand Oaks, CA: Sage.

Wolcott, H.F. (2009) *Writing Up Qualitative Research* (3rd edn). Newbury Park, CA: Sage.

Yin, R.K. (1989) *Case Study Research: Design and Methods*. London: Sage.

Yin, R.K. (2010) *Qualitative Research from Start to Finish*. London: Guilford Press.

Znaniecki, F. (1968) *The Method of Sociology*. New York: Octagon Books.

Index